Legalines

Editorial Advisors:
Gloria A. Aluise
Attorney at Law
David H. Barber
Attorney at Law
Robert A. Wyler
Attorney at Law

Authors:
Gloria A. Aluise
Attorney at Law
David H. Barber
Attorney at Law
Daniel O. Bernstine
Professor of Law
D. Steven Brewster
C.P.A.
Roy L. Brooks
Professor of Law
Frank L. Bruno
Attorney at Law
Scott M. Burbank
C.P.A.
Jonathan C. Carlson
Professor of Law
Charles N. Carnes
Professor of Law
Paul S. Dempsey
Professor of Law
Jerome A. Hoffman
Professor of Law
Mark R. Lee
Professor of Law
Jonathan Neville
Attorney at Law
Laurence C. Nolan
Professor of Law
Arpiar Saunders
Professor of Law
Robert A. Wyler
Attorney at Law

WILLS, TRUSTS & ESTATES

Adaptable to Fifth Edition of Dukeminier Casebook

By Gloria A. Aluise
Attorney at Law

HARCOURT BRACE LEGAL AND PROFESSIONAL PUBLICATIONS, INC.
EDITORIAL OFFICES: 111 W. Jackson Blvd., 7th Floor, Chicago, IL 60604
Legalines
REGIONAL OFFICES: Chicago, Dallas, Los Angeles, New York, Washington, D.C
Distributed by: **Harcourt Brace & Company** 6277 Sea Harbor Drive, Orlando, FL 32887 (800)787-8717

SERIES EDITOR
Astrid E. Ellis, J.D.
Attorney At Law

PRODUCTION COORDINATOR
Sanetta Hister

SEVENTH PRINTING—2000

Printed in the United States of America.

SHORT SUMMARY OF CONTENTS

TABLE OF CONTENTS AND SHORT REVIEW OUTLINE

I. A FOUNDATION FOR ESTATE PLANNING: SOCIETY'S CONTROL OF INHERITANCE

A. PROLOGUE

The material in this outline covers wills, trusts, future interests, and estate and trust administration. Each of these topics relates to the social process by which private wealth is transmitted and allocated, and is critical to a comprehensive understanding of the estate planning process.

B. INHERITANCE AND ITS LIMITATIONS

1. **T. Jefferson.** "The earth belongs in usufruct to the living; the dead have neither power nor rights over it."

2. **2 W. Blackstone, Commentaries.** "The permanent right of property, vested in the ancestor himself, was not a ***natural***, but merely a ***civil*** right." "Wills . . . and rights of inheritance . . . are all creatures of civil or municipal laws."

3. **Supreme Court.** In *Irving Trust Co. v. Day*, 314 U.S. 556 (1942), the Supreme Court held that rights of succession to the property of a deceased are entirely a statutory creation. Nothing in the Constitution forbids a legislature from limiting or even abolishing the power of testamentary disposition over property.

4. **Taking Property Without Just Compensation--Hodel v. Irving,** 481 U.S. 704 (1987). Hodel v. Irving

   a. **Facts.** Pursuant to an 1889 act of Congress, tracts of land reserved for the Sioux Indian Nation were allotted to individual Sioux, though held in trust by the United States, and were allowed to pass to the allottees' heirs. Succeeding generations of Sioux divided their predecessors' tracts into increasingly tiny undivided fractional interests, which often yielded pennies in annual rent. Congress responded by enacting section 207 of the Indian Land Consolidation Act of 1983, which provided that any undivided fractional interest representing less than 2% of a tract's acreage, and which had earned less than $100 in the preceding year, would escheat to the tribe rather than descend by intestacy or devise. Three Sioux who would have inherited such interests but for the operation of section 207 filed an action for injunctive and declaratory relief in federal court, claiming that section 207 violated the Fifth Amendment by taking private property without just compensation.

   The District Court found that the plaintiff heirs did not have any vested property interest which would be entitled to constitutional protection, and accordingly denied relief. The Eighth Circuit reversed, holding that: (i) the heirs or devisees had standing to assert the decedents' right to control the disposition of their property, and (ii) the taking of that right without compensation violated the Fifth Amendment.

b. **Issue.** Does a federal statute barring inheritance of Indian land allotments and providing for escheat to the tribe effect a taking of decedents' property without just compensation in violation of the Fifth Amendment?

c. **Held.** Yes. Judgment affirmed.

1) The fact that section 207 has deprived those tribal members of fractional interests that they would otherwise have inherited is sufficient injury in fact to satisfy the case or controversy requirement of Article III of the United States Constitution.

2) The original version of section 207 of the Indian Land Consolidation Act of 1983 effects a taking of property without just compensation in violation of the Fifth Amendment. It entirely abolishes both the descent and devise of these property interests even when the passing of the property to an heir might result in the consolidation of property.

3) The government has considerable latitude, under the Just Compensation Clause of the Fifth Amendment, in regulating property rights in ways that may adversely affect the owners.

4) There is no set formula for determining when justice and fairness require that economic injuries caused by public action be compensated by the government, rather than remaining disproportionately concentrated on a few persons. Instead, the question whether such action results in a taking of property under the Fifth Amendment is examined by engaging in essentially ad hoc, factual inquiries in which several factors—such as the economic impact of the regulation, its interference with reasonable investment-backed expectations, and the character of the governmental action—have particular significance.

5) Although the state and federal governments have broad authority to adjust the rules governing the descent and devise of property without implicating the guarantees of the Just Compensation Clause of the Fifth Amendment, the complete abolition of both the descent and devise of a particular class of property may constitute a taking within the meaning of that clause. Under these facts, both descent and devise are abolished even where the governmental purpose sought to be advanced, consolidation of ownership of Indian lands, does not conflict with the further descent of the property.

Shriners Hospitals for Crippled Children v. Zrillic

5. **Statutory Restriction of Charitable Gifts--Shriners Hospitals for Crippled Children v. Zrillic,** 563 So. 2d 64 (Fla. 1990).

a. **Facts.** Romans (T) executed her will on May 5, 1986 and died on July 19, 1986. T limited her daughter's, Lorraine Zrillic's (P's), inheritance to several boxes of antiques. The residue of T's estate was devised to Shriners (D). P, pursuant to state statute, requested an order in the circuit court avoiding the charitable devise. Section 732.803 provides that where a testator dies leaving lineal descendants or a spouse and her will leaves all or part of her estate to a charitable institution, the devise shall be entirely avoided if one or more of the descendants or a spouse, who would receive any interest in the devise if avoided, files a written notice to this effect within four months after the date letters are issued, unless the will was executed at least six months before the testator's death. Both D and T's personal representatives defended on equal protection grounds. The circuit court ruled the statute unconstitutional. The district court of appeal reversed, finding that the statute did not violate either the state or federal constitutions. D petitions for certiorari.

b. **Issues.**

1) Is a statute that allows descendants to avoid charitable devises reasonably necessary to limit the property rights guaranteed by Article I, section 2 of the Florida Constitution?

2) Does a statute that allows descendants to avoid charitable devises violate the equal protection guarantees of Article I, section 2 of the Florida Constitution and the Fourteenth Amendment of the United States Constitution?

c. **Held.** 1) No. 2) Yes.

1) Historically, statutes that restricted charitable gifts were promulgated to restrict the exercise of ecclesiastical jurisdiction over personal property and the attendant abuses. Over time society's attitude has come to favor charitable gifts and devises and such dispositions are held valid wherever possible. It remains reasonable for dependent family members to be protected, and the Florida Constitution and other statutes do so, providing for homestead exemptions, the elective share, family allowance, and protection against fraud, duress, mistake, and undue influence.

2) Section 732.803 fails to protect against windfalls for lineal descendants who have had no contact with the decedent or who have been neglectful or abusive, and fails to protect against specifically limited legacies.

3) The statute is not reasonably necessary to accomplish the asserted state goals at the cost of offending property interests protected by the Florida Constitution.

4) Section 732.803 creates a limited class of testators. It is underinclusive. It does not protect against overreaching by lawyers, doctors, nurses, or others who may influence a testator. There is no basis to believe that testators need more protection against charities than against other greedy people.

5) The classification is overinclusive because it voids gifts of many testators who were not improperly influenced or who do not have family members who need protection.

6) The statute does not draw a rational distinction; it is not reasonably related to a legitimate governmental purpose.

d. **Dissent.** This is a matter for the legislature to decide. The facts of this case are not attractive to the application of the statute, but the statute might serve another series of events.

Shapira v. Union National Bank

6. **Partial Restraints on Marriage Permissible--Shapira v. Union National Bank,** 39 Ohio Misc. 28, 315 N.E.2d 825 (1974).

a. **Facts.** The will of the decedent, David Shapira, M.D., bequeathed the residue of his estate to his son, Daniel Jacob Shapira, provided that he marry a Jewish girl both of whose parents are Jewish at the time of the testator's death. If after seven years from the testator's death, the son is unmarried or married to a non-Jewish girl, then his share should go to the State of Israel. Daniel Jacob Shapira (P), who is 21 years old and unmarried, brings a petition in the Court of Common Pleas for a declaratory judgment, arguing that the condition upon his inheritance is unconstitutional, contrary to public policy, and unenforceable because of its unreasonableness.

b. **Issues.**

1) Is a partial restraint on marriage in a will a violation of the right to marry protected by the Fourteenth Amendment?

2) Is a partial restraint on marriage which imposes only reasonable restrictions valid and not contrary to public policy?

c. **Held.** 1) No. 2) Yes. Petition denied.

1) P is correct that the right to marry is constitutionally protected from restrictive state legislative action. Here, however, the court is not asked to enforce any restriction upon P's constitutional right to marry; rather, the court is asked to enforce the testator's restriction upon his son's inheritance. The right to receive property is a creature of the law and is not a constitutionally guaranteed right. Hence, upholding the partial restraint imposed by the testator will not violate the Constitution.

2) Nor does such a restraint violate public policy. If the condition were that the beneficiary not marry anyone, the restraint would be general or total and would be held contrary to public policy. A partial restraint on marriage which imposes only reasonable restrictions is valid, and not contrary to public policy. The weight of authority in the United States is that gifts conditioned upon the beneficiary's marrying within a particular religious class or faith are reasonable. It is the conclusion of this court that the conditions contained in the testator's will are reasonable restrictions upon marriage and valid.

C. THE PROBATE PROCESS

1. **Introduction and Terminology.** The general steps in the probate process are (i) opening the estate by offering the will for probate, (ii) collecting the decedent's assets, (iii) paying any family allowance and setting aside homestead and exempt personal property, (iv) paying creditors' claims and tax bills, and (v) distributing the assets of the estate upon the probate court entering a decree of distribution.

a. **Executor, administrator.** The executor is a personal representative named in a will. The administrator is a personal representative appointed by the court to administer the estate of an intestate. There are various types of administrators:

1) **Administrator:** person originally appointed when the decedent dies intestate.

2) **Administrator with the will annexed (administrator c.t.a.):** person appointed when the decedent dies testate but no executor is named in the will.

3) **Administrator of goods not administered (administered d.b.n.):** person appointed to succeed an original administrator.

4) **Administrator c.t.a.d.b.n.:** person appointed to succeed an executor or an administrator c.t.a.

5) **Special administrator:** person appointed to preserve the assets pending qualification of the regular administrator.

b. **Other terminology.** The terminology used in decedents' estates and trusts originated primarily in England, where common law courts had jurisdiction over real property and ecclesiastical courts had jurisdiction over personal property. Each group developed a distinct terminology that has carried over to this day. Some key terms are defined below.

1) **Succession.** Succession is the process of becoming beneficially entitled to the property of a decedent.

2) **Intestate succession.** Intestate succession occurs where the decedent leaves no valid will, so that his property passes to those of his relatives named in a state statute (called the intestate law).

3) **Statute of descent.** A statute of descent is an intestate law which applies only to real property. Intestate real property is said to pass by descent.

4) **Statute of distribution.** A statute of distribution is an intestate law which applies only to personal property. Intestate personal property is said to pass by ***distribution***.

5) **Statute of descent and distribution.** A statute of descent and distribution is an intestate law which applies to both real and personal property.

6) **Heir.** A person entitled by statute to the land of the intestate is called the heir or heir at law.

   a) **Expectant heir.** An expectant heir is one who expects to take by inheritance.

   b) **Prospective heir.** A prospective heir is one who may inherit but may be excluded. This category includes heirs presumptive and heirs apparent.

(1) **Heir presumptive.** An heir presumptive is a person who will inherit if the potential intestate dies immediately, but who will be excluded if relatives closer in relationship are born.

(2) **Heir apparent.** An heir apparent is one who is certain to inherit unless excluded by a valid will.

7) **Next of kin (or distributee).** The next of kin, or distributee, is that person (or persons) who is, or may be, entitled to the personal property of an intestate. This person is said to ***inherit*** the personal property.

8) **Ascendant or ancestor.** An ascendant or ancestor is a person related to an intestate or to a claimant to an intestate share in the ascending lineal line.

9) **Descendant.** A descendant is a person related to an intestate or to a claimant to an intestate share in the descending lineal line.

10) **Collateral.** A collateral is a relative who traces relationship to an intestate through a common ancestor but who is not in his lineal line of ascent or descent.

a) **Collaterals of the half blood.** A collateral of the half blood is a person related to an intestate through only one common ancestor.

11) **Affinity.** Relationship by marriage is called affinity.

12) **Consanguinity.** Relationship by blood is called consanguinity.

13) **Escheat.** Property escheats to the state if no relatives of the intestate are entitled to inheritance.

14) **Will.** A will is an expression, either written or oral, of a person's intention concerning the disposition of property at death. A person who dies leaving a valid will is said to die ***testate***.

15) **Devise.** A devise is a clause directing the disposition of real property in a will, and the person who is named to take the real property is called the devisee.

16) **Legacy.** A legacy is a clause in a will directing the disposition of money.

17) **Bequest.** A bequest is a clause in a will directing the disposition of personal property other than money.

18) **Attested, holographic, and nuncupative wills.** An attested will is a will signed by a witness. A holographic will is a will entirely in the handwriting of the testator. A nuncupative will is an oral will.

19) **Codicil.** A codicil is a testamentary instrument ancillary to a will.

20) **Probate.** Probate is the procedure by which a transaction alleged to be a will is established judicially as a valid testamentary disposition, and also applies to the act of approving the will after probate has taken place.

2. **Is Probate Necessary?** One of the primary functions of the probate process is to provide evidence of transfer of title to the decedent's heirs or devisees. However, in view of the costs and delays of probate, one may wish to avoid probate by transferring title to property during life. Three common ways of avoiding probate are (i) taking title in joint tenancy, (ii) creating a trust during life, and (iii) designating a payable-on-death beneficiary in a life insurance contract or other contract. Statutes in all states permit heirs to avoid probate where the amount of property involved is small.

3. **A Summary of Probate Procedure.**

   a. **Opening probate.** Primary or domiciliary jurisdiction obtains in the jurisdiction where the decedent was domiciled at the time of death. Ancillary administration obtains if property is located in another jurisdiction. Each state has a detailed statutory procedure for issuance of letters testamentary or letters of administration. The majority of states require prior notice to interested parties before the appointment of a personal representative or probate of a will. Under the Uniform Probate Code ("UPC"), the representative also has a duty to publish a newspaper notice for creditors once each week for three weeks.

   b. **Supervising the representative's actions.** The probate court approves the inventory and appraisal, payment of debts, family allowance, granting of options on real estate, borrowing of funds, personal representative's commissions, attorneys' fees, preliminary and final distributions, and discharge of the personal representative.

   c. **Closing the estate.** A representative is not discharged from fiduciary duties until the court grants discharge.

4. **Contest of Wills.**

   a. **Grounds for contest.** A will contest poses the issue of whether the document offered for probate is a valid will. While most will contests involve the issues of testamentary capacity or undue influence, a will contest may also be based on defective execution, revocation of the will by the testator, lack of testamentary intent, fraud, and mistake.

D. PROFESSIONAL RESPONSIBILITY

No lawyer should prepare a will unless he considers himself competent to do so.

1. **Interested Will Beneficiaries Have Cause of Action Against Attorney--Ogle v. Fuiten,** 102 Ill. 2d 356, 466 N.E.2d 224 (1984). Ogle v. Fuiten

   a. **Facts.** The wills of Oscar and Alma Smith contained provisions bequeathing their respective property to the other spouse if the other spouse survived by 30 days; if both died from a common disaster, the estate was to be divided between the Ogles (Ps). The wills were construed in an earlier proceeding where it was held that because Oscar died suddenly of a stroke, and his wife, Alma, died 15 days later from a lingering illness, and neither will contained any other dispositive provisions, their estates passed by intestacy to persons other than Ps.

In a two-count complaint against the estate of attorney Fuiten and his former law partner, Ps alleged that Fuiten had negligently drafted wills for the Smiths, who were Ps' uncle and aunt, and alternatively, that D failed to properly perform his contract with the Smiths to fulfill their testamentary intentions, and in so doing, failed to benefit Ps. Ds moved to dismiss for failure to state a cause of action. The circuit court allowed the motion, and Ps appealed. The appellate court reversed and remanded.

b. **Issue.** Does the fact that wills are determined to be valid preclude a negligence action based on an attorney's having drafted wills that do not comport with the testator's intent that certain beneficiaries take under those wills?

c. **Held.** No. Appellate court judgment affirmed.

1) A cause of action should not be dismissed on the pleadings unless it clearly appears that no set of facts can be proved that will entitle plaintiffs to recover.

2) Privity is not a prerequisite to an action by a nonclient against an attorney.

3) Cases in California and other jurisdictions have permitted intended beneficiaries to recover from an attorney for his negligence in preparing a will or advising the testator.

4) The complaint sufficiently stated traditional elements of negligence in tort by virtue of the defendant attorney's having prepared wills in such a manner that the intended testamentary beneficiaries failed to benefit at all upon the occurrence of certain contingencies.

5) The complaint sufficiently stated traditional elements of a third-party beneficiary breach of contract theory by virtue of the attorney's having been retained to draft wills not only for the benefit of the testators, but also for the benefit of the intended contingent beneficiaries, with the wills as actually drafted in fact permitting a circumstance by which the intended beneficiaries failed to take anything under the wills.

II. INTESTACY: AN ESTATE PLAN BY DEFAULT

A. INTESTATE SUCCESSORS: SPOUSE AND DESCENDANTS

All states have statutes of descent and distribution that govern the distribution of the property of a person who dies without a will, or who does not make a complete distribution of the estate.

1. **Spouse.** Under common law, a spouse was not an heir and the decedent's property passed by intestacy to descendants. Today, the surviving spouse takes an intestate share of the decedent's estate in all jurisdictions. If the decedent is survived by a spouse and by descendants (children, grandchildren, etc.), in most states the spouse takes one-third or one-half of the decedent's estate. If the decedent is survived by a spouse but not by descendants or parents, in many states the spouse inherits the entire estate.

   a. **Simultaneous Death.** A person cannot take as an heir or will beneficiary unless he survives the decedent for at least an instant of time. However, it is often difficult to determine whether the person survived the decedent (*e.g.,* when the person and decedent are both fatally injured in an accident). All jurisdictions except Louisiana and Ohio have enacted the Uniform Simultaneous Death Act (or its Uniform Probate Code equivalent, the 120-hour survival rule). Under the Act, where the title to property or the devolution thereof depends upon priority of death and there is no sufficient evidence that the parties have died otherwise than simultaneously, the property of each person shall be disposed of as if he had survived. If there is sufficient evidence that one party survived the other, even for a brief period of time, the Act does not apply.

      1) **Evidence of survival--Janus v. Tarasewicz,** 135 Ill. App. 3d 936, 482 N.E.2d 418 (1985). Janus v. Tarasewicz

         a) **Facts.** This declaratory judgment action arose out of the deaths of a husband and wife who died after ingesting Tylenol capsules laced with cyanide. Stanley Janus was pronounced dead shortly after he was admitted to the hospital. However, Theresa Janus was placed on life support systems for almost two days before being pronounced dead. Claiming that there was no sufficient evidence that Theresa Janus survived her husband, Stanley's mother (P) brought this action for the proceeds of Stanley's $100,000 life insurance policy which named Theresa as the primary beneficiary and P as the contingent beneficiary. Metropolitan Life Insurance Company (D) paid the proceeds to Tarasewicz (D), who is Theresa's father and the administrator of her estate.

         The trial court found sufficient evidence that Theresa survived Stanley. P and the administrator of Stanley's estate appealed, contending that there is not sufficient evidence to prove that both victims did not suffer brain death prior to their arrival at the hospital.

b) **Issue.** In a factually disputed case of whether one spouse survived the other, is the appellate court's review limited to whether the trial court's finding was against the manifest weight of the evidence?

c) **Held.** Yes. Judgment affirmed.

(1) A civil case is governed by the law as it exists when a judgment is rendered, not when the facts underlying the case occur.

(2) Even though the *Haymer* case, which set forth standards for determining when legal death occurs, was decided after the deaths in issue, the trial court properly applied the *Haymer* standards. Furthermore, application of those standards was not unfair since the treating physicians had made pertinent diagnoses at the time of the deaths and the parties presented evidence relevant under the standards.

(3) Survivorship is a fact that must be proven by a preponderance of the evidence by the party whose claim depends on survivorship.

(4) In cases where survivorship is determined by the testimony of lay witnesses, the burden of sufficient evidence may be met by evidence of a positive sign of life in one body and the absence of any such sign in the other.

(5) In cases where the death process is monitored by medical professionals, their testimony as to the usual and customary standards of medical practice are highly relevant when considering what constitutes a positive sign of life and what constitutes a criterion for determining death.

(6) The appellate court's task on review of a factually disputed case is to determine whether the trial court's finding was against the manifest weight of the evidence. The finding here that the wife survived her husband was not against the manifest weight of the evidence.

2. **Descendants.**

a. **Taking by representation: per stirpes distribution.** In all jurisdictions, after the spouse's share is set aside, children and issue of deceased children take the remainder of the property to the exclusion of everyone else. Thus, if the intestate is survived by children and grandchildren, the grandchildren will take a share of the estate only if they are children of a deceased child of the intestate. Grandchildren take only by representation.

1) **Majority rule—per capita with representation.** UPC section 2-103 provides that if the issue of the decedent "are all of the same degree of kinship to the decedent they take equally, but if of unequal degree, then those of more remote degree take by representation." Thus, each descendant at the ***first generational level at which there are***

living takers takes one share, and the share of each deceased person at the generational level is divided among his descendants by representation. This form of distribution is called "per capita with representation," but in many jurisdictions it is referred to as "per stirpes."

2) **Minority rule—strict per stirpes.** A few states apply a "strict per stirpes" rule. Under this rule, the stirpital shares are always determined at the first generational level, even if there are no living takers at that level.

b. **Posthumous children.** Today, in many states, a child conceived during the father's lifetime but born after his death is considered his child for inheritance purposes.

c. **Adopted children.** In all states that have enacted statutes governing inheritance rights of adopted children, an adopted child has the same inheritance rights as a natural child.

1) **Loss of inheritance rights from or through natural parents--Hall v. Vallandingham,** 540 A.2d 1162 (Md. App. 1988).

Hall v. Vallandingham

a) **Facts.** Earl Vallandingham died in 1956, survived by his widow, Elizabeth, and their four children. Two years later, Elizabeth married Jim Killgore, who adopted the children. Earl's brother William died childless, unmarried, and intestate. His sole heirs were his surviving brothers and sisters and the children of brothers and sisters who predeceased him. Earl's four natural children (Ps) alleged that they were entitled to the distributive share of their natural uncle William's estate that their natural father would have received had he survived. The circuit court found that Ps were not entitled to inherit from decedent because of their adoption by their stepfather after the death of their natural father and the remarriage of their natural mother. Ps appeal.

b) **Issue.** Do children adopted after the death of a natural parent lose all rights of inheritance from or through that natural parent?

c) **Held.** Yes. Judgment affirmed.

(1) Every state possesses the power to regulate the manner by which property within its dominion may be transmitted by will or inheritance and to prescribe who can receive that property. The state may deny the privilege altogether or may impose whatever restrictions upon the grant it deems appropriate.

(2) An adopted child is entitled to all the rights and privileges of a biological child insofar as the adoptive parents are concerned, but adoption does not confer upon the adopted child more rights and privileges than those possessed by a natural child. To allow dual inheritance would bestow upon an adopted child a superior status.

(3) An adopted child may not inherit from or through its natural parents. Once a child is adopted, the rights of both the natural parents and the relatives are terminated.

(4) Because an adopted child has no right to inherit from the estate of a natural parent who dies intestate, it follows that the same child may not inherit through the natural parent by way of representation.

2) **Equitable Adoption.** The doctrine of "equitable adoption," based on estoppel principles, allows a stepchild to inherit from the foster parent just as though the child had been adopted. The basis of the estoppel is the foster parent's conduct in failing to perform the agreement to adopt. The doctrine only works against the foster parent. Thus, if there is an unperformed agreement to adopt and the stepchild dies intestate, the foster parents do not inherit from the child.

O'Neal v. Wilkes

a) **No valid adoption--O'Neal v. Wilkes,** 439 S.E.2d 490 (Ga. 1994).

(1) **Facts.** O'Neal (P) filed a petition in equity seeking a declaration of virtual adoption. P was given to the Cooks by her aunt in 1961. P lived with the Cooks and after they were divorced, continued to live with Mr. Cook until 1975 when P was married. She was educated by Cook and he identified her children as his grandchildren. When Cook died, Cook's administrator, Wilkes, refused to recognize P's asserted interest in Cook's estate. A jury found P had been virtually adopted. The court granted a judgment n.o.v., finding that P's aunt was without authority to contract for P's adoption. P appeals.

(2) **Issue.** Does an aunt have authority to contract for her niece's adoption if she is not the legal guardian?

(3) **Held.** No.

(a) Although P's father had never acknowledged P and his consent to the adoption was not necessary, P's aunt was not P's "legal guardian."

(b) Even though P's aunt had P at the time of the adoption, P's aunt was not given legal custody by court order; even if she had been "legal custodian," under Georgia law, a custodian does not have the right to consent to a child's adoption.

(4) **Dissent.** Equity considers that done which ought to have been done. This court has held that an agreement to adopt a child, so as to make the child an heir on the adopting person's death, performed on the part of the child, is enforceable upon the death of the adopting person as to property undisposed of by the will. P has fully performed the alleged contract over a lifetime.

d. **Children born out of wedlock.** In all states today, a child born out of wedlock inherits from his natural mother and the mother's kind, and they can inherit from and through the child. While the rules respecting inheritance from the father vary, most states have adopted the provisions in UPC section 2-109, which permit paternity to be established by evidence of the subsequent marriage of the parents, by an adjudication during the life of the father, or by clear and convincing proof after his death.

e. **Transfers to minors.** Minors do not have the legal capacity to manage property. There are three alternatives available to parents of minors for property management: guardianship, custodianship, and trusteeship. The latter two are available only to persons who die testate, creating these arrangements by will. If a parent dies intestate, leaving property to a minor child, a guardian of the property must be appointed by a court.

f. **Advancements.** At common law and in a number of states today, any lifetime gift to a child is presumed to be an advancement of the child's intestate share, to be taken into account in distributing the intestate's property at death. Many states have statutes governing advancements. Most of these statutes provide that an advancement can be made to any heir and not just a child or other descendant. The most important effect of these statutes is to reverse the common law presumption: in many states, a lifetime gift to an heir can be treated as an advancement only if (i) expressly declared as such in a writing signed by the donor, or (ii) acknowledged as such in a writing signed by the donee.

g. **Cryogenically-preserved sperm--Hecht v. Superior Court,** 20 Cal.Rptr.2d 275 (1993). Hecht v. Superior Court

1) **Facts.** Kane left frozen sperm specimens for his girlfriend Hecht (P), with whom Kane had lived for five years before his death. He indicated in a letter that he hoped P would have his child. He bequeathed only a piece of land to his two adult children, whom he considered financially secure. After Kane's suicide, his children filed separate will contests alleging lack of mental capacity and undue influence by P. The children requested Kane's special administrator to file a petition to order Kane's sperm destroyed. The administrator also filed petitions to have the sperm distributed and for the court to determine whether any children conceived from Kane's sperm would be entitled to distribution under instructions accompanying Kane's will. P contended that the sperm was either an inter vivos gift or a gift causa mortis. The court ordered the sperm destroyed. P petitioned and the trial order was stayed pending a hearing.

2) **Issues.**

a) Did decedent have sufficient right of possession or ownership of the sperm so as to bring it within the jurisdiction of the probate court?

b) Does the public policy of California prohibit the artificial insemination of P because she is an unmarried woman or because Kane is deceased?

3) **Held.** a) Yes. b) No.

a) Other authorities have, in considering the legal status of pre-embryos, determined that sperm is "gametic material" that can be used for reproduction. At the time of Kane's death, he had an interest in the nature of ownership to the extent that he had decision-making authority as to the use of his sperm for reproduction. Such interest is sufficient to constitute property within the meaning of the relevant probate statute.

b) This court has interpreted state civil law to afford both married and unmarried women a vehicle for obtaining semen for artificial insemination without fear that a donor may claim paternity. The donor was determined to have a statutory vehicle for donating semen without fear of liability for child support. Thus, we are not operating in a legal vacuum and are free to establish policies relative to an unmarried woman's access to artificial insemination. There is no support for the argument that California public policy prohibits P's artificial insemination because of her status.

c) Respondents do not establish, with their argument that posthumous conception would create orphaned children with state authorization, a state interest sufficient to justify interference with P's and decedent's desire to conceive a child. There is no California statute that contains a public policy statement that reveals an interest that could justify infringing on gamete-providers' decisional authority.

B. INTESTATE SUCCESSORS: ANCESTORS AND COLLATERALS

When the intestate is survived by descendants, parents and collaterals do not take in any jurisdiction. When there are no descendants, after deducting the spouse's share, the intestate's property is usually distributed to parents. In nearly all states, if the intestate is not survived by a spouse, descendants, or parents, the estate passes to the descendants of the intestate's parents, *i.e.*, to the decedent's brothers and sisters (and the descendants of deceased brothers and sisters, per stirpes).

1. **Half bloods.** In most states, a relative of the half blood (*e.g.*, a half-brother) is treated the same as a relative of the whole blood.

2. **Escheat.** If there are no heirs, the property of the decedent escheats to the state in all jurisdictions.

C. BARS TO SUCCESSION

1. **Misconduct.**

In re Estate of Mahoney

a. **Killing decedent--*In re* Estate of Mahoney,** 126 Vt. 31, 220 A.2d 475 (1966).

1) **Facts.** The decedent, Howard Mahoney, died intestate after being shot to death by his wife, Charlotte Mahoney, who was convicted of manslaughter and sentenced to prison. The decedent was survived only by Charlotte and his father and mother. The trial court entered a judgment decreeing the residue of the decedent's estate to his father and mother in equal shares. Charlotte appeals.

2) **Issue.** Can a widow convicted of manslaughter for the death of her husband inherit from his estate?

3) **Held.** Yes. Judgment reversed.

a) There are three separate lines of cases dealing with this issue: (i) some states hold that legal title passes to the slayer and may be retained in spite of the crime; (ii) some states hold that legal title does not pass to the slayer because of the principle that no one should be permitted to profit by his own wrong; and (iii) some states hold that legal title passes to the slayer but equity holds him to be a constructive trustee for the heirs or next of kin of the decedent.

b) We adopt the third line of cases. However, in this case, the trial court did not decree the estate to the widow and then make her a constructive trustee of the estate for the benefit of the parents; rather, the court below decreed the estate directly to the parents. We reverse. The trial court was bound to follow the statutes of descent and distribution and decree the estate to the widow.

c) Further, jurisdiction to impose a constructive trust rests with the chancery court, not the probate court. Accordingly, we remand this case so that application may be made to the chancery court for purposes of imposing a constructive trust and for determination of whether the death of the husband was voluntary manslaughter or involuntary manslaughter. If no such application is made, then the probate court shall assign to the widow the interest in the estate of her deceased husband.

b. **Adultery and desertion.** States may disqualify a parent as an heir if the parent has failed or refused to support the child or has abandoned the child during his minority. In a few states, a spouse is disqualified from dower, inheritance, or an elective share if the spouse abandoned the decedent and committed adultery.

2. **Transfer of Interest in Decedent's Estate.** A person may be barred from succeeding to a decedent's estate because he has released, transferred, or disclaimed his interest.

a. **Release of expectancy.** A child's release to his parent during the parent's lifetime is binding if given for fair consideration.

b. **Transfer of expectancy.** An expectancy is merely the possibility of inheriting property and, as such, it cannot be transferred, though a purported transfer of an expectancy for consideration may be enforceable in equity.

c. **Disclaimer.** It has always been held that a beneficiary can disclaim any testamentary gift. If a beneficiary makes a valid disclaimer, the disclaimed interest passes as though the disclaimant predeceased the testator. If a person disclaims, and the disclaimer is not "qualified," *i.e.,* the person has not made an irrevocable and unqualified refusal of an interest in property under Internal Revenue Code section 2518 procedures, gift tax liability results. The disclaimer must be made within nine months after the interest is created or after the donee reaches age 21, whichever is later.

III. CAPACITY AND WILL CONTESTS

A. MENTAL CAPACITY, UNDUE INFLUENCE, AND FRAUD

1. Mental Capacity.

a. **Why require mental capacity?** Mental capacity is required for the protection of society and for the protection of the decedent's family and the decedent himself.

b. **Test of mental capacity.** The decedent must know: (i) the nature and extent of his property; (ii) the persons who are the natural objects of his bounty; (iii) the disposition he is making; and (iv) how these elements relate so as to form an orderly plan for the disposition of his property.

c. **Insane delusion.** An insane delusion is a false conception of reality. It is one to which the testator adheres against all evidence and reason to the contrary.

1) **Insane delusions about men--*In re* Strittmater,** 53 A.2d 205 (N.J. 1947). *In re* Strittmater

a) **Facts.** Strittmater (T) never married. She lived with her parents until their death and was devoted to them and they to her. Four years after their death, she wrote that her father was "a corrupt, vicious, and unintelligent savage," typical of the majority of his sex, and on a photograph of her mother, she inscribed, "moronic she-devil." T's dealings with her attorney, over a period of years, were normal. T became a member of the National Women's Party and volunteered one day a week for at least two years. In her will, she left her estate to the party, as had been her expressed intention. T died one month after her will was executed. The will was admitted to probate. Two cousins challenged the will, alleging it was a product of T's insanity.

b) **Issue.** May a will that was executed by a person with sane delusions about men be admitted to probate?

c) **Held.** No.

(1) T's female physician opined T suffered from a split personality.

(2) T had been a member of the party for 11 years when she wrote: "It remains for feminist organizations like [the party] to make exposure of women's 'protectors' and 'lovers' for what their vicious and contemptible selves are."

(3) I think it was her paranoiac condition, especially her insane delusions about the male, that led her to leave

her estate to the party. Probate should be set aside.

In re Honigman

2) **Insane delusion resulting from irrational belief in nonexistent facts--*In re* Honigman,** 8 N.Y.2d 244, 168 N.E.2d 676 (1960).

a) **Facts.** Prior to his death, the decedent, Frank Honigman, told friends and strangers alike that he believed his wife was unfaithful. This suspicion became an obsession, although he was normal and rational in other respects. The decedent, a man of 70 who had undergone a number of operations, once commented that he was sick in the head and that he knew something was wrong with him. The decedent instructed his attorney to prepare a will cutting off his wife from any of his estate, leaving her life use of her minimum statutory share, with directions to pay the principal upon her death to his surviving brothers or sisters and to the descendants of any predeceased brother or sister, per stirpes. At the trial, the proponents of the will adduced evidence which, they argued, showed a reasonable basis for the decedent's belief. This included an anniversary card sent by a Mr. Krause to the decedent's wife; a letter; evidence that whenever the phone rang the decedent's wife would answer it; and evidence that Mr. Krause came over to the decedent's house one night while the decedent was out. When the will was offered for probate, the decedent's widow (P) filed objections. A trial was conducted on the issue of whether the deceased was of sound mind and memory at the time he signed the will. The jury answered in the negative. The appellate court reversed. This appeal followed.

b) **Issue.** If a person believes facts which are against all evidence and probability and conducts himself, however logically, upon the assumption of their existence in making his will, does he suffer from an insane delusion so as to defeat testamentary capacity?

c) **Held.** Yes. Judgment of the appellate court is reversed and a new trial ordered.

(1) The general rule is that if a person persistently believes supposed facts, which have no real existence except in his perverted imagination and against all evidence and probability, and conducts himself, however logically, upon the assumption of their existence, he is, so far as they are concerned, under a morbid delusion. Such a person is essentially mad or insane on those subjects.

(2) Here, the issue of the decedent's sanity was an issue for the jury to resolve. There was sufficient evidence to justify placing this issue before the jury: the decedent's repeated suspicions of P's unfaithfulness; his belief of P's misbehaving by hiding male callers under her bed and by hauling men from the street up to her bedroom by the use of sheets; and so forth.

(3) The proponents argue that even if the decedent was laboring under a delusion, other reasons support the validity of the will. We disagree. A will is invalid where its dispository provisions might have been caused or affected by the delusion.

(4) Finally, we hold that the Dead Man's Statute—which excludes the testimony of a witness concerning a personal communication between the witness and the deceased—was misconstrued to permit the testimony of P when an objection to her testimony had been properly raised.

d) **Dissent.** The evidence adduced utterly failed to prove that the testator was suffering from an insane delusion or lacked testamentary capacity. Much of the evidence was improperly admitted, as the court itself notes, by reason of the Dead Man's Statute.

2. **Undue Influence.** A will or a gift in a will may be set aside if it was the result of undue influence—mental coercion that destroyed the testator's free agency and forced him to embody someone else's intention in his will in place of his own.

a. **Subjective test.** The test of whether a testator has been subjected to undue influence is a subjective one, measured at the time of execution of the will. The evidence must establish: (i) that undue influence was exerted on the testator; (ii) that the effect of the influence must have been to overpower the mind and will of the testator; and (iii) that the influence must have produced a will or a gift in the will that expresses the intent not of the testator but of the one exerting the influence, and that would not have been made but for the influence.

b. **Requirement of proof showing substitution of a plan testamentary disposition--Lipper v. Weslow,** 369 S.W.2d 698 (Tex. 1963).

Lipper v. Weslow

1) **Facts.** The testatrix, Mrs. Sophie Block, executed a will written by her son, Frank Lipper, a lawyer, 22 days before she died. Lipper bore malice against his deceased half-brother, who was excluded from the will. This resulted in Lipper receiving a larger share under the will than he otherwise would have received. Lipper lived next door to the decedent and had a key to her home. After signing the will, the decedent told one witness that she was leaving her estate to her son and daughter and that her other son, Julian A. Weslow, and his children would be excluded because they never showed any attention to her. The will provided a lengthy explanation as to why Julian was excluded from the will largely due to the "unfriendly and distant attitude" the decedent felt had been accorded to her. The children of Julian Weslow (Ps) contest the will, charging Frank Lipper and Irene Lipper Dover (Ds) with undue influence. At trial, a jury found that the will of the decedent was procured by undue influence. Ds appeal, contending that there is no evidence to support this finding.

2) **Issue.** Must a person contesting a will on the basis of undue influence supply proof of the substitution of the plan of testamentary disposition by another as the will of the testatrix?

3) **Held.** Yes. Judgment is reversed and rendered for Ds.

a) The contestants have established a confidential relationship, the opportunity, and perhaps a motive for undue influence. However, they must go forward and prove in some fashion that the will as written resulted from the defendant substituting his mind and will for that of the testatrix. Proof of vital facts of undue influence must be provided: the substitution of a plan of testamentary disposition by another as the will of the testatrix.

b) Here, the evidence shows that the decedent was of sound mind, of strong will, and in excellent physical condition. A person of sound mind has the legal right to dispose of her property as she wishes, with the burden on those attacking the disposition to prove that it was the product of undue influence. The decedent had a legal right to do what she did whether we think she was justified or not. We conclude that there was no evidence of probative force to support the verdict of the jury.

In re Will of Moses

c. **Undue influence arising out of attorney-client relationship--*In re* Will of Moses,** 227 So. 2d 829 (Miss. 1969).

1) **Facts.** The decedent, Fannie Taylor Moses, during her second marriage, became friends with Clarence Holland, an attorney. Prior to her death, she suffered from heart trouble, had a breast removed because of cancer, and became an alcoholic. Three years prior to her death, she made a will devising virtually all of her property to Holland. This will was drafted by a lawyer who had no connection with Clarence Holland, nor did Holland know about the will. The decedent's eldest sister (P) attacked the will on the ground of undue influence. The trial court found for P. Holland appeals.

2) **Issue.** Does a presumption of undue influence exist where a sexual relationship between attorney and client coexists with the attorney-client relationship?

3) **Held.** Yes. Judgment is affirmed.

a) It is argued that even if Holland, the decedent's attorney, occupied a fiduciary relationship on the date of execution of the will, the presumption of undue influence is overcome since the decedent had the independent advice and counsel of an attorney. We disagree. The evidence here shows that the attorney who drafted the will was little more than a scrivener, and that there was no meaningful independent advice or counsel touching upon the area in question.

b) Here, the intimate nature of this relationship is relevant to the question of undue influence to the extent that its existence warranted an inference of undue influence, extending and augmenting that which flowed from the attorney-client relationship. This is particularly true when it is considered that Holland will personally benefit from the will as drafted.

4) **Dissent.** There is not one iota of evidence in the record that Holland even knew of the will, much less that he participated in the preparation or execution of it. The evidence is to the contrary. The decedent prepared her will on the advice of independent counsel whose sole purpose was to advise her and prepare the will exactly as she wanted it.

d. **Undue influence a question of fact where testator is easily swayed.** Under the facts in *In re Kaufmann's Will*, 20 A.D.2d 464, 247 N.Y.S.2d 664 (1964), *aff'd,* 15 N.Y.2d 825, 257 N.Y.S. 2d 941 (1965), the decedent, Robert Kaufmann, a millionaire by inheritance, lived with Walter Weiss for some eight years, during which time Robert, in successive wills, increased Walter's share of his estate. Upon Robert's death, his brother Joel sued to have the final will, drafted in 1958, set aside on the ground of undue influence. In his deposition, Walter denied that a homosexual relationship existed between the two men. After two jury trials, both finding undue influence, the court of appeals affirmed, stating that "where, as here, the record indicates that testator was pliable and easily taken advantage of, that there was a long and detailed history of dominance and subservience between them, that testator relied exclusively upon proponent's knowledge . . . and proponent is willed virtually the entire estate, we consider that a question of fact was presented concerning whether [there had been undue influence]."

e. **No-contest clauses.** A no-contest clause in a will provides that any person who contests the will shall forfeit all interests he otherwise would have received under that will. If a beneficiary contesting the will is successful, the no-contest clause fails with the will. In most states and under the UPC, a beneficiary who unsuccessfully contests the will does not forfeit the legacy if the court finds that the beneficiary challenged the will in ***good faith*** and on the basis of ***probable cause***. A minority view gives full effect to no-contest clauses even if the losing contestant had probable cause for challenging the will. A challenge based on an action brought to construe the will, on jurisdictional grounds, or on the appointment of an executor, or to the accounting made by that person, is not considered a contest to the will that would result in a forfeiture under a no-contest clause.

3. **Fraud.**

a. **Definition.** Fraud consists of (i) false statements of material facts, (ii) known to be false by the party making the statements, (iii) made with the intention of deceiving the testator, (iv) which actually deceive the testator, and (v) which cause the testator to act in reliance on such statements.

1) **Fraud in the execution.** This type of fraud (also known as fraud in the factum) includes cases where the testator was tricked into signing a document not knowing it to be a will, and cases where one will is substituted for another.

2) **Fraud in the inducement.** This type of fraud includes those cases where the testator is fraudulently induced into making the will (*e.g.,* in return for a false promise of care).

b. **Constructive trust imposed where testator prevented from executing will--Latham v. Father Divine,** 299 N.Y. 22, 85 N.E.2d 168 (1949).

Latham v. Father Divine

1) **Facts.** The complaint brought by Ps (first cousins of decedent) alleged the following facts: The will of the decedent, Mary Sheldon Lyon, gave almost her whole estate to Father Divine, leader of a religious cult (D), two corporate defendants (Ds), and to Patience Budd, one of Father Divine's active followers (D). After making the

will, the decedent expressed a desire to revoke the will and to execute a new will by which the Ps would receive a substantial portion of the estate. The decedent, shortly before her death, had attorneys draft a new will for her with Ps receiving a substantial sum, but before she could execute this will, Ds by undue influence and physical force prevented the deceased from executing the will. The complaint brought by Ps alleged that Ds conspired to kill, and did kill, the deceased by means of a surgical operation performed by a doctor engaged by Ds without the consent or knowledge of any relatives of the deceased. The will the decedent did sign was probated under a compromise agreement in a proceeding in which Ps were not parties. The trial court upheld the complaint but the appellate court dismissed it on grounds of insufficiency. Ps appeal.

2) **Issue.** When an heir or devisee in a will prevents the testator from providing for one for whom he would have provided but for the interference of the heir or devisee, will such heir or devisee be deemed a trustee of the property received by him to the extent that the defrauded party would have received had not the deceased been interfered with?

3) **Held.** Yes. Judgment of the appellate court is reversed.

a) The general rule is that where an heir or devisee in a will prevents the testator from providing for one for whom he would have provided but for the interference of the heir or devisee, such heir or devisee will be deemed a trustee, by operation of law, of the property, real or personal, received by him from the testator's estate, to the amount or extent that the defrauded party would have received had not the intention of the deceased been interfered with.

b) This is not a proceeding to probate the will nor is it an attempt to accomplish a revocation of the earlier will. The complaint alleges that by force and fraud Ds kept the decedent from making a will in favor of Ps. We cannot say as a matter of law that no constructive trust can arise therefrom.

c) A constructive trust will be erected whenever necessary to satisfy the ends of justice. Here, the probated will has full effect but equity, in order to defeat the fraud, raises a trust in favor of those intended to be benefitted by the testator and compels the legatee to turn over the gift to them.

IV. EXECUTION: FORMS AND FORMALITIES

A. EXECUTION.

1. **Attested Wills.** The standard form of a will is one that is signed by the testator and witnessed by two witnesses pursuant to a formal attestation procedure.

   a. **Requirements of due execution.** For a will to be valid and admissible to probate, the testator must meet the formal requirements of due execution imposed by statutes of the appropriate state. These requirements vary from state to state, and generally include requiring the testator to sign at the end of the will and in the presence of all attesting witnesses. The testator might also be required to publish the will, *i.e.,* declare to the witnesses that the instrument is her will.

   b. **Requirement that both witnesses be present--*In re* Groffman,** 1 W.L.R. 733 (1969). *In re* Groffman

      1) **Facts.** The decedent, Charles Groffman, one evening while sitting in his lounge, asked David Block, the solicitor who prepared his will, and Julius Leigh, a friend, to witness his will. Block led the decedent out of the lounge into the dining room where the decedent took out his will, which had already been signed by the decedent. The decedent asked Block to sign the will and Block did so. Mr. Leigh, however, was left behind and was not present when Block signed. Block returned to the lounge, leaving the decedent in the dining room. Mr. Leigh went to the dining room and signed his name beneath Block's. In the meantime, Block had remained in the lounge. The son of the decedent (P) and Block (P), both executors under the will, propound the will to be probated. The widow of the decedent contests the will, contending that it was not validly acknowledged in the presence of two or more witnesses present at the same time.

      2) **Issue.** For a will to be valid, must it be signed by the testator in the presence of two or more witnesses present at the same time with the witnesses signing the will in the presence of the testator?

      3) **Held.** Yes. Probate denied.

         a) The Wills Act states that no will shall be valid unless it shall be in writing and executed in the manner hereafter mentioned: It shall be signed at the end by the testator or some other person in his presence and by his direction; and such signature shall be made or acknowledged by the testator in the presence of two or more witnesses present at the same time, and such witnesses shall attest and shall subscribe the will in the presence of the testator, but no form of attestation shall be necessary.

b) Here, there was no acknowledgment or signature by the testator in the presence of two or more witnesses at the same time. The arguments put forth—that there was sufficient acknowledgment since the attesting witnesses had an opportunity to see the will if they had wished to and that there was no break in the continuity of the transaction—are without merit. I am bound to pronounce against this will.

2. **Competency of Witnesses.** Witnesses must be competent. This generally means that at the time the will is executed the witness must be mature enough and of sufficient mental capacity to understand and appreciate the nature of the act he is witnessing and to be able to testify in court should this be necessary.

a. **Interested witnesses.** At common law, if an attesting witness was also a beneficiary of a will, the witness-beneficiary was not a competent witness and the will was denied probate. Today, however, most jurisdictions have interested witness statutes, which provide that if an attesting witness is also a beneficiary, the gift to the witness is void but the witness is a competent witness and the will may be probated.

Estate of Parsons

b. **Requirement of disinterestedness--Estate of Parsons,** 103 Cal. App. 3d 384, 163 Cal. Rptr. 70 (1980).

1) **Facts.** Three persons signed the will of the decedent, Geneve Parsons: Evelyn Nielson, Marie Gower (D), and Bob Warda, a notary public. Two of them, Nielson and Gower, were named in the will as beneficiaries. After the decedent's death, her will was admitted to probate. Nielson then filed a disclaimer of her bequest in the will. Thereafter, the assignees of the decedent's first cousin once removed and other first cousins once removed (Ps) claimed an interest in the estate on the ground that the devise to Gower was invalid. The trial court rejected that argument, and Ps appeal.

2) **Issues.**

a) Is a subscribing witness to a will who is named in the will as a beneficiary a disinterested subscribing witness as required by statute?

b) Is a subsequent disclaimer effective to transform an interested witness into a "disinterested" one?

3) **Held.** a) No. b) No. Judgment reversed.

a) Probate Code section 51 provides that a gift to subscribing witnesses is void unless there are two other disinterested witnesses to the will. Ps contend that a subsequent disclaimer is ineffective to transform an interested witness into a disinterested one. They assert that because there was only one disinterested witness at the time of attestation, the devise to D is void by operation of law. D, however, points to language in Probate Code section 190.6 that states "in every case, the disclaimer shall relate back for all purposes to the date of creation of the interest."

b) At common law a party to an action, or one who had a direct interest in its outcome, was not competent to testify in court because it was thought that an interested witness would be tempted to perjure himself in favor of his interest. If any one of the requisite number of attesting witnesses was also a beneficiary, then the entire will would fail. Parliament, in 1752, enacted a statute that saved the will by providing that the interest of an attesting witness was void; under such legislation, the competence of a witness to testify is restored by invalidating his gift. The majority of jurisdictions have similar statutes; section 51 falls into this category.

c) The essential function of a subscribing witness is performed when the will is executed. We believe section 51 looks in its operation solely to that time. It operates to insure that least two of the subscribing witnesses are disinterested.

d) Because we hold that section 51 looks solely to the time of execution and attestation of the will, it follows that a subsequent disclaimer will be ineffective to transform an interested witness into a disinterested one within the meaning of that section. D's reliance on section 190.6 is misplaced: that section serves to equalize the tax consequences of disclaimers as between heirs at law and testamentary beneficiaries.

3. **Recommended Method of Executing a Will.** The law of the decedent's domicile at death determines the validity of the will insofar as it disposes of personal property. The law of the state where real property is located determines the validity of the disposition of real property. Hence, the will should be executed so that it will be admitted to probate in all jurisdictions involved.

4. **Self-Proving Affidavit.** The great majority of states have adopted a self-proving affidavit procedure in which the testator and the witnesses, after executing the will, execute in front of a notary public an affidavit reciting that all of the requisites for due execution have been complied with. If the witnesses are dead or cannot be located or have moved far away, a self-proving affidavit permits the will to be probated.

5. **Safeguarding a Will.** An attorney's retention of a client's will may have the appearance of soliciting business, which is an unethical practice. Many states have statutes permitting deposit of wills with the clerk of the probate court.

6. **Mistake in Execution of a Will--*In re* Pavlinko's Estate,** 394 Pa. 564, 148 A.2d 528 (1959).

In re Pavlinko's Estate

a. **Facts.** The decedent, Vasil Pavlinko, by mistake signed the will of his wife, Hellen, and Hellen by mistake signed the will of her husband, Vasil. The lawyer who drew up the wills and his secretary signed as witnesses. A brother of Hellen, who was the residuary legatee of both wills, offered for probate as the will of the decedent, Vasil Pavlinko, the will that purported to be the will of Hellen Pavlinko, but which was signed by her husband. The trial court refused to probate the will. This appeal followed.

b. **Issue.** Will a court reform a will to allow probate where there is a mistake in execution of the will in that one party mistakenly signs the will of another?

c. **Held.** No. Judgment affirmed.

1) The Wills Act provides in clear language that every will shall be in writing and shall be signed by the testator at the end thereof. The court below correctly held that the paper that recited that it was the will of Hellen Pavlinko could not be probated as the will of Vasil Pavlinko and was a nullity.

2) To decide in favor of the residuary legatee, almost the entire will would have to be rewritten. Here, the paper signed was not the will of Vasil Pavlinko. He had executed no will and there was nothing to be reformed. He therefore died intestate and his property descends as at law. Were we to rewrite wills or make exceptions to the clear provisions of the Wills Act, the Act would become meaningless and would encourage fraudulent claims.

d. **Dissent.** The majority does not make a serious effort to effectuate the intent of the testator. The fact that some of the provisions in the will cannot be executed does not strike down the residuary clause, which is meaningful and stands independently. Some of the provisions are not effective, but their ineffectuality in no way bars the legality and validity of the residuary clause, which is complete in itself.

7. **Conditional Wills.** A conditional will is one that becomes operative if a stated event occurs.

8. **Statutory Wills.** Several states have authorized "statutory wills," which are short wills, with the wording spelled out in a statute. The will provides spaces for the testator to fill in the names of the beneficiaries. Statutory wills must be signed and attested in the same manner as any attested will.

9. **Holographic Wills.** A holographic will is one written in the testator's hand and signed by the testator; attesting witnesses are not required. About half of the states permit holographic wills. Under the UPC, a holographic will is valid, whether or not witnessed, if the signature and the material provisions are in the handwriting of the testator.

In re Will of Ranney

a. **Self-proved wills--*In re* Will of Ranney,** 589 A.2d 1339 (N.J. 1991).

1) **Facts.** Ranney (T) executed a four-page will before a notary and two witnesses. T acknowledged that the instrument was his will and he wanted the witnesses to act as witnesses. T signed the will on the unnumbered fourth page, and the witnesses simultaneously signed a self-proving affidavit on the fifth page. All parties believed they were complying with statutory attestation requirements. All signatures were notarized and the fifth page was stapled to the fourth. The attestation clause refers to the execution of the will in the past tense and states that each witness "signed the Will as witnesses." Upon T's death, the will was admitted to probate; T's wife contested,

claiming that the will failed to comply literally with the statutory formalities. The superior court ruled that the will did not contain the signatures of two witnesses. The appellate division reversed and found the affidavit to be a part of the will, and, therefore, the witnesses had signed. The supreme court granted T's wife's petition for certification.

2) **Issue.** Should an instrument purporting to be a last will and testament that includes the signature of two witnesses on an attached self-proving affidavit, but not on the will itself, be admitted to probate?

3) **Held.** Yes. Affirmed.

a) We do not agree with the appellate division that a will containing witnesses' signatures only on a self-proving affidavit literally complies with attestation requirements. The court's rationale was that an affidavit and an attestation clause are sufficiently similar to justify the conclusion that signatures on an affidavit, like signatures on the attestation clause, satisfy the requirement that the signatures be on the will. This conclusion fails to consider the basic differences between a subsequently-executed, self-proving affidavit and an attestation clause.

b) Attestation clauses (i) provide "prima facie evidence" that the will was signed by the testator in the presence of witnesses; (ii) permit probate when a witness forgets the circumstances of execution or dies before the testator; and (iii) express the present intent of the attestant to act as witness.

c) Self-proving affidavits are sworn statements that the will has been executed and has already been witnessed. The affidavit performs all the functions of the attestation clause and permits probate without requiring either witness to appear.

d) Here, affiants, intending to act as witnesses, signed the affidavit immediately after witnessing T's execution of the will.

e) Nothing in statutory language or history suggests that the legislature contemplated a subsequently-executed affidavit as a substitute for the attestation clause. The legislature did indicate its intention that subsequently-executed, self-proving affidavits be used solely in conjunction with duly executed wills. In the instant case, the affidavit does not comply with statutory requirements.

f) In limited circumstances, however, a will that "substantially complies" with statutory requirements may be admitted to probate. Other states, scholars, and treatises have determined that "substantial compliance better serves the goals of statutory formalities by permitting probate of formally-defective wills that nevertheless represent the intent of the testator."

g) Formalities in execution of wills (i) are meant to insure that the instrument reflects the testator's uncoerced intent; (ii) perform the function of providing uniformity in the organization, language, and content of a will; and (iii) provide a ritual that underscores the seriousness of the occasion. These purposes are often frustrated when rigid insistence on literal compliance invalidates a will that is the deliberate and voluntary act of the testator.

h) The variation of the UPC adopted by the state legislature in 1977 minimizes the formalities of execution: (i) witnesses are not required to sign in the presence of the testator and each other; (ii) a beneficiary who acts as witness is no longer prevented from taking; and (iii) unwitnessed holographic wills may be admitted to probate. Thus, we believe the legislature did not intend that a will should be denied probate because the witnesses signed in the wrong place.

i) Because an affidavit serves a unique function, we are reluctant to permit the signatures on an affidavit to both validate the signatures on the will and to render the will self-proving. However, if the witnesses, with the intent to attest, sign a self-proving affidavit, but do not sign the will or an attestation clause, clear and convincing evidence of their intent should be adduced to establish substantial compliance with the statute.

In re Estate of Johnson

b. Testamentary provisions not in handwriting of testator--*In re* Estate of Johnson, 129 Ariz. 307, 630 P.2d 1039 (1981).

1) Facts. The will of the decedent, Arnold H. Johnson, was on a printed will form available in various office supply stores. It contained certain printed provisions followed by blanks where the testator could insert any provisions he might desire. Barton Lee McLain and Marie Ganssle (Ps), two beneficiaries under the will, petitioned for formal probate of the instrument. The personal representative of the estate objected to the petition and filed a motion for summary judgment on the grounds that the instrument was invalid as a will, in that it was not attested by any witnesses, and that it did not qualify as a holographic will since the material provisions thereof were not in the handwriting of the testator. Ps filed a cross-motion for summary judgment, urging that the document constituted a holographic will. The trial court granted the motion of the personal representative. Ps appeal.

2) Issue. May an instrument be probated as a holographic will where it contains words not in the handwriting of the testator if such words are essential to the testamentary disposition?

3) Held. No. Judgment affirmed.

a) A will that does not comply with the statutory requirements for a will may still be valid as a holographic will, whether or not witnessed, if the signature and the material provisions are in the handwriting of the testator. An instrument may not be probated as a holographic will where it contains words not in the handwriting of the testator if such words are essential to the testamentary disposition. However, the mere fact that a testator used a blank form does not invalidate what would otherwise be a valid will if the printed words may be entirely rejected as surplusage.

b) Here, the only words that establish the requisite testamentary intent on the part of the decedent are found in the printed portion of the form. Though the decedent used the word "estate," this word alone is insufficient to indicate an *animus testandi.*

4) **Concurrence.** I concur in the decision because established legal principles indicate that the trial court did not err in refusing to admit the document to probate. However, the result in this case—which defeats the intent of the testator—justifies reappraisal of the statutorily expressed requirements of a holographic will in light of practical considerations.

c. **Informal will--Kimmel's Estate,** 123 A. 405 (Pa. 1924). Kimmel's Estate

1) **Facts.** A letter mailed by Kimmel, decedent, (D) to two of his children, who were named as beneficiaries therein, was admitted to probate. D died the afternoon of the day he wrote the letter. One of D's heirs objected to the admission and now appeals.

2) **Issues.**

a) May an informal letter be testamentary in character?

b) Is the signature "Father" sufficient to comply with the Wills Act?

3) **Held.** a) Yes. b) Yes. Decree affirmed and appeal dismissed.

a) Where a testator's purpose was to make a posthumous gift, we have held deeds, letters, powers of attorney, and an informal letter of requests as wills.

b) D's contingency here, "if enny thing hapens," was still existing when he died suddenly, and the question of testamentary intent is one of law for the courts.

c) D's words make it difficult to determine that he meant anything other than a testamentary gift, and his act of sending the letter to the persons for whom the gift was intended give further support to that determination.

d) The signature "Father" was intended as a complete signature. It was the method employed by D in signing all such letters and was mailed by D as a finished document.

B. REVOCATION OF WILLS

1. **Methods of Revocation.** A will may be revoked by one of three methods:

(i) By operation of law. If a testator gets married or divorced after executing a will, this change in status may revoke, by operation of law, all or part of the will.

(ii) By a later will or codicil. In these instances, language that expressly revokes the prior will should be included. Alternatively, a later will may revoke a prior will if there are inconsistent provisions in the later will that impliedly revoke the earlier will.

(iii) By a physical act of destruction. Generally, burning, tearing, or obliterating a material part of the will revokes it. Another person can do the tearing or burning if in the testator's presence and at his direction.

2. **Probate of Lost or Destroyed Wills.** In the absence of a statute, the fact that a will is lost, or is destroyed without the consent of the testator, does not prevent its probate, provided its contents are proved. Most states require proof of contents by testimony of persons who had knowledge of the contents of the will, as by having read the will or having heard it read. States that have statutes restricting the probate of lost or destroyed wills have narrowly construed them in order to permit probate.

3. **Revocation by Writing or Physical Act.** Under the UPC, a will or any part thereof is revoked (i) by a subsequent will which revokes the prior will or part of it expressly or by inconsistency; or (ii) by being burned, torn, canceled, obliterated, or destroyed, with the intent and for the purpose of revoking it by the testator or by another person in his presence and by his direction.

Harrison v. Bird

a. **Presumption will destroyed--Harrison v. Bird,** 621 So. 2d 972 (Ala. 1993).

1) **Facts.** Speer, decedent (D), executed a will naming Harrison as the main beneficiary. D later called her attorney, who had the original will, to revoke the will. The attorney and his secretary tore up the will and wrote a letter to D confirming this and enclosing the torn pieces. He informed D she was without a will. Upon D's death, the letter was found, but not the torn pieces. Letters of administration were granted to Bird. Harrison filed the copy of the revoked will for probate. The circuit court ruled (i) the will was not revoked; (ii) there could be no ratification of the destruction of the will as it had not been done pursuant to strict statutory requirements; and (iii) based on the fact that the pieces were not found, there was a presumption that D revoked the will herself. The court found this presumption had not been rebutted by Harrison and the duplicate was not D's will. The court held that D's estate should be administered as an intestate estate. Harrison appeals.

2) **Issue.** Was the evidence presented sufficient to rebut the presumption that D destroyed her will with the intent to revoke it?

3) **Held.** No. Affirmed.

(a) Even though a duplicate exists that was not in a D's possession, if D had possession of her will before her death, and the will is not found after her death, a presumption arises that D revoked her will and all duplicates.

(b) Harrison argued that the facts that D's attorney destroyed the will outside of D's presence, D had possession of the pieces, and such pieces were not found, are not sufficient to invoke the presumption of revocation. This argument is without merit.

b. **Attempted revocation by writing on paper upon which will is written--Thompson v. Royall,** 163 Va. 492, 175 S.E. 748 (1934).

Thompson v. Royall

1) **Facts.** On September 4, 1932, the decedent, Mrs. Knoll, signed a will consisting of five sheets of legal paper. On September 19, 1932, at the request of the decedent, her attorney and her executor took the will and codicil to her home, where she told the attorney, in the presence of her executor and another, to destroy both. But instead of destroying them, she decided to retain them as memoranda. Upon the back of the manuscript cover, in the handwriting of her attorney, signed by the decedent, there was written: "This will null and void and to be held only by (the executor) instead of being destroyed as a memorandum for another will if I desire to make same." The same notation was made on the back of the codicil, except that the name of the attorney was substituted for that of the executor. The jury found that the instruments were the last will and testament of the decedent. From an order sustaining this verdict and probating the will, this appeal was taken.

2) **Issue.** Must written words used for revocation by cancellation of a will be so placed as to physically affect the written portion of the will and not merely the blank parts of the paper on which the will is written?

3) **Held.** Yes. Judgment affirmed.

a) A will must be revoked as prescribed by statute, either by (i) some writing declaring an intention to revoke and executed in the same manner as a will or by (ii) cutting, tearing, burning, obliterating, canceling, or destroying the same with the intent to revoke.

b) Here, the notations made on the back of the will are not wholly in the handwriting of the testatrix, nor are her signatures attested by subscribing witnesses. Hence, under the statute they are ineffectual as "some writing declaring an intention to revoke."

c) Nor are the words sufficient to revoke the will by cancellation by physical act. The statute contemplates marks or lines across the written parts of the instrument or a physical defacement or some mutilation of the writing itself with the intent to revoke. If written words are used for the purpose, they must be placed as to physically affect the written portion of the will, not merely the blank parts of the will on which the will is written. The attempted revocation is therefore ineffectual.

c. **Partial revocation by physical act.** Most statutes authorize partial as well as total revocation of a will by physical act. Extrinsic evidence is generally admissible to show whether the testator intended only a partial revocation. In the absence of a statute expressly allowing partial revocation, several states refuse to recognize partial revocation by a physical act. In these jurisdictions, where the testator attempts to revoke a portion of the will, the act is given no effect. Thus, if testator crosses out a bequest to Tom, Tom takes the bequest despite the attempted cancellation. If the destroyed portion cannot be recreated by extrinsic evidence, only the destroyed portion fails; the remainder of the will is given effect.

4. **Dependent Relative Revocation and Revival.** The doctrine of dependent relative revocation is an equitable doctrine under which a court may disregard a revocation if the court finds that the act of revocation was premised on a mistake of law or fact and would not have occurred but for the testator's mistaken belief that another disposition of property was valid. The requirements of this doctrine are as follows:

(i) It must be shown that the testator at the time of revocation intended to make a new testamentary disposition which for some reason was ineffective.

(ii) It must be shown that there was an otherwise valid revocation.

(iii) It must be shown that the testator's intent was premised on a mistaken belief as to the validity of the new disposition.

(iv) It must be shown that invalidation of the revocation would be consistent with the testator's probable intent.

Carter v. First United Methodist Church of Albany

a. **Presumption against intestacy--Carter v. First United Methodist Church of Albany,** 271 S.E.2d 493 (Ga. 1980).

1) **Facts.** Tipton's, decedent's (D's) 1963 will was found at D's death among her personal papers together with a handwritten instrument dated May 22, 1978, captioned as a will but unsigned and unwitnessed. Pencil marks had been made through the property dispositions of the 1963 will. The superior court found D had indicated to her attorney that she wished to change her will but that she did not intend to revoke the 1963 will by scratchings. The 1963 will was admitted to probate. The caveator, Carter, appeals.

2) **Issue.** Was sufficient evidence presented to rebut the statutory presumption of revocation and to give rise to a presumption in favor of the propounder under the doctrine of dependent relative revocation?

3) **Held.** Yes. Affirmed.

a) We agree with First Methodist's contention that the Georgia statute which provides that intention to revoke will be presumed from the obliteration or canceling of a material portion of the will is inappropriately applied in this case.

b) The doctrine of dependent relative revocation, one of presumed intention, has as its purpose to effect the testator's intent. The mere fact that a testator intended to make a new ill, or made one which failed of effect, will not alone, in every case, prevent a cancellation or obliteration of a will from operating as a revocation. If it is clear that the cancellation and the making of the new will were parts of one scheme, and the revocation of the old will was so related to the making of the new will as to be dependent on it, then if the new will is not made, or is invalid, the old will, though canceled, should be given effect.

c) The stipulation that the 1963 will and the 1978 document were found together shifted the burden to Carter to prove that D would have preferred intestacy. The presumption against intestacy stands unrebutted.

b. **Doctrine applicable where later will revoked under mistaken belief that doing so reinstates prior will--Estate of Alburn,** 18 Wis. 2d 340, 118 N.W.2d 919 (1963). Estate of Alburn

1) **Facts.** The decedent, Ottilie L. Alburn, executed a will in Milwaukee, Wisconsin, in 1955 and left it with her attorney, George R. Affeldt. Thereafter, the decedent moved to Kankakee, Illinois, and in 1959 executed another will while residing there. She then moved to Fort Atkinson, Wisconsin, where she instructed her brother, Edwin Lehmann, to dispose of the Kankakee will, which she had torn up. He did so. Olga Lehmann, the wife of Edwin, testified that the decedent told her that she wanted the Milwaukee will to stand. A sister of the deceased, Adele Ruedisili, brought a petition for appointment of a special administrator, alleging that the deceased died intestate. Thereafter, a grandniece of the decedent, Viola Henkey, filed a petition for the probate of the Milwaukee will, and Lulu Alburn and Doris Alburn filed a petition for probate of the Kankakee Will. The county court heard all three petitions and held that the decedent destroyed the Kankakee will under the mistaken belief that by so doing she would revive the Milwaukee will. The court applied the doctrine of dependent relative revocation and held that the Kankakee will was admitted to probate. Ruedisili appeals.

2) **Issue.** Where a testator revokes a later will under the mistaken belief that by doing so she is reinstating a prior will, may the doctrine of dependent relative revocation be invoked to render the revocation ineffective?

3) **Held.** Yes. Judgment affirmed.

a) We are committed to the doctrine of dependent relative revocation. The usual situation for application of this doctrine arises where a testator executes one will and thereafter attempts to revoke it by making a later testamentary disposition which for some reason proves ineffective.

b) However, the doctrine has been applied to the unusual situation in which a testator revokes a later will under the mistaken belief that by doing so she is reinstating a prior will. In this situation, the doctrine of dependent relative revocation is invoked to render the revocation ineffective. The doctrine is based upon the testator's inferred intention. It is held that the destruction of the later document is intended to be conditional where it is accompanied by the express intent of reinstating a former will and where there is no explanatory evidence.

c) Here, we find that the trial court was correct in finding that the decedent had revoked the Kankakee will under the mistaken belief that she was thereby reinstating the prior Milwaukee will. The decedent's statement to Olga Lehmann that she wished her Milwaukee will to stand, the inference that she did not wish to die intestate, and the fact that she took no steps following the destruction of the Kankakee will to make a new will are sufficient evidence that she destroyed the Kankakee will under the mistaken belief that the Milwaukee will would control the disposition of her estate. Applying the doctrine of dependent relative revocation, therefore, the trial court was correct in holding that the attempted revocation of the Kankakee will was ineffective and admitting the will to probate.

4) **Comment.** Wisconsin law on revival of wills precluded the Milwaukee will from being revived.

c. **Revival.**

1) **Common law.** The common law rule, still adhered to in several states, is that no part of a will is effective until the death of the testator. Therefore, if Will #2 (which expressly revokes Will #1) is itself revoked before testator's death, Will #1 alone remains in effect and is operative upon testator's death. Destruction of Will #2 operates to "revive" Will #1.

2) **Modern law.** In most jurisdictions, a will, once revoked, is not revived unless republished by (i) reexecution or (ii) a later codicil under the doctrine of republication by codicil. Thus, revocation of a later will that contained language revoking an earlier will does not, by itself, revive the earlier will or any of its provisions. Under the UPC and in a substantial minority of states, destruction of Will #2 and its language of revocation may operate to revive Will #1, depending upon testator's intent. Such intent is established by testator's statements and by reference to all of the circumstances of the case.

5. **Revocation by Operation of Law: Change in Family Circumstances.** A change in family circumstances may revoke a will by operation of law. The law in these instances presumes an intent to revoke on the part of the testator.

a. **Marriage.** At common law, a marriage following the execution of a will had no effect on the will, but marriage followed by birth was held to revoke the will. Most states no longer follow the common law rule.

1) **States without statutes.** About half of the states have no statute dealing with the effect of marriage on a previously executed will. In most of these states marriage, by itself, does not affect the will. In a minority of states, however, the courts apply the common law rule noted above.

2) **States with statutes.** In most of the states having statutes dealing with the effect of marriage on a will, the will is only partially revoked. The marriage revokes the will only to the extent of providing the new spouse with an intestate share. After distribution of the spouse's intestate share, the will operates to distribute the remaining assets. In a minority of states, marriage after the execution of a will revokes the will in its entirety. Note that in either case, the will is not partially or totally revoked if (i) the will makes provision for the new spouse, (ii) the will provides that the spouse's omission was

intentional, or (iii) it appears that the will was made in contemplation of marriage.

b. **Divorce.** With regard to divorce, a majority of states have enacted statutes that hold a divorce partially revokes a will in that it automatically revokes the provisions of a will in favor of the former spouse. The will is read as though the former spouse predeceased the testator.

C. COMPONENTS OF A WILL

1. **Integration of Wills.** Integration of a will concerns the problem of what pages should constitute the will. Typically, the problem arises where the pages of a will have not been fastened together.

2. **Republication by Codicil.** Republication by codicil means an implied restatement or rewriting of the language of a valid will as of the time of republication. Republication by codicil has sometimes been used to validate a prior invalid will.

3. **Incorporation by Reference.** Pages that cannot be integrated because they were not present at the will's execution nevertheless may be given effect under the doctrine of incorporation by reference. This doctrine recognizes that a duly executed will may by appropriate reference incorporate into itself any extrinsic document or writing even though the other document was not properly executed. The following requirements must be met:

(i) The document must have been in existence at the time the will was executed;

(ii) The will must expressly refer to the document in the present tense;

(iii) The will must describe the document to be incorporated so clearly that there can be no mistake as to the identity of the document referred to; and

(iv) The testator must have intended to incorporate the extrinsic document as part of the overall testamentary plan.

a. **Notebook incorporated by reference--Clark v. Greenhalge,** 582 N.E.2d 949 (Mass. 1991). Clark v. Greenhalge

1) **Facts.** Testatrix (T) executed a will in 1977 which named Greenhalge (D) executor and principal beneficiary of any personal property except that designated by a memorandum known to D or in accord with T's wishes as expressed during T's life. D had helped T draft a document entitled "Memorandum" in 1972; T modified this list of specific bequests from time to time. T wished her friend Clark (P) to have a painting and so listed in a notebook T kept. T's nurses knew of her wish for P to have the painting and knew of the notebook and had observed T write in it. T executed two codicils in 1980; T amended some bequests and ratified her will in all other respects. Upon T's death, D was given T's notebook. D distributed T's property in accord with the will as amended, the 1972 memorandum,

and certain of the provisions in the notebook, including all of the property bequeathed to him in the notebook. However, he refused to give P the painting. P commenced an action to compel D to deliver the painting. The probate court found: (i) T wished P to have the painting, (ii) the notebook was a memorandum within the meaning of T's will, (iii) the notebook was in existence at the time of the codicils, which ratified the language of the will in its entirety, and (iv) the notebook was incorporated by reference into the terms of the will. D appeals.

2) **Issue.** Was T's notebook incorporated by reference into the terms of T's will?

3) **Held.** Yes. Affirmed.

a) A will may incorporate by reference any document not so executed and witnessed if it was in existence when the will was executed and is identified by clear and satisfactory proof as the paper referred to in the will.

b) The cardinal rule in the interpretation of wills is the intention of the testator shall prevail. T's language and the circumstances surrounding the execution of T's will and codicils are used to determine T's intent.

c) T intended to retain the right to alter and amend her bequests of tangible personal property in her will without having to formally amend the will. The mechanism T chose was a memorandum, and the notebook, although not titled "Memorandum," has as its purpose and is in the spirit of T's intent. T is not limited to only one memorandum.

d) Having been in existence at the time T executed her codicils, that republishing of T's intent incorporated the notebook by reference.

Johnson v. Johnson

b. **Validation of inoperative will by holographic codicil--Johnson v. Johnson,** 279 P.2d 928 (Okla. 1954).

1) **Facts.** The will of the decedent, Dexter G. Johnson, was on a single sheet of paper with three typewritten paragraphs. The typewritten portion was not dated, nor did the testator sign the typewritten portion or have it attested by two witnesses. At the bottom of the typewritten portion, the testator wrote in his handwriting a bequest to his brother James for $10. The proponents of the will introduced evidence showing that the testator was a practicing attorney who had prepared many wills; that he had told his insurance counselor that he had a will but it was out of date; that he had told his rental agent that the typewritten instrument was his will and that he wanted his rental agent to witness it; that his rental agent did not do so but later the decedent told him that he had changed his will by codicil and did not need him to sign it as a witness. The trial court refused to admit the instrument to probate. The appellate court affirmed. The proponents appeal.

2) **Issue.** May a valid holographic codicil republish and validate a will which was theretofore inoperative because it was not

signed, dated, or attested according to law?

3) **Held.** Yes. Judgment reversed and the case remanded with directions to enter the will for probate.

a) There is no question that the typewritten instrument was not signed, dated, or attested. A will may be so defective, as here, that it is not entitled to probate, but if testamentary in character it is a will nonetheless.

b) By definition a codicil is a supplement to an existing will made by the testator to alter, enlarge, or restrict its provisions and it must be testamentary in character. A codicil need not be called a codicil; rather, it is the intention to add a codicil that is controlling. Here, the handwritten words are testamentary in character and they make an addition to the provisions of the will already in existence. Further, the codicil meets all the requirements of a valid holographic codicil. It is written, dated, and signed by the testator. The fact that it was written on the same piece of paper as the typewritten will does not invalidate the codicil.

c) The general rule is that a codicil validly executed operates as a republication of the will no matter what defects may have existed in the execution of the earlier document, that the instruments are incorporated as one, and that a proper execution of the codicil extends also to the will. We therefore hold that the valid holographic codicil incorporated the prior will by reference and republished and validated the prior will as of the date of the codicil.

4) **Concurrence.** All rules of construction are designed for the purpose of effectuating the intent of the testator. To hold otherwise would permit a contrary disposition of testator's property against the purpose for which the statutory provisions were aimed.

5) **Dissent.** The typewritten part is not a will and the handwritten part is not a codicil. The testator intended the typewritten portion to be part of his will, not the completed will. I can never subscribe to the proposition that a holographic codicil will validate as a will an instrument that is typewritten, unfinished, undated, unsigned, and unattested. Property may descend by will when the will is executed in conformity with the statutes.

4. **Acts of Independent Significance.** Under the UPC, a will may dispose of property by reference to acts and events which have significance apart from their effect upon the dispositions made by the will. The execution or revocation of a will by another person is such an event (*e.g.*, "I devise Blackacre to the persons named as beneficiaries in my sister's will.")

D. CONTRACTS RELATING TO WILLS

Contracts to make a will, contracts not to revoke a will, and contracts not to make a will are kinds of contracts pertaining to wills. In these instances, the law of contracts applies. A will in violation of a valid contract made by the testator, while it may be probated, will be subject to contractual remedies (*e.g.*, imposition of constructive trust).

1. **Contracts to Make a Will.** Many states have enacted statutes requiring that a contract to make a gift by will be in writing. If the promisor fails to make the promised testamentary gift, the promisee has a cause of action against the promisor's estate for damages for breach of contract. The measure of damages is the value of the property promised to be devised or bequeathed. However, if the case involves a promise to make a devise or bequest of specific property, the usual remedy is to grant a constructive trust for the promisee's benefit.

2. **Contracts Not to Revoke.** These contracts typically arise when a husband and wife have executed joint and mutual wills. A number of states have enacted statutes requiring that any agreement relating to a will, including a contract not to revoke a will, be in a writing executed with certain formalities. The mere execution of reciprocal wills containing identical provisions does not constitute evidence that wills were contractual.

3. **Joint Wills.** A joint will is the will of two or more persons executed as a single testamentary instrument. In contrast to joint wills, reciprocal wills, sometimes called mirror wills, are separate wills of two or more persons which contain reciprocal provisions.

Shimp v. Huff

a. **Elective share in conflict with will contract--Shimp v. Huff,** 556 A.2d 252 (Md. 1989).

1) **Facts.** Shimp (D) executed a joint will with Clara, his first wife, which this court determined in a prior hearing to operate as a binding contract and thereby limit the survivor's right to dispose of property by a testamentary plan different from that in the will. After his first wife's death, D did not execute a new will. Following D's death, his second wife, Lisa Mae, filed an election for her statutory share. The personal representatives refused to pay. Lisa Mae filed suit for declaratory judgment; the circuit court held since the contract beneficiaries' rights arose before the second marriage, they had priority over Lisa Mae. Lisa Mae appeals.

2) **Issue.** May a surviving wife take an elective share when her claims are in conflict with claims under a contract to convey by will?

3) **Held.** Yes. Judgment vacated.

(a) A review of decisions shows that in cases where there is a divorce or separation agreement, where one spouse agrees to devise property to the other, and the decedent has breached the contract by executing a nonconforming will or by dying intestate, the claimants generally proceed under a theory of specific performance. After-acquired rights of third parties are equitable considerations in adjudication. Courts consider such factors as: (i) the surviving spouse's notice of the contract, (ii) length of the marriage, and (iii) public policy concerning the marriage relationship. The outcomes have gone both ways.

(b) Where a decedent has executed a will conforming to the contract, the courts have analyzed the conflicting claims by characterizing the competing claimants as creditors or legatees and applying priority statutes.

(c) We find the conflict should be resolved based on the public policy which surrounds a marriage and underlies an elective share statute. The contract beneficiaries' rights under the contract were limited by the possibility that the survivor might remarry and the subsequent spouse might elect against the will. The contract beneficiaries' claims are subordinate to Lisa Mae's superior right.

V. WILL SUBSTITUTES

A. CONTRACTS WITH PAYABLE-ON-DEATH PROVISIONS

1. **Life Insurance.** The issue in these cases includes whether a beneficiary of a life insurance policy can be changed by will. A majority of courts hold that where the policy requires written notice of change of beneficiary filed with the insurance company, the beneficiary of a life insurance policy may not be changed by will.

Wilhoit v. Peoples Life Insurance Co.

a. **Successor beneficiary not permitted in life insurance contract--Wilhoit v. Peoples Life Insurance Co.,** 218 F.2d 887 (7th Cir. 1955).

1) **Facts.** Roley Wilhoit was the insured of a $5,000 life insurance policy issued by Century Life and reinsured by Peoples Life (D). After Roley's death in 1930, Sarah Wilhoit, his widow and beneficiary, arranged to leave the amount due her on deposit with Peoples Life on specified terms, including that upon her death any remaining funds plus accrued interest would be paid to her brother, Robert Owens. Robert Owens died in 1932 leaving all his property by will to Thomas Owens (D). Sarah Wilhoit died in 1951. Her will purported to leave the funds on deposit with Peoples Life to Robert Wilhoit (P). Both P and Thomas Owens claim the funds; Peoples Life refused to recognize P's claim. The district court granted P's motion for summary judgment, and Thomas Owens appeals.

2) **Issue.** Where the proceeds of a life insurance policy are to be disposed of in accordance with its provisions, may a beneficiary of the policy designate a successor beneficiary to take upon the death of the primary beneficiary?

3) **Held.** No. Judgment affirmed.

a) D relies on cases which have held that the proceeds of a life insurance policy are to be disposed of in accordance with its provisions, and that a beneficiary, if authorized by the policy, may designate a successor beneficiary to take on the death of the primary beneficiary. This contention is without merit if we do not accept the premise that the agreement between Sarah Wilhoit and the company was an insurance contract or an agreement thereto. We reject this premise and hold that the arrangement between the parties was the result of a separate and independent agreement, unrelated to the terms of the policy.

b) Sarah Wilhoit did not take advantage of the investment provision in the insurance policy by which she could have left the proceeds with the company on the terms and conditions stated therein. Instead, she accepted the proceeds and surrendered the policy. Only later did she by letter make her own proposal, which was accepted by the company on conditions which differed materially from those contained in the policy. We agree with P, therefore, that the provision in the agreement by which Robert Owens was to take the funds in the event of her death was an invalid testamentary disposition.

c) Finally, it is not immaterial to take into consideration the intentions of the parties. Here, Sarah Wilhoit in her will specifically devised the funds in controversy to P. It thus appears plain that she did not intend the funds to go to the successors of Robert Owens but that, after his death, she thought she had a right to dispose of the funds as she saw fit. While we recognize that the intention of the parties is not controlling, we think that it is entitled to some consideration.

b. Change of beneficiary of life insurance policy by will--Cook v. Equitable Life Assurance Society, 428 N.E.2d 110 (Ind. App. 1981).

Cook v. Equitable Life Assurance Society

1) **Facts.** Decedent Douglas Cook had purchased a whole life insurance policy in 1953 naming his wife at that time, Doris, as the beneficiary. In 1965, Douglas and Doris were divorced. The divorce decree made no provision regarding the insurance policy. After the divorce Douglas ceased paying the premiums on his life insurance policy, and the insurance company notified him in 1965 that his whole life policy was automatically converted to a paid-up term policy. The policy contained a provision allowing the owner to change the beneficiary by written notice provided that the change is endorsed on the policy by the insurance company. In 1965, Douglas married Margaret, and a son, Daniel, was born to them. In 1976, Douglas made a holographic will in which he bequeathed his insurance policy to his wife and son.

Decedent's insurer brought an interpleader action to determine whether decedent's former wife, Doris, the named beneficiary on the life insurance policy, or decedent's widow and child, Margaret and Daniel, to whom decedent had bequeathed such insurance policy in a holographic will, were entitled to the proceeds of decedent's policy. The circuit court entered summary judgment in favor of the former wife, and the widow and child appeal.

2) **Issue.** Can a beneficiary of a life insurance policy be changed by the testator's intent as expressed in his will?

3) **Held.** No. Judgment affirmed.

a) An insured's attempt to change the beneficiary of a life insurance policy by will, without more, is ineffectual.

b) It is in the interest of insurance companies to require and to follow specified procedures in the change of beneficiaries so that they may pay benefits to persons properly entitled to them without subjecting themselves to claims by others of whose rights they had no notice or knowledge. These procedures are also in the interest of beneficiaries themselves, since insurance companies will not feel obligated to withhold payment until a will has been probated, in fear of litigation which might result from having paid the wrong party.

c) Substantial compliance with the requirements of an insurance policy will be sufficient to change a beneficiary as long as the insured has done everything in his power to effect such a change. Under these facts, there is no indication that Douglas took any action in the 14 years between his divorce from Doris and his death, other than the making of the will, to change the beneficiary of his life insurance policy from Doris to Margaret and Daniel. If Douglas had wanted to change the beneficiary, he had ample time and opportunity to comply with the policy requirements.

d) Public policy requires that the insurer, insured, and beneficiary should be able to rely on the certainty that policy provisions pertaining to the naming and changing of beneficiaries will control except in extreme situations.

2. **Nontestamentary Transfers at Death.** Under the UPC, written agreements to pay, after the death of the decedent, money or other benefits to a person designated by the decedent in either the instrument or a separate writing are deemed to be nontestamentary.

Estate of Hillowitz

a. **Investment club proceeds--Estate of Hillowitz,** 238 N.E.2d 723 (N.Y. 1968).

1) **Facts.** Hillowitz's executors (Ps) brought a discovery proceeding in surrogate court against Hillowitz's widow (D) to have determined whether Hillowitz's investment club contract to have Hillowitz's share paid to his widow upon his death was an invalid attempt to make a testamentary disposition of property. The surrogate court ruled for D; the appellate division for Ps. D appeals.

2) **Issue.** Is a partnership agreement which provides that, upon the death of one partner, his interest shall pass to the surviving partner or partners, resting in contract, valid?

3) **Held.** Yes. Reversed.

a) There is no difference between a contract providing for surviving partner(s) and one providing for a surviving widow.

b) This is a third-party beneficiary contract, performable at death, and it need not conform to the requirements of the statute of wills.

c) Other such contracts include (i) a contract to make a will, (ii) an inter vivos trust in which the settlor reserves a life estate, and (iii) an insurance policy.

B. JOINT TENANCY AND MULTIPLE-PARTY BANK ACCOUNTS

1. **Types of Accounts.** Multiple-party bank accounts include joint and survivor accounts, payable-on-death accounts, agency accounts, and savings account trusts.

2. **Joint Bank Account: Lack of Donative Intent--Franklin v. Anna National Bank of Anna,** 140 Ill. App. 3d 533, 488 N.E.2d 1117 (1986).

Franklin v. Anna National Bank of Anna

   a. **Facts.** The executor of decedent's estate brought an action against the bank alleging that funds in a joint savings account were the property of the estate. The bank interpleaded decedent's sister-in-law, Cora Goddard, who asserted her right to the money as a surviving joint owner.

   Decedent had had eye surgery and, according to Goddard, was losing his eyesight. Goddard subsequently moved in with decedent to help him. Goddard claims that she and decedent went to the bank to have his money put in both their names so she could get money when they needed it. She alleges that "he wanted me to have this money if I outlived him." Goddard testified that she did not deposit any money in the savings account to which she and the decedent had signed a signature card. She made no withdrawals, though she once took decedent to the bank so he could make a withdrawal. Later in the year, Enola Franklin began to care for decedent. Decedent sent Franklin to the bank to deliver a handwritten letter signed by decedent in which he attempted to change the name of the joint tenant to Franklin. The bank, however, would not remove a signature from a signature card based on a letter. Thus, the most recent signature card the bank had for the savings account was signed by decedent and Goddard.

   The trial court found that Goddard was the sole owner of the funds in the savings account by right of survivorship as surviving joint tenant, and that no part of the funds became part of decedent's estate. Franklin argues that decedent did not intend to make a gift of the savings account to Goddard. After remand by the appellate court, the circuit court entered judgment for Goddard, and the executor appealed.

   b. **Issue.** Does evidence of lack of donative intent at the time of creation of a joint tenancy sever the joint tenancy?

   c. **Held.** Yes. Judgment of the circuit court reversed.

      1) The instrument creating a joint tenancy account presumably speaks the whole truth. In order to go behind the terms of a joint tenancy agreement, one claiming adversely thereto has the burden of establishing by clear and convincing evidence that a gift was not intended.

2) The form of a joint tenancy agreement is not conclusive regarding the intention of the depositors between themselves.

3) Evidence of lack of donative intent must relate back to the time of creation of the joint tenancy. The decision of the donor, made subsequent to the creation of the joint tenancy, that he did not want the proceeds to pass to the survivor would not, in itself, be sufficient to sever the joint tenancy.

4) It is proper to consider events occurring after creation of the joint account in determining whether the donor actually intended to transfer his interest in the account at his death to the surviving joint tenant.

5) Evidence that, nine months after adding his sister-in-law's name to his savings account, the decedent had attempted to remove her name and substitute another and that decedent had written letters to the bank indicating that he might lose his sight and be unable to transact his own banking business, established that decedent had made his sister-in-law a signatory of the joint account for his own convenience, in case he could not get his money, and not with the intent to effect a present gift. It does not appear that Goddard ever exercised any authority or control over the joint account. Such evidence thus established that, upon decedent's death, money in the joint account was the property of decedent's estate.

3. Stock Certificates Held in Joint Tenancy. In *Blanchette v. Blanchette*, 362 Mass. 518, 287 N.E.2d 459 (1972), Robert Blanchette worked for AT&T and began to buy shares of stock in the company. When he acquired the shares, he told his wife, Marie (P), that he put them in both their names as joint tenants. The certificates were issued at his request: "Robert L. Blanchette & Mrs. Marie A. Blanchette, Joint Tenants." He executed assignments to himself and Marie "as Joint Tenants with rights of survivorship and not as Tenants in Common." Robert never told P that she owned half the stock. The certificates were kept in the wardrobe of their bedroom up to the time they separated; at that time P demanded one of the two bankbooks but did not ask for any of the stock. No evidence existed that she made any claim to the stock before the parties' divorce. P brought a petition in connection with the divorce to determine her interest in the stock. The petition was referred to a master, who held that Robert never at any time indicated that he intended to transfer any present interest in the stock to his wife. The master found that the words "joint tenants" were used because this was the only form of issuance authorized by the company that would approximate Robert's desire to make his wife his beneficiary if he died. On appeal, the court determined that certificates of stock held in joint tenancy between a husband and wife may be paid to the wife upon the death of the husband without the arrangement being declared testamentary and void.

The court found that the intention was clear that the husband was to have sole control during his life and that whatever should remain at his death, if the wife survived, should ripen into full ownership by her. The finding that no present gift was intended would have the effect of frustrating the intention of the parties by rendering their arrangement testamentary and void. The court avoided this result by finding a present gift of a future interest, subject to a reserved life estate in the husband and subject to his power to revoke his wife's interest.

C. JOINT TENANCIES IN LAND

A joint tenancy or a tenancy by the entirety in land is a common method of avoiding the cost and delay of probate. Upon the death of one joint tenant or tenant by the entirety, the survivor owns the property absolutely. A joint tenant cannot devise his share by will. If a joint tenant wants to give his share to someone other than the cotenant, he must sever the joint tenancy during life, converting it into a tenancy in common. A creditor of a joint tenant must seize the joint tenant's interest during life. At death the joint tenant's interest expires and there is nothing for the creditor to reach.

D. DEEDS OF LAND

Deeds that reserve a life estate in the grantor with a right to revoke the conveyance during the lifetime of the grantor are deemed to be testamentary in character and should not be used.

1. **Instrument Declared Void Where Grantor Reserves Life Estate with Unlimited Power to Sell--Wright v. Huskey,** 592 S.W.2d 899 (Tenn. 1979).

Wright v. Huskey

a. **Facts.** Sallie Wright (P) executed an instrument which conveyed about 56 acres of land to her daughter Elva McNutt and her son-in-law Ernest Turnbow, as tenants in common, subject to the reservation that P would retain a life estate in the property with the right to sell all or part of the property without McNutt or Turnbow signing the deed. After delivery of the instrument, Turnbow remarried and later died, leaving Sharon Turnbow Huskey (D) as his only child and sole heir at law. D learned that P was planning to sell the property and filed in the register's office a notice of lis pendens identifying the property. P then filed this lawsuit to clear title to the property and to cancel the notice of lis pendens. The trial court held for P, finding that the instrument was a deed which conveyed a present vested remainder to the grantees with the reservation of the absolute power to revoke the conveyance of the remainder interest by sale during the life of the grantor, and held that the grantor holds a life estate in the realty with the absolute power to sell the property. D appeals.

b. **Issue.** Is an instrument where a grantor reserves a life estate in property with unlimited power to sell it testamentary in character and thus void as not complying with the statutory requirements necessary to constitute a valid will?

c. **Held.** Yes. Judgment reversed.

1) The instrument before the court expressly reserves in the grantor a life estate with the right to sell. In other cases, the instruments were held to be deeds conveying a present interest but reserving a life estate in the grantor. But in those cases the grantor did not reserve the right to revoke the conveyance during his lifetime.

2) In determining whether an instrument is testamentary in character or a deed, the intent of the grantor is controlling. In order

that it be held a deed it must convey an interest to take effect in praesenti, though the enjoyment rest in futuro. Here, P testified by deposition that the purpose of the instrument was to defeat any claim her husband might assert against the property by a divorce proceeding or as her survivor, and still reserve use of the property with the unlimited right to sell. The stated purpose shows that she did not intend to grant a present interest. We hold that when a grantor reserves a life estate with unlimited power to sell, she retains the fee—no interest in praesenti passes to the grantee—and the instrument is not a deed. Being testamentary in character and not complying with the requirements for a will, the instrument is void.

E. REVOCABLE TRUSTS

1. **Introduction.** A revocable trust is one where the settlor retains the power to revoke, alter, or amend the trust and the right to trust income during his lifetime. All jurisdictions recognize the validity of a trust in which the settlor reserves the power to revoke during life.

2. **Retention of Control by Settlor.** If the settlor retains numerous powers and lacks the true trust "intent," the trust may be ruled illusory. However, as long as the trust creates some interests in some category of beneficiaries, courts will recognize a valid nontestamentary trust even though the settlor retains extensive powers.

Farkas v. Williams

a. **Creation of valid inter vivos trust notwithstanding control retained by settlor/trustee--Farkas v. Williams**, 5 Ill. 2d 417, 125 N.E.2d 600 (1955).

1) **Facts.** Albert B. Farkas, who died intestate, purchased on four occasions during his life the stock of Investors Mutual, Inc., instructing it, by means of a written application, to issue the stock in his name "as trustee for Richard J. Williams." Farkas also signed separate declarations of trust, all of which were identical except as to dates. In each of these declarations, Farkas reserved to himself as settlor the following powers: (i) the right to receive during his lifetime all cash dividends; (ii) the right at any time to change the beneficiary or revoke the trust; and (iii) upon sale or redemption of any portion of the trust property, the right to retain the proceeds therefrom for his own use. Coadministrators of the estate (Ps) bring this action to have declared their legal rights in the four stock certificates. The circuit court found that the declarations were testamentary in character and, not having been executed with the formalities of a will, were invalid, and directed that the stock be awarded to Ps as assets of the estate of Albert Farkas. The appellate court affirmed. Williams and Investors Mutual (Ds) appeal.

2) **Issues.**

a) Does the fact that the interest of a beneficiary is contingent upon a certain state of facts existing at the time of the settlor's death indicate that no present interest is acquired in the subject matter of a trust, and hence render a trust instrument testamentary in character?

b) Does the retention of power by a settlor to sell or redeem stock and keep the proceeds for his own use, to change the beneficiary, and to revoke the trust indicate that the settlor has retained such control over the subject matter of a trust so as to render a trust instrument testamentary in character?

3) **Held.** a) No. b) No. Reversed and remanded.

a) Williams acquired a present interest in the subject matter of the intended trusts. Farkas, immediately after execution of these instruments, could not deal with the stock the same as if he owned the property absolutely. As trustee, Farkas is held to have intended to take on those obligations that are expressly set out in the instrument, as well as those fiduciary obligations implied by law.

(1) The fact that the trust instrument provides that "the decease of the beneficiary before my death shall operate as a revocation of this trust" does not change the result. The disposition is not testamentary and the intended trust is valid even though the interest of the beneficiary is contingent upon the existence of a certain state of facts at the time of the settlor's death.

(2) Admittedly, absent this provision, Williams's interest would have been greater. But to say that his interest would have been greater is not to say that he did not have a beneficial interest during the lifetime of Farkas.

b) Farkas did not retain such control over the subject matter of the trust as to render the trust instruments testamentary in character. The retention by the settlor of the power to revoke, even when coupled with a reservation of a life interest in the trust property, does not render the trust inoperative for want of execution of a will.

(1) A more difficult problem is posed by the fact that Farkas is also trustee and as such is empowered to vote, sell, and otherwise deal in and with the subject matter of the trusts. Here, the control reserved is not as great as in those cases where the power is reserved to the owner as settlor, for as trustee he must conduct himself in accordance with standards applicable to trustees generally. Williams would have had an enforceable claim against Farkas's estate were Farkas to have improperly dissipated the stock.

(2) Another factor in determining whether an inter vivos trust exists is the formality of the transaction. Here, the stock certificates in question were issued in Farkas's name as trustee for Williams. He thus manifested his intention in a solemn and formal manner.

In re Estate and Trust of Pilafas

b. **Inter vivos trust revoked--*In re* Estate and Trust of Pilafas,** 836 P.2d 420 (Ariz. 1992).

1) **Facts.** Decedent (D) executed a trust appointing himself trustee. The agreement directed that upon D's death, a portion of the trust estate would be distributed to eight nonprofit organizations (Os). The remaining portion was to be held in various trusts. Two of D's children were explicitly omitted. The trust included a revocation/amendment provision which D exercised twice. On the occasion of the second amendment in 1987, after D's divorce, D simultaneously executed a will which gave the residue of his estate to the trust. Subsequently, D's relationships with his children (Cs) improved. During the last month of his life, D indicated to his attorney his intention to revise his estate plan to include all his children. D's attorney had given D the originals of the trust, the amendments, and the will immediately after they were executed. Upon D's death, D's son unsuccessfully searched D's house for the documents. Cs testified D fastidiously saved important documents and that D was a man of direct action who had been known to tear or discard papers that offended him. D's son filed a petition for appointment of a special administrator and a special trustee, a petition for adjudication of intestacy and determination of revocation of trust, and asked the court to authorize him to transfer all trust assets to D's estate. Os objected, seeking a determination D had revoked neither his will nor the trust. The trial court granted Cs' motion for summary judgment. Os appeal.

2) **Issues.**

a) Did appellees present sufficient evidence that D revoked his will?

b) Did the trial court err in determining D effectively revoked his inter vivos trust?

3) **Held.** a) Yes. Affirmed. b) Yes. Reversed.

a) Cs' argument relies on the common law principle that if a will is last seen in a testator's possession and cannot be found after his death, there is a presumption that the testator destroyed the will.

b) Cs submitted affidavits tending to prove (i) D took possession of his will, (ii) he meticulously kept important papers, and (iii) a diligent search did not uncover the will. Os offered no evidence to rebut.

c) A trust, unlike a will, involves the present transfer of a property interest to beneficiaries. These interests can only be taken from the beneficiaries (i) in accord with a trust provision, (ii) by their own acts, or (iii) by a court decree.

d) D's trust provided for revocation only by written instrument.

e) In accord with the Restatement (Second) of Torts, section 330, and accompanying commentary, we hold that D could only revoke his trust in the manner provided for in the trust instrument. If a settlor reserves a power to revoke the trust by a transaction inter vivos, for example, by a notice to the trustee, he cannot revoke his trust by his will.

c. **Creditors may reach trust assets over which the settlor had control at the time of his death--State Street Bank & Trust Co. v. Reiser,** 7 Mass. App. Ct. 633, 389 N.E.2d 768 (1979).

State Street Bank & Trust Co. v. Reiser

1) **Facts.** The decedent, Wilfred A. Dunnebier, created an inter vivos trust with the power to amend or revoke the trust, and conveyed to the trust the capital stock of five closely held corporations. Immediately following the execution of the trust, the decedent executed a will under which he left his residuary estate to the trust he had established. Thereafter, the decedent applied to the State Street Bank & Trust Co. (P) for a loan, which was later granted. Approximately four months after he borrowed the money, the decedent died and his estate had insufficient assets to pay the entire indebtedness due the Bank. P seeks to reach the assets of the inter vivos trust.

2) **Issue.** Where a settlor places property in trust, may the settlor's creditors reach those assets owned by the trust over which the settlor had control at the time of his death?

3) **Held.** Yes. So ordered.

a) We hold that where a person places property in trust and reserves the right to amend and revoke, or to direct disposition of principal and income, the settlor's creditors may reach, in satisfaction of the settlor's debts to them, those assets owned by the trust over which the settlor had such control at the time of his death as would have enabled the settlor to use the trust assets for his own benefit.

b) Assets which pour over into such a trust as a consequence of the settlor's death over which the settlor did not have control during his life are not subject to the reach of creditors.

3. **Testamentary "Pour-Over" into an Inter Vivos Trust.** Pour-over wills are useful to establish an inter vivos trust which later merges into the estate after the death of the settlor. The settlor sets up a revocable inter vivos trust naming X as trustee. The settlor then transfers to X his stocks and bonds. The settlor then executes a will devising the residue of his estate to X, as trustee, to hold under the terms of the inter vivos trusts.

a. **Uniform Testamentary Additions to Trusts Act.** This Act validates a testamentary gift to any preexisting trust evidenced by a writing, provided the trust is sufficiently described in the testator's will. This is so whether the preexisting trust was created by the testator or by a third person and whether it was modifiable or in fact modified. The size and extent of the trust corpus during the testator's lifetime is likewise immaterial. The Act specifically validates gifts to either funded or unfunded life insurance trusts, even where the testator has reserved all rights of ownership in the policies.

Clymer v. Mayo

b. **Effect of divorce on validity of dispositions to former spouse made by revocable inter vivos trust--Clymer v. Mayo,** 393 Mass. 754, 473 N.E.2d 1084 (1985).

1) **Facts.** Clara Mayo (decedent) died in 1981. She had been married to James Mayo from 1953 to 1978. The couple had no children, and decedent's sole heirs at law are her parents. As a consequence of a $300,000 gift to the couple from decedent's parents in 1971, she and James executed new wills and indentures of trust in 1973 wherein each spouse was made the other's principal beneficiary. Under the terms of decedent's will, James was to receive her personal property. The residue of her estate was to "pour over" into the inter vivos trust she created that same day.

Decedent's trust instrument named herself and John Hill as trustees. As the donor, decedent retained the right to amend or revoke the trust at any time by written instrument delivered to the trustees. In the event that James survived decedent, the trust estate was to be divided into two parts. Trust A was the marital deduction trust. The balance of decedent's estate, or the entire estate if James did not survive her, composed Trust B. Trust B provided for five specific bequests. After those gifts were satisfied, the remaining trust assets were to be held for the benefit of James for life. Upon James's death, the assets in Trust B were to be held for the benefit of the nephews and nieces of decedent living at the time of her death. When all of these nephews and nieces reached the age of 30, the trust was to terminate and its remaining assets were to be divided equally between Clark University and Boston University.

The Mayos divorced on January 3, 1978. The court incorporated into the decree a stipulation of the parties' property settlement. Under the terms of that settlement, James waived any right, title or interest in decedent's securities, savings accounts and certificates, retirement fund, furniture, and art.

The administrator of decedent's estate petitioned for instructions on the effect of decedent's divorce on the estate's administration. Decedent's parents brought actions for declaratory and equitable relief to preclude James from participating in the estate and to remove the administrator. The probate and family court dismissed the parents' action, and appeal was taken.

2) **Issues.**

a) Did decedent create a valid trust despite the fact that it was not funded until her death?

b) Does a statute which revokes any disposition to a former spouse made by will apply to revoke dispositions to the former spouse made by a revocable inter vivos trust which has no funding or practical significance until decedent's death?

3) **Held.** a) Yes. b) Yes. Judgment affirmed in part, reversed in part, and remanded.

a) In light of the Massachusetts statute governing "pour-over" devises, decedent's inter vivos trust executed contemporaneously with her will was valid despite the fact that the trust did not receive funding until decedent's death.

b) Probate courts are empowered to terminate or reform a trust in whole or in part where its purposes have become impossible to achieve and the settlor did not contemplate continuation of the trust under new circumstances.

c) Decedent's former husband could not take under the trust established by decedent, inasmuch as such transfer was intended by its terms to qualify for a marital deduction for federal estate tax purposes, and such objective became impossible after the parties' divorce. Therefore the trust was effectively terminated.

d) Reference to an existing trust in a will's pour-over clause is not of itself sufficient to incorporate that trust by reference without evidence that testator intended such result.

e) The Massachusetts statute which operated to revoke any disposition to a former spouse "made by the will" was also applicable to revoke dispositions to a decedent's divorced husband made in a revocable inter vivos trust executed contemporaneously with her will, inasmuch as such trust had no funding or practical significance until decedent's death.

f) Inasmuch as decedent had no siblings, and thus had no nephews or nieces who were blood relations, decedent's bequest in the indenture of trust to "nephews and nieces of the donor" created a latent ambiguity. The trial court therefore properly considered extrinsic evidence to determine that decedent intended the bequests to go to the nephews and nieces of her former husband.

g) The statute which operated to revoke any testamentary disposition to a former spouse did not apply to revoke decedent's bequest in indenture of trust to her former husband's nieces and nephews.

4. Use of Revocable Trusts in Estate Planning.

a. Consequences during life of settlor. During the life of the settlor, a revocable trust may be used to relieve the settlor of the burdens of financial management, to deal with the contingency of the settlor's incompetency, and to clarify title and ownership of assets. There are no federal tax advantages in creating a revocable trust, since trust income is taxable to the settlor regardless of to whom it is paid.

b. Consequences at death of settlor. Upon the death of the settlor, a revocable trust can be used to avoid probate. Under a revocable trust continuing after the settlor's death, income and principal can be disbursed to the beneficiaries without significant delay. In contrast to probate, there is no short-term statute of limitations applicable to revocable trusts to cut off the rights of creditors. A revocable trust avoids publicity since it is not recorded in a public place. To avoid ancillary probate over real property located outside the domiciliary state, land in another state can be transferred to a revocable inter vivos trust. In some states, the law might permit a funded revocable trust to defeat a spouse's elective share in certain circumstances. The settlor of an inter vivos trust of personal property may choose the state law that is to govern the trust. In practice, it is more difficult to set aside a revocable trust than a will on grounds of lack of mental capacity and undue influence. As noted above, there are no federal tax advantages to a revocable trust. Finally, a revocable trust which becomes irrevocable upon the death of one spouse can thereby control the surviving spouse's disposition of property.

5. **Durable Power of Attorney.** The durable power of attorney, like the revocable trust, is useful in planning for incapacity.

Cruzan v. Director, Missouri Department of Health

6. **Health-Care Directives--Cruzan v. Director, Missouri Department of Health,** 497 U.S. 261 (1990).

a. **Facts.** Nancy Cruzan was in an automobile accident that left her in a persistent vegetative state; she exhibited motor reflexes, but showed no indication of significant cognitive function. Nancy's parents (Ps) asked hospital employees to terminate artificial nutrition and hydration procedures. The employees refused to do so without a court order. The trial court determined Nancy had a fundamental right under state and federal Constitutions to refuse or direct the withdrawal of death-prolonging procedures. The court found Nancy had expressed thoughts to a housemate that she would not wish to continue to live unless she was "halfway normal," and, thus, she would not wish to continue her nutrition and hydration. The state supreme court reversed. The Supreme Court granted certiorari.

b. **Issue.** Does an incompetent patient have a right under the United States Constitution to require a hospital to withdraw life-sustaining treatment?

c. **Held.** No. Affirmed.

1) A review of cases from many states demonstrates that the common law doctrine of informed consent is viewed as generally encompassing the right of a competent individual to refuse medical treatment. Beyond that, the cases agree and disagree in their approaches to the issue of an individual's "right to die." In this case of first impression, we do not attempt to cover every phase of the subject and focus only on the prohibitions of the United States Constitution.

2) Determination of whether an individual's constitutional rights have been violated must be made by balancing her liberty interests under the Due Process Clause against the relevant state interests.

3) The United States Constitution would grant a competent person a constitutionally protected right to refuse lifesaving hydration and nutrition.

4) An incompetent person, however, is not able to make an informed and voluntary choice to exercise a hypothetical right to refuse treat-

ment or any other right. Such a "right" must be exercised for her, if at all, by a surrogate, as Missouri law has determined. Missouri has also established a procedural safeguard to assure that the surrogate's action conforms as best it may to the patient's wishes as expressed by the patient while competent. The state requires that clear and convincing evidence be offered of the incompetent's wishes as to the withdrawal of treatment.

5) The United States Constitution does not forbid the establishment of this procedural requirement.

6) Even in the case of a competent individual, a state has an interest in the protection and preservation of human life. In the case of an incompetent person, this interest is heightened.

7) The clear and convincing standard, as with any standard of proof embodied in the Due Process Clause, is to instruct the fact finder concerning the degree of confidence our society thinks he should have in the correctness of factual conclusions for a particular type of adjudication, and serves as a societal judgment about how the risk of error should be distributed between litigants.

8) An erroneous decision here not to withdraw life-sustaining treatment results in maintenance of the status quo; an erroneous decision to terminate is not susceptible of correction.

9) We do not think the Due Process Clause requires the states to repose judgment in these matters with anyone but the patient herself; there is no automatic assurance that the view of close family members will be the same as the patient's.

d. Concurrence (Scalia, J.). I would have preferred that we had announced the federal courts have no business in this field.

7. Termination of Medical Treatment. A living will contains directives concerning termination of medical treatment. It provides that a signer's life shall not be artificially prolonged by extraordinary measures where there is no reasonable expectation of recovery from extreme physical or mental disability.

8. Disposition of Decedent's Body. All states have enacted Uniform Anatomical Gift Acts, which permit a person to give his or her body to any hospital, physician, or medical school for research or transplantation.

VI. WILLS: CONSTRUCTION PROBLEMS

A. ADMISSION OF EXTRINSIC EVIDENCE: AMBIGUITY, MISTAKE, AND OMISSION

1. **Admissibility of Extrinsic Evidence.** In general, extrinsic evidence is not admissible to change the plain meaning of a will. Some jurisdictions do not apply this rule rigidly but invoke a presumption that can be overcome with strong evidence of a contrary meaning. Parol evidence may be admissible to resolve ambiguities in a will.

   a. **Latent ambiguities.** A latent ambiguity exists when the language of the will, though clear on its face, is susceptible to more than one meaning when applied to the extrinsic facts. In these cases, parol evidence is admissible to resolve the ambiguity.

   b. **Patent ambiguities.** A patent ambiguity exists where the uncertainty appears on the face of the will. The traditional view is that parol evidence is not admissible to clarify a patent ambiguity. The modern trend is to admit parol evidence in these instances as well.

Mahoney v. Grainger

   c. **No extrinsic evidence to correct drafter's mistake--Mahoney v. Grainger,** 186 N.E. 86 (Mass. 1933).

      1) **Facts.** Upon Sullivan's (T's) death, her only heir at law was her aunt. However, shortly before T's death, T executed a will, instructing her attorney to leave the residue of her estate to her 25 cousins and "let them share equally." The language of the residue clause read: "I give, demise and bequeath to my heirs at law living at the time of my decease, absolutely; to be divided among them equally, share and share alike." The probate court denied a petition for distribution to the first cousins. Certain cousins appeal.

      2) **Issue.** Are T's statements regarding T's understanding of "heirs at law" admissible?

      3) **Held.** No. Decree affirmed.

         a) A testator's statements are admissible only insofar as they tend to give evidence where testamentary language is not clear in its application to facts. Where no doubt exists as to the property bequeathed or the identity of the beneficiary, there is no room for extrinsic evidence.

         b) There is no doubt as to the meaning of "heirs at law." A draftsman's mistake does not authorize a court to reform or alter a duly executed and allowed will.

Fleming v. Morrison

   d. **Failure to comply with statutory requirements--Fleming v. Morrison,** 72 N.E. 499 (Mass. 1904).

1) **Facts.** T executed a sham will leaving all of his property to Fleming in an effort to get her to sleep with him. Goodridge attested as a witness. Later, two additional witnesses attested to T's signature. The will was admitted to probate. Contestants appeal.

2) **Issue.** Has the proponent of the will proved the necessary *animus testandi*?

3) **Held.** No. Reversed; instrument disallowed.

   a) T indicated to his attorney that the will was a sham.

   b) It is competent to contradict by parole the solemn statements contained in an instrument that is a will, that it has been signed as such by the person named as testator, and attested and subscribed by persons signing as witnesses.

   c) If the *animus testandi* does not exist when a will is signed or acknowledged before, or attested and subscribed by, each of the necessary three witnesses, the statutory requirements have not been complied with.

   d) Here, if acknowledgement of *animus testandi* of a signature not originally made with that *animus* is enough, if T had acknowledged the instrument subsequently before three witnesses, the will would have been duly executed. But T did not; two witnesses are insufficient.

e. **Extrinsic evidence not admissible to show error of a scrivener--Connecticut Junior Republic v. Sharon Hospital,** 188 Conn. 1, 448 A.2d 190 (1982).

Connecticut Junior Republic v. Sharon Hospital

1) **Facts.** The will of the decedent, Richard Emerson, set up trusts for a designated person for life, remainder to seven named charities. Thereafter, he executed a codicil to his will deleting six of the seven charities and substituting 11 different charities. Thereafter, the decedent instructed his attorney to amend his will and codicil in such a manner as to qualify the trusts as charitable annuity trusts. The attorney drafted a second codicil that made the requested changes but also, by mistake, reinstated the prior charities and deleted the later charities. The decedent signed the second codicil without realizing the change in beneficiaries. The probate court admitted the second codicil to probate, refusing to permit introduction of extrinsic evidence as to the scrivener's mistake. The superior court affirmed. The later charities inadvertently deleted from the second codicil (Ps) appeal.

2) **Issues.**

   a) Should the same evidentiary rules apply to proceedings to admit a will to probate and will construction proceedings?

   b) Is extrinsic evidence showing a scrivener's error admissible in a proceeding to admit a will to probate?

3) **Held.** a) Yes. b) No. The judgment of the trial court is affirmed.

a) Ps contend that courts have made a distinction between proceedings to admit a will to probate and will construction proceedings, holding that extrinsic evidence showing a scrivener's error is admissible in the former but not in the latter proceeding. Our cases, however, do not distinguish between the two types of proceedings. Nor are we inclined to establish a rule which would effectuate such a distinction. To do so would transform probate proceedings into mere semantic exercises. Disappointed beneficiaries could merely rephrase their argument to allege that the scrivener did not follow instructions and thus the will should not be admitted to probate since it does not represent the testator's true intention. This would tend to produce needless litigation. We believe the better course is to have the same evidentiary rules apply to both types of proceedings.

b) We also agree with the trial court that parol evidence may not be admitted to show that the scrivener erred in drafting the codicil or that testator mistakenly signed it. While it is true that extrinsic evidence may be admitted to identify the devisee or legatee named, or the property described in a will, or to make clear the doubtful meaning of language in a will, it is never admissible for the purpose of showing an intention not expressed in the will itself. Construction of a will must be derived from the words in it, not from extrinsic evidence.

4) **Dissent.** The majority would disallow extrinsic evidence of a scrivener's error for two reasons: the existing case law and risk of subverting the Statute of Wills. Neither reason is persuasive. With regard to the first, the law upon which the majority relies is ancient and moreover pertains to cases that sought to reform wills by adding new provisions. Here Ps seek to delete unintended testamentary bequests, surely a less problematical confrontation with the Statute of Wills. With regard to the second, there is no greater risk of judicial error in the case of a scriveners's error than in the case of fraud or undue influence.

f. **Correcting mistakes.** If the alleged mistake involves the reasons that led the testator to make the will (or the reasons for making or not making a particular gift), and the mistake was not fraudulently induced, no relief is granted. Some courts have recognized an exception if the mistake appears on the face of the will, and the disposition the testator would have made but for the mistake can at least be inferred from the instrument. Cases in which such relief is granted are rare because it is unlikely for the mistake and the alternate disposition to appear on the face of the instrument. If a provision was mistakenly omitted from the will, or a provision contained in the will is not what the testator intended, parol testimony is generally not admissible to show the existence of the mistake and what the testator intended to provide had the mistake not been made. Thus, mistakes of omission generally cannot be corrected, nor can a mistake in describing a beneficiary or item of property.

Estate of Russell

g. **Extrinsic evidence admissible to ascertain circumstances under which will was made--Estate of Russell,** 69 Cal. 2d 200, 444 P.2d 353 (1968).

1) **Facts.** The decedent, Thelma Russell, died leaving a validly executed holographic will written on a small card that bequeathed everything she owned to Chester Quinn, a close friend, and to Roxy Russell, her pet dog,

which was alive on the date the will was executed but predeceased the testator. The reverse side of the card bequeathed a $10 gold piece and diamonds to Georgia Nan Russell Hembree (P), the niece and only heir at law of the testator. P brought a petition for determination of heirship, alleging that Roxy was a dog, that the Probate Code enumerates those entitled to take by will and that dogs are not included, that the gift of half of the estate to Roxy is void, and that P, as the testator's sole heir at law, is entitled to half. At the hearing, P introduced without objection extrinsic evidence that Roxy was the testator's dog. Quinn, through his attorney, introduced evidence of his relationship with the testator, and documentary evidence consisting of testator's address book and a certain quitclaim deed, all of which was admitted over objection. The trial court held that it was the intention of the testator that Quinn was to receive her entire estate excepting the gold coin and diamonds bequeathed to P and that Quinn was to care for the dog in the event of the testator's death. The court held that the language in the will indicated that Quinn was to use whatever portion of the estate as might be necessary to care for and maintain the dog. P appeals.

2) **Issue.** May extrinsic evidence of the circumstances under which a will is made be considered in ascertaining what the testator meant by the words used in a will?

3) **Held.** Yes. Judgment reversed.

a) When the language of a will is ambiguous or uncertain, resort may be had to extrinsic evidence in order to ascertain the intention of the testator. A latent ambiguity is one that is not apparent on the face of the will but is disclosed by some fact collateral to it, whereas a patent ambiguity is an uncertainty that appears on the face of the will. We think it is self-evident that in the interpretation of a will, a court cannot determine whether the terms of the will are clear and definite in the first place until it considers the circumstances under which the will was made. Extrinsic evidence of the circumstances under which a will is made may be considered by the court in ascertaining what the testator meant by the words used in the will.

b) Here, extrinsic evidence offered by P to raise and resolve the latent ambiguity as to Roxy and to establish that Roxy was a dog was properly considered in order to ascertain what testator meant by the words of the will. However, viewing the will in light of the surrounding circumstances, the trial court erred in holding that the testator intended to make an absolute gift of her entire estate to Quinn. A disposition in equal shares to two beneficiaries cannot be equated with a disposition of the whole to one of them, who may use whatever portion on behalf of the other. We conclude that the testator intended to make a disposition of all of the residue of the estate to Quinn and the dog in equal shares. As a dog cannot be the beneficiary under a will, the attempted gift to Roxy is void. Hence, that portion of the estate remains undisposed of by the will and passes to the heirs at law. We conclude that the residue of the estate should be distributed in equal shares to Quinn and P.

h. **Liability for drafting ambiguous will.** If, in preparing a will pursuant to testator's instructions, the attorney omits a clause that makes a gift to a beneficiary, the attorney is liable to the intended beneficiary for the amount the beneficiary would have received under the will had the clause not been negligently omitted. Case law, however, has held that an attorney is not liable for drafting an ***ambiguous*** document.

B. DEATH OF BENEFICIARY BEFORE DEATH OF TESTATOR: LAPSE

When a beneficiary predeceases the testator, the beneficiary's bequest will lapse (and pass through the residuary estate or through intestacy) in the absence of an antilapse statute, which specifies substitute takers.

1. **UPC Section 2-601.** Under this section, if a devisee does not survive the testator by 120 hours, then he is treated as having predeceased the testator, unless the will contains some explicit language dealing explicitly with simultaneous deaths.

2. **UPC Section 2-605.** Under this section, if a devisee who is a grandparent or a lineal descendant of a grandparent (i) is dead at the time of execution of the will, (ii) fails to survive the testator, or (iii) is treated as if he had predeceased the testator, then the issue of a deceased devisee who survive the testator by 120 hours take in place of the deceased devisee. If they are all of the same degree of kinship they take equally, but if they are of unequal degree then those of more remote degree take by representation.

3. **Lapse Statutes.** The states' lapse statutes vary widely as to their scope. In many states, the lapse statute applies only if the predeceasing beneficiary was a child or other descendant of the testator. Under the UPC and in several non-UPC states, the statute applies if the predeceasing beneficiary was a grandparent or a lineal descendant of a grandparent of the testator. In nearly all states, the lapse statute operates only if the predeceasing beneficiary left descendants who survived the testator. Such descendants take the gift by substitution. In most states, the lapse statutes do not apply if the gift is contingent on the beneficiary's surviving the testator.

In re Estate of Ulrikson

a. **Antilapse statute automatically applies unless contrary intent--*In re* Estate of Ulrikson,** 290 N.W.2d 757 (Minn. 1980).

1) **Facts.** A proceeding was instituted in a contest over the construction of a residuary clause of a will. The sole issue is whether the antilapse statute applies where the residuary estate is given to a brother and sister, "and in the event that either one of them shall predecease me, then to the other surviving brother or sister," but in fact both brother and sister predecease the testator, the brother leaving issue. The decision of the probate court that the antilapse statute was applicable was affirmed by the district court. Application for leave to appeal was granted.

2) **Issue.** Does the antilapse statute apply if there is no contrary intent expressed in the will?

3) **Held.** Yes. Judgment affirmed.

a) The law prefers testacy over intestacy.

b) The antilapse statute applies unless a contrary intention is indicated by the will.

c) The antilapse statute was applicable in the absence of a clear intention to the contrary where the residuary estate was devised to a brother and sister, "and in the event that either one of them shall predecease me, then to the other surviving brother or sister," but in fact both the brother and sister predeceased the testator, the brother leaving issue. The words of survivorship are effective only if there are survivors. Since there are no survivors in this case, the antilapse statute is free to operate.

d) The fact that testator made a $1,000 bequest to each of her nieces and nephews did not establish that she expressed an intention to treat her legal heirs equally and thus contrary to the antilapse statute. The fact that the brother and sister of the testator, both of whom predeceased her, were preferred in the residuary clause of the will and that two persons outside her bloodline, the nieces by marriage, were also given $1,000 specific bequests supports application of the antilapse statute.

4. Rule of Construction that "And" be Read as "Or" to Effectuate Testator's Intent--Jackson v. Schultz, 38 Del. Ch. 332, 151 A.2d 284 (1959). Jackson v. Schultz

a. Facts. The children of Bessie Bullock (Ps) contracted to sell to the defendant a house formerly owned by their stepfather, Leonard Bullock, contending that title passed to them through the will of their stepfather. The will bequeathed all property to Bessie Bullock "and of whatever nature and kind, to her and her heirs and assigns forever." Bessie Bullock, however, predeceased the testator. The defendant contends that since Bessie Bullock predeceased the testator, Ps took nothing under their stepfather's will, arguing that the words "her heirs and assigns forever" were words of limitation defining the quantity of the estate devised and that, as such, the heirs took nothing by way of substitution, since the devisee predeceased the testator. Defendant further contends that where the word "and" appears before the words "heirs and assigns," the same rule applies, in contrast to where the word "or" appears, which has been deemed to designate those who will take by way of substitution. Ps move for summary judgment requesting the court to grant a decree of specific performance under the contract.

b. Issue. Will the words "and" or "or" be substituted for each other in arriving at a proper construction of a will for the purpose of carrying out an obvious testamentary purpose of a testator?

c. Held. Yes. Ps' motion for summary judgment is granted.

1) Defendant contends that when a devise is made to a named person "his heirs and assigns forever," the heirs as such normally take nothing by way of substitution if the devisee predeceases the testator, such expression being deemed one of limitation defining the quantity of the estate devised, and that this rule has been applied in cases where the word "and" appears before the clause "heirs and assigns." However, when the word "or" is used following a primary devise,

the subsequent reference to "heirs" or the like has been deemed to designate those who will take by way of substitution in the event that the primary devisee predeceased the testator and a lapse is thereby avoided.

2) It has also been held, however, that the words "or" and "and" may be substituted for each other in arriving at a proper construction of a will, "and" having been read as "or" for the purpose of carrying out an obvious testamentary purpose.

3) Here, the evidence indicates that the testator's father was survived by his son (the testator, Leonard Bullock), a brother, and a stepson, all of whom entered into an agreement designed to insure that, in the event of Leonard's death during the settlement of his father's estate, his share would go to his wife, Bessie. This agreement clearly demonstrates the testator's intent that his share of his father's estate should go to his wife. Additionally, the will of the testator should be read not only to carry out his intention but construed, if possible, to avoid not merely intestacy but total escheat.

4) A decree for specific performance should normally be granted in a land purchase case unless to do so would require a buyer to accept a defective title subject to attack by an adverse interest not before the court. Here, there is a solid basis for sustaining Ps' claim to a fee simple title in the land here involved. I adopt the rule of construction that permits "and" to be read as "or" when to do so will carry out the testator's intent. Here, the evidence sustains a ruling that the will be construed as making a substitutionary devise over to Ps.

5. **Rule of Construction Held Inapplicable.** In *Hofing v. Willis*, 31 Ill. 2d 365, 201 N.E.2d 852 (1964), the court held that while there is some support for the proposition that the phrase "and to their heirs" could be considered as words of purchase by reading the word "and" as "or," the presence of the words "and assigns" makes such a construction unacceptable. The court stated that it is hardly reasonable to suppose that the grantor would create a substitutionary gift and at the same time designate the assigns of the named takers to take by way of substitution.

Dawson v. Yucus

6. **No Class Gift--Dawson v. Yucus,** 239 N.E.2d 305 (Ill. 1968).

a. **Facts.** T's duly executed will devised her one-fifth interest in certain farm lands to two nephews, each taking one-half. One nephew died prior to T's death. Wilson (P) filed suit to construe the will, alleging the devise was a class gift and that P, survivor of the class, was entitled to the entire one-fifth interest. P later conveyed the interest he allegedly received as survivor to the two children of the deceased nephew and they were substituted as plaintiffs. The trial court found for Ds. Ps appeal.

b. **Issue.** Was a class gift to the nephews created in T's will?

c. **Held.** No. Affirmed.

1) A class gift is a gift of an aggregate sum to a body of persons uncertain in number at the time of the gift, to be ascertained at a future time, and who are all to take in equal or in some other definite proportions, the share of each being dependent for its amount upon the ultimate number of persons.

2) Here, there were two named individuals, making certain the number of beneficiaries and their share. The shares do not depend upon the number who survive T.

3) T used no class gift language, *i.e.*, "nephews," "cousins," "descendants," etc. and the will contained a survivorship gift of the residue of her estate; no survivorship gift was created in the clause devising the farmland.

7. **Gift to Class and Named Individual Who Predeceases the Testator--*In re* Moss**, [1899] 2 Ch. 314, *aff'd,* [1901] A.C. 187 (H.L.). *In re* Moss

a. **Facts.** Walter Moss (T) bequeathed his interest in the *Daily Telegraph* newspaper in trust to pay the income to Elizabeth Moss (his wife) for life and, upon her death, in trust for Elizabeth Jane Fowler (his niece) and the children of Emily Walter (his sister) who shall attain the age of 21, to be divided equally among them as tenants in common. T left the residue of his estate to his wife. Elizabeth Jane Fowler died in 1891; T died in 1893. Elizabeth Moss (T's widow) died in 1897, leaving her residuary estate to William George Kingsbury (P). She was survived by the five children of Emily Walter (Ds), all older than 21. P claims that the share of T's estate bequeathed to Elizabeth Jane Fowler lapsed upon her death during T's lifetime and became part of T's and Elizabeth Moss's residuary estates. Ds claim that the bequest to Elizabeth Jane Fowler and them was a gift to a class, of which they are the surviving members. The trial court held for P. Ds appeal.

b. **Issue.** Where a gift by will is to a class and a named individual equally, so that the testator contemplates the named individual taking the same share that each member of the class will take, does the testator intend that the whole shall pass by his gift to the surviving members of the class if any member of the class survives, even though the named individual does not?

c. **Held.** Yes. Judgment reversed.

1) (Lindley, M.R.) The question we have to decide is: Who are the persons entitled to T's share in the *Daily Telegraph* newspaper? One view, adopted by the trial court, is that the share that Elizabeth Jane Fowler would have taken if she were alive—one-sixth—has lapsed and fallen into the residuary estate. I decline to follow this view. Whether you follow the definition that a gift to A and the children of B may in effect be a gift to a class if the testator treats the legatees as a class or whether you call them a number of persons who are to be treated as a class is quite immaterial. Here, the intention of the testator was that the share should go to such of the children as shall be living. The alternative view takes the share away where it was never intended to go.

2) (Romer, L.J.) When a testator gives property to A and a class of persons—say the children of B—in equal shares, he intends that the whole property shall pass by his gift if any one of the children of B survive him even though A does not. Generally, when the testator gives property to be shared at a particular period equally between a class properly so called and an individual, then what the testator must be taken to mean is that you are to see which part of that aggregated body is to share in that property at the time it comes for distribution. Hence, a gift by will to a class and a named individual equally, so that the testator contemplates the individual taking the same share that each member of the class will take, is prima facie evidence of a gift to a class. Here, Elizabeth Jane Fowler was only intended to share as one of a class, and, inasmuch as she did not survive, the rest of the class takes the whole of the property.

C. CHANGES IN PROPERTY AFTER EXECUTION OF WILL: SPECIFIC VS. GENERAL DEVISES

1. **Ademption.** If specifically devised property is not in the testator's estate at the time of death (*e.g.*, it was sold by the testator or destroyed), the gift is adeemed. This is known as ademption by extinction. The doctrine only applies to specific devises and bequests; general legacies are not affected.

Wasserman v. Cohen

a. **Ademption by extinction--Wasserman v. Cohen,** 606 N.E.2d 901 (Mass. 1993).

1) **Facts.** Drapkin created an inter vivos trust funded at execution, and retained the right to add property by inter vivos transfer and will and amend, revoke, and withdraw property from the trust. A trust provision ordered Cohen, trustee, to convey a building to P. However, Drapkin had sold the building prior to her death and had never conveyed her interest in the property to the trust. P brought an action for declaratory judgment, requesting the trustee pay her the proceeds of the sale of the building. The probate judge dismissed the action. P applied for direct appellate review.

2) **Issue.** Does the doctrine of ademption by extinction apply to the specific gift of real estate contained in a revocable inter vivos trust?

3) **Held.** Yes. Affirmed.

a) When a testator disposes during her lifetime of the subject of a specific legacy in her will, that devise is held to be adeemed.

b) A trust, particularly when executed as part of an estate plan, should be construed according to the same rules traditionally applied to wills.

2. **Abatement.** Abatement is the process of reducing testamentary gifts in cases where the estate assets are not sufficient to pay all claims against the estate and satisfy all bequests and devises. At common law, all gifts of personal property abate before dispositions of real property. Today, in most states, the distinction between real and personal property has been abolished, and statutes provide a general order in which the types of gifts are abated.

   a. **UPC section 2-608.** Under this section, a specific devisee has the right to a general pecuniary devise equal to the net sale price of devised property sold by a conservator.

3. **Exoneration of Liens.** The doctrine of exoneration of liens, followed by most jurisdictions, holds that where a will makes a specific disposition of property that is subject to a mortgage or other encumbrance, it is presumed that the testator wanted the debt to be paid out of the residuary estate, so that the property passes free and clear of the encumbrance.

   a. **UPC section 2-609: nonexoneration.** Under this section, a specific devise passes subject to any security interest existing at the date of death, without right of exoneration, regardless of a general directive in the will to pay debts.

4. **Satisfaction.** Satisfaction applies where a testator makes an inter vivos transfer to a beneficiary after executing the will, with the intention of making the testamentary gift inoperative. At common law, a gift to a child of the testator is presumptively in partial or total satisfaction of any gifts made to the child in a previously executed will.

   a. **UPC section 2-612: ademption by satisfaction.** Under this section, property that a testator gave in his lifetime to a person is treated as a satisfaction of a devise to that person, in whole or in part, only if the will provides for deduction of the lifetime gift, or the testator declares in a contemporaneous writing that the gift is to be deducted from the devise.

5. **Stock Splits.** Under the majority rule, a specific beneficiary is entitled to additional shares of stock produced by a stock split, but is not entitled to additional shares of stock produced by a stock dividend. Under the UPC, the specific beneficiary of corporate securities is entitled to additional or other securities of the same entity—*i.e.,* both stock splits and stock dividends.

VII. RESTRICTIONS ON THE POWER OF DISPOSITION: PROTECTION OF THE FAMILY

A. RIGHTS OF THE SURVIVING SPOUSE

1. **Introduction to Marital Property Systems.** In the United States, two basic marital property systems exist, the common law system of separate property and the system of community property.

   a. **Common law system.** Under the common law system, husband and wife own separately all property each acquires (except those items one spouse has agreed to put into joint ownership with the other). Nearly all of the common law jurisdictions have enacted elective share statutes designed to give the surviving spouse some protection against disinheritance. These statutes give the spouse an election to take a statutory share (usually one-third or one-half) of the decedent's estate in lieu of taking under the decedent's will.

   b. **Community property system.** Under community property, husband and wife own all acquisitions from earnings after marriage in equal undivided shares. In eight states (Arizona, California, Idaho, Louisiana, Nevada, New Mexico, Texas, and Washington) a community property system exists. In general, none of the community property states has an elective share statute. Each spouse has the power of testamentary disposition over only his or her one-half community interest. The surviving spouse automatically owns one-half of the community estate upon the other spouse's death.

2. **Rights of Surviving Spouse to Support.**

   a. **Social security.** The worker has no right to shift the survivor's benefit to a person other than the spouse (though benefits may be paid to a deceased retired worker's dependents as well as to the worker's spouse).

   b. **Private pension plans.** The Retirement Equity Act of 1984 requires that pensions paid under covered private pension plans must be paid as a joint and survivor annuity to the worker and his or her spouse, unless the nonworker spouse consents to some other form of payment of the retirement benefit.

   c. **Homestead.** Nearly all states have statutes that secure some interest in the family home to the surviving spouse and minor children, free of the claims of creditors. These homesteads are known as probate homesteads.

   d. **Personal property set-aside.** Related to the homestead laws are statutes that exempt certain items of tangible personal property from execution or levy in satisfaction of creditors' claims.

   e. **Family allowance.** Also, in many states, the surviving spouse or minor children are entitled to petition for a family allowance to provide for their maintenance during the period in which the decedent's estate is in administration.

f. **Dower and curtesy.** Dower was the provision the law made for a widow out of the husband's property. Upon the husband's death, the widow was entitled to a life estate in an undivided one-third of the husband's lands. A husband had a comparable interest in his wife's lands. Upon a wife's death her husband's curtesy right gave him a life estate in all (not just an undivided one-third) of the lands of which the wife was seised during marriage. However, a husband's curtesy estate (unlike dower) arose only if issue were born to the marriage.

1) **Property subject to dower.** A wife had dower in all lands of which her husband was seised of an estate of inheritance during marriage. Thus, dower applied to lands owned by the husband at the time of the marriage as well as to land acquired during the marriage. In effect, dower applied to all lands owned by the husband at death and also to lands conveyed during the marriage without his wife's joinder.

2) **Testamentary effect.** Dower and curtesy rights could be asserted regardless of the decedent's will. Thus, a wife's dower interest in her husband's land was not affected by the fact that the husband had devised the land to another. To this extent, then, each spouse's power of testamentary disposition over property was limited by the other's dower or curtesy right.

3) **Present status of dower and curtesy.** Most states have abolished dower and curtesy in favor of elective share statutes.

3. **Rights of Surviving Spouse to a Share of Decedent's Property.**

a. **Elective share and its rationale.** The majority of states give the surviving spouse an elective share of the deceased spouse's real and personal assets. The spouse can elect to either take under the deceased spouse's will or renounce the will and take a statutory share of the estate (usually one-third or one-half). Section 2-203 of the UPC provides a schedule to determine the elective share percentage determined by the length of the marriage.

b. **No advancement against spouse's share--King v. King,** 613 N.E.2d 251 (Ohio 1992). King v. King

1) **Facts.** Husband (H) executed a will leaving all real property and certain personal property to Wife (W) and remaining personal property to his children from a prior marriage (Cs). H later deeded real estate to W, telling her he did not want it to go through his estate. Upon H's death, W elected to take against the will. Cs filed for declaratory judgment, asking the court to find H's inter vivos gift was an advancement. The trial court found for W. Cs appeal

2) **Issue.** Was H's inter vivos gift of real estate an advancement against W's share, thereby reducing W's portion of the remaining assets W would receive by her election?

3) **Held.** No. Affirmed.

a) An advancement is an irrevocable gift made during a person's lifetime to an heir, by way of anticipation of the portion of the estate which the heir would receive in the event of the person's death intestate.

b) When a spouse takes a statutory share, she takes as if the testator had died intestate.

c) However, the relevant statute provides that the value of any advancement will be counted against an intestate share only if it is declared to be an advancement. These methods of proof are exclusive.

In re Estate of Cooper

c. **No forced share in homosexual relationship--*In re* Estate of Cooper,** 592 N.Y.S.2d 797 (1993).

1) **Facts.** Upon Cooper's (T's) death, the bulk of his estate was left to his former lover. Petitioner (P), who had a homosexual relationship with T, petitioned the court to allow him to elect against the will. T's executrix (E) opposed and applied to dismiss P's action. The court found for E. P appeals.

2) **Issue.** Is a homosexual relationship a "spousal relationship" such that a survivor is entitled to a right of election against the decedent's will pursuant to the relevant statute?

3) **Held.** No. Affirmed.

a) The statute permits a surviving spouse the right of election.

b) A "surviving spouse" is defined as a husband or wife, but even if it were not, the language of a statute is generally construed according to its natural and most obvious sense in accord with its ordinary and accepted meaning.

c) The traditional definition contemplates the survivor of a union between members of the opposite sex, and we see no reason to reject that.

d) Any equal protection analysis in the instant case is to be measured by the rational basis standard, *i.e.*, the legislation is valid if the classification drawn is rationally related to a legitimate state interest.

e) The Supreme Court of Minnesota rejected same sex petitioners' argument that a prohibition on same sex marriages denied them equal protection, holding: "the institution of marriage as a union of man and woman, uniquely involving the procreation and rearing of children within a family . . . [is] 'fundamental to the very existence and survival of the race.' This historic institution manifestly is more deeply founded than the asserted contemporary concept of marriage and societal interests for which petitioners contend." [Baker v. Nelson, 191 N.W.2d 185 (Minn. 1980)] The Supreme Court dismissed petitioners' appeal for want of a substantial federal question. "Such a dismissal is a holding that the constitutional challenge was considered and rejected." [Hicks v. Miranda, 422 U.S. 332 (1960)]

d. **Revocable inter vivos trust--Seifert v. Southern National Bank of South Carolina,** 409 S.E.2d 337 (S.C. 1991).

Seifert v. Southern National Bank of South Carolina

1) **Facts.** Husband created a revocable inter vivos trust in favor of his daughters from a former marriage (Ds). At his death the trust was worth $800,000. The trust provided that at Husband's death a separate trust containing $150,000 was carved out for Widow (P), who received a life interest in the income and who could invade the principal for medical purposes only. Under Husband's will, P received a one-half life interest in the marital home, of which she already owned half, and the residue of the estate was transferred to Ds' trust. P requested her elective share, but the will was designed so there were no assets in the estate other than the life interest in the house, personal property, and the residue. P filed a complaint in probate court. The matter was removed to circuit court and transferred to the Master-in-Equity. P instituted this declaratory judgment action.

2) **Issue.** Should the proceeds of the revocable inter vivos trust be included in Husband's estate for purposes of calculating P's elective share?

3) **Held.** Yes. Reversed and remanded.

a) Where a spouse seeks to avoid payment of the elective share by creating a trust over which substantial control is retained, the trust may be declared invalid as illusory and the trust assets will be included in the decedent's estate for calculation of the elective share.

b) The trust was completely revocable. The trustee's role was "custodial" and the settlor retained extensive powers. The trust was illusory and, therefore, invalid.

e. **Property subject to the elective share.**

1) **UPC section 2-201: right to elective share.** Under this section, the surviving spouse has a right of election to take an elective share to one-third of the "augmented estate" under certain conditions.

2) **UPC section 2-202: augmented estate.** This section defines the properties to be included in the augmented estate. Nonprobate assets—such as life insurance policies, pension plans, bonds, and bank accounts—frequently pass to beneficiaries outside of the will. As a result, instances arise where the surviving spouse may receive too great a share of the decedent's estate, or too little. Under the UPC, the spouse's one-third share from the augmented estate includes the following:

a) The probate estate less funeral expenses, claims, and various family allowances;

b) The value of property gratuitously transferred during the marriage without the consent of the spouse by arrangements that are, in effect, will substitutes; and

c) Property acquired by the surviving spouse from the decedent.

Sullivan v. Burkin

3) **Surviving spouse's statutory share of assets of inter vivos trust created by deceased spouse--Sullivan v. Burkin,** 390 Mass. 864, 460 N.E.2d 571 (1984).

a) **Facts.** Mary Sullivan (P), a widow who exercised her statutory right to take a share of her husband's estate, brought an action seeking determination that the assets held in inter vivos trust created by her husband during marriage should be considered as part of the estate in determining that share. The husband had executed a deed of trust under which he transferred real estate to himself as sole trustee. The net income of the trust was payable to him during his life and the trustee was instructed to pay to him all or such part of the principal of the trust estate as he might request in writing periodically. He retained the right to revoke the trust at any time. On his death, the successor trustee was directed to pay the principal and any undistributed income equally to George and Harold Cronin (Ds) if they should survive him, which they did. The husband died while still trustee of the inter vivos trust. He left a will in which he stated that he intentionally neglected to make any provision for his wife and grandson. He directed that, after payment of debts, expenses, and all estate taxes levied by reason of his death, the residue of his estate should be paid over to the trustee of the inter vivos trust. The Probate Court rejected P's claim and entered judgment dismissing the complaint. Appeal was taken.

b) **Issue.** Are the assets of an inter vivos trust to be considered in determining the portion of the estate of the deceased to which a widow may claim her statutory share?

c) **Held.** No. Judgment affirmed.

(1) A trust with remainder interests given to others on the settlor's death is not invalid as a testamentary disposition simply because the settlor retained a broad power to modify or revoke the trust, the right to receive income, and the right to invade principal during his life.

(2) The fact that the settlor of a trust with remainder interests given to others on the settlor's death is the sole trustee does not make the trust testamentary.

(3) Whether or not decedent established an inter vivos trust in order to defeat P's right to take her statutory share of the assets placed in trust, and even though decedent had a general power of appointment over the trust assets, P obtained no right to share in the assets of that trust when she made her statutory election.

(4) In the future, as to any inter vivos trust created or amended after the date of this opinion, the estate of decedent, for purposes of the surviving spouse's statutory share, shall include the value of assets held in an inter vivos trust created by the deceased spouse as to which he alone retained power during his life to direct disposition of those trust assets for his benefit, as, for example, by the exercise of a power of appointment or by revocation of the trust.

f. **Source of elective share.** The UPC provides that values included in the augmented estate that pass or have passed to the surviving spouse are applied first to satisfy the elective share and to reduce any contributions due from other recipients of transfers included in the augmented estate.

1) **Renunciation of a will by a court to increase interest to surviving spouse--*In re* Estate of Clarkson,** 193 Neb. 201, 226 N.W.2d 334 (1975).

In re Estate of Clarkson

a) **Facts.** The will of the decedent, Joseph Clarkson, bequeathed one-fourth of the value of his estate to the First National Bank of Omaha, as trustee for his wife, Evelyn Clarkson, in the event that she survived him. The will further provided that in the event she failed to exercise the trust's general testamentary power of appointment upon her death, the remaining assets would be distributed in a specified way to the couple's children by prior marriages. The will was made at a time when Mrs. Clarkson was incompetent and hence unable to exercise the power of appointment. A guardian ad litem filed a report recommending that the probate court renounce the provision made for Evelyn Clarkson under the will and that she take by descent and distribution. The probate court declined to do so. The guardian appealed, and the district court reversed, finding that an estate in fee title would be of greater value than a beneficial interest in a trust. The executor appeals.

b) **Issue.** Should a court elect to renounce a will so that the share to an incompetent surviving spouse has greater pecuniary value?

c) **Held.** Yes. The judgment of the district court is affirmed.

(1) The majority view provides that the election should be made that is in the best interests, advantage, and welfare of the incompetent person. The so-called minority view provides that the best interests of the incompetent will be served by electing the method that is the most valuable to the surviving spouse; this usually means that the one having the greater pecuniary value is the one selected.

(2) Here, we find no considerations other than the monetary value of the estate. The estate in fee is of much greater value than a beneficial interest in a trust. We agree that the best interest of the surviving spouse requires taking the estate in fee with full incidents of ownership, notwithstanding that the title would vest in her guardian (who would have fiduciary limitations on its disposal).

d) **Dissent.** The minority view adopted by the court is too restrictive. It places too much emphasis upon monetary considerations, with a possible detriment to the personal welfare, comfort and best interest of the incompetent. Where, as here, the trust provisions in a will for the welfare of an incompetent are at least equal to, or better than, the statutory provisions, the testator's property should ordinarily be permitted to pass under the will.

Briggs v. Wyoming National Bank

g. Waiver--Briggs v. Wyoming National Bank, 836 P.2d 263 (Wyo. 1992).

1) **Facts.** The Briggs signed an agreement creating Mrs. Briggs' living trust when she executed her will. The trust contained a "no contest" provision to which Mr. Briggs consented. The Briggs had been married for 20 years during their later years in life and had maintained separate ownership of property acquired before the marriage and separate accounts. Upon Mrs. Briggs' death, Mr. Briggs (P) filed a petition to take his elective share of the $900,000 estate and commenced a declaratory judgment action to declare the trust agreement invalid, to include the trust assets in the probate estate, and to declare the beneficiaries' rights. The court entered summary judgment for the trustee and beneficiaries, declaring the trust agreement valid and its provisions enforceable, except for the no contest clause. The parties appeal.

2) **Issues.**

a) Is the waiver valid?

b) If the waiver is valid, is the no contest clause valid?

3) **Held.** a) Yes. b) Yes. Affirmed in part; reversed in part.

a) A waiver must be manifested in some unequivocal manner. P was advised to consult an attorney. He refused, affirmatively stating he consented to Mrs. Briggs' wishes, and voluntarily signed the agreement. He cannot now effectively complain he did not understand what he was doing.

b) The no contest clause does not violate Wyoming's elective share statute, which expressly provides that the right of election of a surviving spouse may be waived by a written waiver.

4) **Dissent.** The decision is made on allegations and not facts established after a trial. There were sufficient disputed questions of material fact to make summary judgment improper.

4. Rights of Surviving Spouse in Community Property.

a. Introduction. In all of the community property states, if an intestate is not survived by descendants, the intestate's one-half share of the community estate passes to the surviving spouse. Because the other half of the community estate belongs to the surviving spouse, the surviving spouse succeeds to the entire estate. In several states, the surviving spouse takes the entire community estate even if the decedent was survived by descendants. In others, the decedent's one-half community share is inherited by his descendants.

b. Classification of assets as community or separate property. This classification is important for tax reasons since under the federal tax law the entire value of a spouse's separate property but only one-half of the community property is included in the deceased spouse's gross estate.

c. **Putting the survivor to an election.** Under the widow's election, an estate planning device, the deceased spouse's will purports to dispose of the entire community property and not just an undivided one-half share, giving the surviving spouse an election, such that if the surviving spouse lays claim to her community interest, she loses the testamentary gifts in her favor. On the other hand, where the testator disposes only of his separate property and his one-half share of community property, the surviving spouse may claim both her share of community property and her devise under the will.

5. **Migrating Couples and Multistate Property Holdings.**

a. **Migration from separate property state to community property state.** Only two states, California and Idaho, give the surviving spouse a remedy in these situations, through the concept of quasi-community property. Quasi-community property is property acquired by one spouse while domiciled in another state which would have been classified as community property had it been acquired while the spouse was domiciled in the community property state. Real property located in another state does not constitute quasi-community property. Upon the death of the acquiring spouse, one-half of the quasi-community property belongs to the surviving spouse; the other half is not subject to testamentary disposition by the decedent.

b. **Migration from community property state to separate property state.** In general, such a change does not affect the preexisting rights of the husband or wife. Community property continues to be community property when the couple and the property move to a separate property state.

c. **Uniform Disposition of Community Property Rights at Death Act.** Under this Act, one-half of the property to which the Act applies is the property of the surviving spouse and is not subject to testamentary disposition by the decedent. This Act has been adopted in about a dozen states.

6. **Spouse Omitted from Premarital Will.**

a. **States without statutes.** The states are divided on the effect of marriage on a previously executed will. In about half the states, marriage by itself does not affect the will. *Rationale:* The new spouse is given adequate protection by dower or elective share statutes (or, in a community property state, by the community property system).

b. **Statutory solutions.** About half the states have statutes under which the testator's subsequent marriage has an effect on the will. In most of these states, the will is only partially revoked. The marriage revokes the will only to the extent of providing the new spouse with an intestate share. After distribution of the spouse's intestate share, the will operates to distribute the remaining assets. These are sometimes referred to as "pretermitted spouse" statutes. Note that the above statutes often provide that the will is not partially or totally revoked if (i) the will makes provision for the new spouse, (ii) the will provides that the spouse's omission was intentional, or (iii) it appears that the will was made in contemplation of marriage.

Estate of Shannon

c. **Spouse omitted from premarital will--Estate of Shannon,** 274 Cal. Rptr. 338 (1990).

1) **Facts.** Shannon (T) executed his will in 1974, naming his daughter sole beneficiary and executrix. T married in 1986 and died in 1988; T made no changes in his will, which was admitted to probate. T's wife (W) petitioned the probate court to determine heirship. The petition was denied. W appeals. During the pendency of the appeal, W died and W's son was substituted as appellant.

2) **Issue.** Was W a pretermitted spouse?

3) **Held.** Yes. Reversed and remanded.

a) The relevant statute provides that if a testator fails to provide in his will for a surviving spouse who married the testator after the execution of testator's will, the omitted spouse shall receive a share.

b) None of the exceptions that would preclude W from sharing in T's estate apply. T's failure to provide does not appear from the will to be intentional. No evidence shows T provided for W outside the will. W did not execute an agreement to waive her share.

c) The exclusionary clause, without more, is insufficient to avoid the statutory presumption of revocation of the will as to the omitted spouse based upon public policy.

B. RIGHTS OF ISSUE OMITTED FROM THE WILL

Pretermitted child statutes are designed to protect children who have been accidentally omitted from the will. In most states, the statute operates only in favor of children born or adopted after the will's execution. In other states, the pretermitted child statute applies to children alive when the will was executed as well as to afterborn and after-adopted children.

Azcunce v. Estate of Azcunce

1. Child Born After Will But Before Codicil--Azcunce v. Estate of Azcunce, 586 So. 2d 1216 (Fla. 1991).

a. **Facts.** T executed a will which established a trust for the benefit of his spouse and his then-born children; there was no provision for after-born children. T subsequently executed a codicil which republished the terms of the will. Petitioner (P) was born after this first codicil but before a second, which, again, republished the will and first codicil and made no mention of after-born children. T died of a heart attack at age 38. P petitioned for a statutory share as a pretermitted child. The trial court denied the petition. P appeals.

b. **Issue.** May a child who is born after the execution of her father's will, but before the execution of a codicil to said will, take a statutory share under Florida's pretermitted child statute when the will and codicil fail to provide for such child and all the other statutory requirements for pretermitted child status are otherwise satisfied?

c. **Held.** No. Affirmed.

1) Under the statute, prior to the second codicil, P was a pretermitted child, a child born after the making of the will who had not received a portion of T's property by way of advancement.

2) The second codicil expressly stated that it republished the original will and first codicil. Thus, P's pretermitted status was destroyed.

3) If T had wished to provide for P, presumably, he would have done so in the second codicil. P was, in effect, disinherited.

4) There is no ambiguity in the will and codicils which would authorize the taking of parole evidence.

2. **No Malpractice Suit Without Priority--Espinosa v. Sparber, Shevin, Shapo, Rosen & Heilbronner,** 612 So. 2d 1378 (Fla. 1993).

Espinosa v. Sparber, Shevin, Shapo, Rosen & Heilbronner

a. **Facts.** After T's daughter was born, T contacted his attorney (D) and indicated his desire to include P in his will. D drafted a will and restructured the trust. However, because of a disagreement between P and D, P never signed the second will. Instead, P executed a second codicil that did not provide for P. P's wife (W) brought a malpractice suit on P's behalf against D. The trial court dismissed for lack of privity and entered summary judgment for D. The court of appeal reversed the dismissal with regard to the estate, affirmed it with regard to P, and certified the question of whether P has standing to bring a legal malpractice action.

b. **Issue.** May a malpractice lawsuit be brought against an attorney who drafted a codicil if the a plaintiff is not in privity with the attorney or an intended third-party beneficiary?

c. **Held.** No. Affirmed.

1) To bring a legal malpractice action, a plaintiff must be in privity with the attorney, where one party has a direct obligation to the other, or an intended third-party beneficiary.

2) Because T is not alive to testify regarding intended third-party beneficiaries, the court is obligated to honor T's intent in conformity with the will contents.

3) T's estate stands in T's shoes and satisfies the privity requirement.

VIII. TRUSTS: CREATION, TYPES, AND CHARACTERISTICS

A. INTRODUCTION

1. **Background.** The trustee of a trust owns the legal interest of the trust property while the beneficiary owns the equitable interest.

2. **The Settlor.** The settlor is the person who creates the trust. A trust created during the settlor's lifetime is an inter vivos trust. A trust created in the settlor's will is a testamentary trust.

3. **The Trustee.** The trustee may be a third party or a beneficiary. Failure to name a trustee will not defeat a trust; a court will appoint a trustee.

4. **The Beneficiaries.** Beneficiaries hold equitable interests. They have a personal claim against the trustee for breach of trust, and equitable claims on the trust property itself.

5. **Use of Trusts in Estate Planning.** Trusts can be used to avoid the probate process. Also, trusts can be used to secure certain tax advantages and for property management, including transferring property to minors or incompetents.

6. **A Trust Compared with a Legal Life Estate.** In most cases, creating a trust with the donee as life beneficiary is preferable to giving the donee a legal life estate, since resolution of various administrative problems with the estate is facilitated by having a trustee.

B. CREATION OF A TRUST

1. **Intent to Create a Trust.** While the settlor must have the intent to create a trust, no particular words need to be used. Where the grantor conveys property to a grantee to hold for the use and benefit of another, this is a sufficient manifestation of an intention to create a trust.

Jimenez v. Lee

a. **Application--Jimenez v. Lee,** 274 Or. 457, 547 P.2d 126 (1976).

1) **Facts.** In 1945, the paternal grandmother of Betsy Lee Jimenez (P) purchased a $1,000 U.S. Savings Bond registered in the name of P and/or Jason Lee (D), the father of P, and/or Dorothy Lee, the mother of P, to be used for P's educational needs. In 1956, Mrs. Adolph Diercks gave $500 to P and made identical gifts to D's other two children. Mrs. Diercks deposited the $1,500 in a savings account in the names of D and his three children. Thereafter, D cashed the savings bond and invested the proceeds in common stock of the Commercial Bank of Salem, Oregon, with the shares registered as "Jason Lee, Custodian . . . for Betsy Lee [P]." At the same time, D closed the joint savings account and invested $1,000 of the proceeds in Commercial Bank stock, taking this stock as custodian for his children. P contends that the gifts for her educational needs created trusts in each instance and that the trusts survived D's investment of the trust assets in the Commercial Bank stock. P

brought an action for an accounting. The trial court held for D. P appeals.

2) **Issues.**

a) To create a trust relationship, is it essential to expressly direct that the subject matter of a gift be held in trust?

b) Does a trustee have the responsibility to administer a trust solely in the interest of the beneficiary of the trust and to prove that any expenditures made were made for trust purposes?

3) **Held.** a) No. b) Yes. Case reversed and remanded.

a) It is undisputed that the gifts were made for the educational needs of P. While the respective donors did not expressly direct D to hold the subject matter of the gift in trust, this is not essential to create a trust relationship. It is enough if the transfer of the property is made with the intent to vest the beneficial ownership in a third person. This was clearly shown in the present case.

b) Having decided that a trust was created for the benefit of P, it follows that D's purchase of the Commercial Bank stock as custodian for P was ineffectual to expand D's powers over the trust property from that of trustee to that of custodian. D's attempt to broaden his power violated his duty to the beneficiary to administer the trust solely in the interest of the beneficiary. Here, many of the items that D lists as trust expenditures are either questionable or clearly outside the purpose of an educational trust. The trial court therefore erred in finding that P has received the accounting that she sought and is entitled to no further accounting.

c) The case must be remanded for an accounting to be predicated upon a trustee's duty to account and the trustee's burden to prove that the expenditures were made for trust purposes. In determining whether D has met this strict burden of proof, the trial court must adhere to the rule that all doubts are resolved against a trustee who maintains an inadequate accounting system.

b. **Custodianship under Uniform Transfers to Minors Act.** Under this Act, a gift to a minor may be transferred to a person as custodian for the benefit of the minor. The creation of this custodianship is simpler than the creation of a trust. The custodian is a fiduciary. To the extent that the custodial property is not expended for the minor's benefit, the custodian is required to transfer the property to the minor on his attaining the age of 21 or, if the minor dies before attaining the age of 21, to the estate of the minor.

c. **Precatory language and equitable charges.** Precatory language—such as "To A with the hope that A will care for B"—creates a moral obligation unenforceable at law. Uncertainty can be avoided by specifying that only a moral obligation is desired; *e.g.*, "I wish, but do not legally require, that A will care for B." In contrast, an equitable charge occurs when a testator devises property to a person "subject to" the payment of a certain sum of money to another person.

2. **Necessity of Trust Property.** A trust cannot exist without trust property. Any type of property—contingent remainders, life insurance policies, leasehold interests—will suffice. The key question is whether the particular claim will be called property by a court.

Unthank v. Rippstein

a. **Promise to make gifts in the future--Unthank v. Rippstein,** 386 S.W.2d 134 (Tex. 1964).

1) **Facts.** C.P. Craft wrote a letter to Iva Rippstein (P), promising to pay her $200 a month for the next five years provided he lived that long. In the margin of the letter, he wrote: "I have stricken out the words 'provided I live that long' and hereby and herewith bind my estate to make the $200 monthly payments." Craft died three days after writing the letter. P brought suit against the executors of his estate (Ds) for declaratory judgment adjudicating their liability to pay future installments as they mature. The trial court granted the executors' motion for summary judgment. The court of appeals reversed and rendered judgment for P, holding that the writing in question established a voluntary trust under which Craft bound his property to the extent of the promised payments. Ds appeal.

2) **Issue.** Is a writing promising to make gifts in the future binding as a voluntary trust?

3) **Held.** No. The judgment of the court of appeals is reversed and that of the trial court is affirmed.

a) While the transactions under review are in the form of voluntary trusts, they are governed in general by the rules applicable to gifts. The principal difference between such a trust and a gift lies in the fact that in the case of a gift the thing given passes to the donee, while in the case of a voluntary trust only the equitable or beneficial title passes to the beneficiary.

b) Here, the language of the notation of Craft cannot be expanded to show an intention on the part of Craft to place his property in trust. The most Craft did was to express an intention to make monthly gifts to P accompanied by an ineffectual attempt to bind his estate in futuro; the writing was no more than a promise to make similar gifts in the future and as such is unenforceable.

b. **Resulting and constructive trusts.**

1) **Resulting trust.** A resulting trust is a trust that arises by operation of law in one of two situations: (i) where an express trust fails, or (ii) where one person pays the purchase price for property and causes title to the property to be taken in the name of another person who is not a natural object of the bounty of the purchaser.

2) **Constructive trust.** A constructive trust is the name given the flexible remedy imposed to prevent unjust enrichment. A constructive trustee is under a duty to convey the property to another on the ground that the retention of the property would be wrongful. In general, the requirements for a constructive trust are:

(i) A confidential relationship;

(ii) A promise, express or implied;

(iii) A transfer of property in reliance on the promise; and

(iv) Unjust enrichment of the transferee.

A constructive trust may also be imposed where a promise or confidential relationship is not involved but the court is moved simply to avoid unjust enrichment.

c. **Trust distinguished from debt.** The crucial factor to differentiate between a trust relationship and an ordinary debt is whether the recipient of the funds is entitled to use them as his own and commingle them with his own monies.

1) **Trust based upon interest not in existence--Brainard v. Commissioner,** 91 F.2d 880 (7th Cir. 1937). Brainard v. Commissioner

a) **Facts.** Brainard, a taxpayer, contemplated trading in the stock market. He consulted a lawyer and was advised that it was possible for him to trade in trust for his children and other members of his family. Brainard stated to his wife and mother that he declared a trust, upon certain terms and conditions, of his stock trading for the benefit of his family. He agreed to assume personally any losses resulting from the venture, and to distribute the profits, if any, in equal shares to his wife, mother, and two children after deducting a reasonable compensation for his services. Brainard carried on his trading operations and at the end of the year determined his compensation to be slightly less than $10,000, which he reported in his income tax for that year. The profits remaining were then divided among the members of the family in approximately equal shares, which they reported in their respective income tax returns. The Board of Tax Appeals held that the income in controversy was taxable as part of gross income. Brainard appeals.

b) **Issue.** Can a trust be based upon an interest that had not come into existence at the time the trust is declared and in which no one had a present interest?

c) **Held.** No. Order of the board affirmed.

(1) An interest which has not come into existence or which has ceased to exist cannot be held in trust. A person can make a contract binding himself to create a trust of an interest if he should thereafter acquire it, but such an agreement is not binding as a contract unless the requirements of contract law are complied with. An expectancy cannot be the subject matter of a trust, and an attempted creation, being merely a promise to transfer property in the future, is invalid unless supported by consideration. Here, the taxpayer had no property interest in the profits in stock trading because there were none in existence at the time. His declaration amounted to nothing more than a

promise to create a trust. We therefore must determine whether it complied with the law of contracts.

(2) It is elementary that an executory contract, in order to be enforceable, must be based upon valuable consideration. Here, the declaration was gratuitous. Even if we assume that it was based on love and affection, this would not be sufficient consideration for a promise.

(3) This does not mean, however, that the taxpayer had no right to carry out his declaration after the subject matter had come into existence. The question is, therefore, at what times did the respective earnings that constitute the trust fund come into existence and at what times did the trust attach to them?

(4) Where a person purports to declare himself trustee of an interest not in existence, no trust arises even if the interest later comes into existence, unless there is a manifestation of intention at that later time. Mere silence ordinarily will not be such a manifestation.

(5) Here, the profits in question were not impressed with a trust when they first came into existence. The taxpayer's crediting the profits to the beneficiaries on his books seems to constitute his first subsequent expression of intention to become a trustee of the fund. Before that, the declaration could not have been enforced against him, and his mere silence should not be considered an expression of his intention to establish a trust.

Speelman v. Pascal

2) **Gift made of property not in existence at time of gift--Speelman v. Pascal,** 10 N.Y.2d 313, 178 N.E.2d 723 (1961).

a) **Facts.** In 1952, Gabriel Pascal Enterprises, Ltd. made an agreement with the estate of George Bernard Shaw that granted to the corporation the exclusive rights to prepare and produce a musical play based on Shaw's *Pygmalion* and a motion picture version of the musical. Prior to this agreement, Pascal had produced a nonmusical movie version of the play under rights obtained by Pascal from Shaw during Shaw's life. The new agreement provided that the Shaw estate would receive 3% of the receipts of the musical play and movie. It also provided that the license was to terminate if the licensee did not arrange to have the play produced within certain time periods. At a time when the license still had two years to run, Gabriel Pascal, who died shortly thereafter, wrote, signed, and delivered to Speelman (P) a letter that confirmed that he would give to P 5% of the profits obtained in England and throughout the world and 2% of the profits in the United States. P brought suit to enforce Pascal's promise to pay the share of the profits. The trial court held for P. Mrs. Pascal (D), Pascal's widow, appeals.

b) **Issue.** May a valid present gift be made of property that is not in existence at the time the gift is made?

c) **Held.** Yes. Judgment affirmed.

(1) The question here is: Did the delivery of the letter constitute a valid, complete, present gift to P by way of assignment of a share in future

royalties? We hold that it did. There are many instances of courts enforcing assignments of rights to sums which were expected thereafter to become due to the assignor. In those cases that failed, there had not been such a completed and irrevocable delivery of the subject matter of the gift as to put the gift beyond cancellation by the donor. Here, there was nothing left for Pascal to do in order to make an irrevocable transfer to P of part of Pascal's right to receive royalties from the productions.

3. **Necessity of Trust Beneficiaries.** A trust must have one or more beneficiaries. However, the beneficiaries may be unborn or unascertained when the trust is created. If the beneficiaries are too indefinite to be ascertained at the time the trust becomes effective, the trust may fail, in which case there will be a resulting trust in favor of the settlor, his heirs, or other successors in interest.

   a. **Identification of beneficiaries--Clark v. Campbell,** 82 N.H. 281, 133 A. 166 (1926). Clark v. Campbell

      1) **Facts.** The will of the decedent bequeathed to his trustees articles of personal property "such as books, photographic albums, pictures, statuary, [etc.]" to give to the decedent's friends as the trustees shall select. The lower court reserved the question of whether the enumeration of the chattels was intended to be restrictive or merely indicative of the variety of personal property bequeathed. On appeal, it is argued that the bequest for the benefit of the testator's friends must fail for want of certainty of beneficiaries.

      2) **Issues.**

         a) Does a bequest to a trustee to distribute personal property to a testator's friends constitute a private trust?

         b) Must a private trust have a beneficiary or a class of beneficiaries indicated in the will capable of coming into court and claiming the benefit of the bequest?

      3) **Held.** a) Yes. b) Yes. Case discharged.

         a) At common law, there cannot be a bequest to an indefinite person. There must be a beneficiary or a class of beneficiaries indicated in the will capable of coming into court and claiming the benefit of the bequest. This principle applies to private trusts but not to public trusts and charities. Here, the language of the will, granting the trustees property of the described class to give to the testator's friends as they shall select, clearly discloses an intention to create a private trust.

         b) However, we hold that the will does not provide for definite and ascertainable beneficiaries. It thus cannot be sustained as a private trust. The word "friends," unlike "relations," has no accepted statutory or other controlling limitations and in fact has no precise sense at all. No sufficient criterion is furnished to govern the selection of the individuals from the class.

c) When a gift is impressed with a trust ineffectively declared and incapable of taking effect because of the indefiniteness of the beneficiary, the donee will hold the property in trust for the next taker under the will, or for the next of kin by way of a resulting trust. The trustees therefore hold the property under consideration to be disposed of as part of the residue.

In re Searight's Estate

b. Honorary trusts--*In re* Searight's Estate, 87 Ohio App. 417, 95 N.E.2d 779 (1950).

1) **Facts.** The will of the decedent, George Searight, bequeathed his dog, Trixie, to Florence Hand, and directed his executor to deposit $1,000 to be used by him to pay Hand the sum of 75¢ per day for the care of the dog as long as it shall live. Hand accepted the bequest of Trixie and the executor paid her 75¢ per day for the keep and care of the dog. The trial court held the provision in the will valid. This appeal followed.

2) **Issues.**

a) Is the creation of a trust for the benefit of a specific animal the proper subject of an honorary trust?

b) Does a bequest for the benefit of a specific animal "as long as it shall live" violate the Rule Against Perpetuities?

3) **Held.** a) Yes. b) No. Judgment affirmed.

a) A bequest for the care of a specific animal is an "honorary trust," that is, one binding the conscience of the trustee, since there is no beneficiary capable of enforcing the trust. The modern authorities uphold the validity of such gifts where the person to whom the power is given is willing to carry out the testator's wishes. We hold that the bequest for the care of the dog, Trixie, is not in and of itself unlawful.

b) Nor does the bequest violate the Rule Against Perpetuities. It is to be noted that unless a trust established for specific animals limits the duration of the trust—that is, the time during which the power is to be exercised—to human lives, we will have honorary trusts established for animals of great longevity that possibly could continue longer than the maximum period allowed by the Rule Against Perpetuities. Here, however, the rule is not violated since the money given for the purpose of caring for the animal is limited to $1,000 at 75¢ per day. This sum of money will be fully exhausted in three years and 238 1/3 days. It is thus apparent that the testator provided a time limit for the exercise of the power given to the executor and that such time limit is less than the maximum period allowed under the Rule Against Perpetuities.

4. **Oral Inter Vivos Trusts of Land.** An oral inter vivos trust of personal property is enforceable, but if the subject matter of the oral trust is land, a written instrument is required to make the trust effective. However, some

courts will impose a constructive trust upon property if the transferee stood in a confidential relationship to the transferor.

a. **Oral promise to reconvey land held sufficient to impose a constructive trust--Hieble v. Hieble,** 164 Conn. 56, 316 A.2d 777 (1972). Hieble v. Hieble

1) **Facts.** Mrs. Hieble (P) transferred title of her real estate by deed to her son (D) and to her daughter. The motivation for the transfer was that P feared a recurrence of cancer. She and the grantees orally agreed that the transfer would be temporary; that she would remain in control of the property and pay all expenses and taxes; and that once the illness had passed, the grantees would reconvey the property to P upon request. Five years after the conveyance, P requested that D reconvey his title to her. D refused. P brought suit against D seeking a reconveyance of the property. The trial court held for P. D appeals.

2) **Issue.** Will a constructive trust be imposed upon property where the donee by deed has received realty under an oral promise to hold and reconvey to the grantor but refuses to perform his promise?

3) **Held.** Yes. Judgment affirmed.

a) D has not attacked the court's finding that the agreement was in fact made, nor does he contest the receipt of parol evidence as having violated the Statute of Frauds. Since the finding of facts is not challenged, the conclusion of the court that the parties stood in a confidential relationship must stand unless it is unreasonably drawn. We grant that the bond between parent and child is not per se a fiduciary one; it does generate, however, a natural inclination to repose great confidence and trust.

b) This case comes squarely within the general rule that where the owner of an interest in land transfers it inter vivos to another in trust for the transferor, but no memorandum is signed as required by the Statute of Frauds, and the transferee refuses to perform the trust, the transferee holds the interest upon a constructive trust for the transferor if the transferee at the time of the transfer was in a confidential relationship to the transferor.

5. **Oral Trusts for Disposition at Death.** Where a testator devises property to his executors upon trusts not defined in the will but the existence of which the testator has communicated to the executors before the will's execution, some courts hold that such trusts may be proved by oral evidence. Other courts refuse to follow this line of decisions, holding that the trust has not been sufficiently defined by the will to take effect, and the equitable interest goes by way of resulting trust to the heirs as property of the deceased.

a. **Application--Olliffe v. Wells,** 130 Mass. 221 (1881). Olliffe v. Wells

1) **Facts.** The will of the decedent, Ellen Donovan, left the residue of her estate to Rev. Wells (D) to distribute in such manner as in his discretion shall appear best calculated to carry out the wishes that she had expressed to him or may express to him. The heirs of the

decedent (Ps) brought suit against D, claiming that the residue should be distributed to them. In his answer, D stated that the decedent had stated to him her wish that her estate be used for charitable purposes. D further stated that he desired and intended to distribute the residue for these purposes.

2) **Issue.** Where a will shows the devisee to take legal title only and not the beneficial interest, and the trust is not sufficiently defined by will to take effect, will a court impose a resulting trust on the heirs of the decedent as to the property of the decedent not disposed of by will?

3) **Held.** Yes. Judgment for Ps.

a) It has been held that if a testator devises property to his executors upon trusts not defined in the will, but which, as he states in the will, he has communicated to them before the will's execution, such trusts, if for lawful purposes, may be proved by the admission of the executors or by oral evidence and enforced against them. It has also been held that such trusts may be enforced against the heirs or next of kin.

b) We reject this line of cases. The will upon its face shows that the devisee takes the legal title only and not the beneficial interest, and the trust is not sufficiently defined by the will to take effect. Thus, the equitable interest goes, by way of resulting trust, to the heirs as property of the deceased, not disposed of by will. They cannot be deprived of that equitable interest unless signified in those forms which the law makes essential to every testamentary disposition. A trust not sufficiently declared on the face of the will cannot therefore be set up by extrinsic evidence to defeat the rights of the heirs at law.

C. DISCRETIONARY TRUSTS

In a mandatory trust, the trustee must distribute all the income. In a discretionary trust, the trustee has discretion over payment of either the income or the principal or both.

Marsman v. Nasca

1. Trustee's Duty--Marsman v. Nasca, 573 N.E.2d 1025 (Mass. 1991).

a. **Facts.** Testator was survived by her second husband (H), for whom she provided in a trust. Trustee (T) was directed to pay quarterly income to H and, after having considered H's sources of income, to pay principle for H's comfortable support and maintenance. H obtained title by operation of law to the Wellesley home owned as tenants by the entirety, but testator also indicated in her will her intent to convey the property to H. Upon Testator's death, Farr, the attorney, met with H. H was forced to reduce his style of living dramatically and to apply for a mortgage to pay bills. Farr was aware of H's status because he replied to an inquiry of the mortgage bank and H had asked Farr for money on one occasion. Farr asked H to support his need in writing and wrote to H that Farr thought the trust language was "broad enough to permit a distribution of principle." H never asked again from the date of Testator's death in 1971 until H was admitted to a nursing home in 1983. Farr had given him only $300 beyond the income of the trust. H remarried in 1972 and executed a simple will drafted by Farr, leaving most of H's property to his wife (P). By 1974, H could not meet expenses and conveyed his home to Testator's daughter by a former marriage and her husband. The daughter took over the mortgage payments, taxes, insurance, and major repairs. H retained a life estate. Farr had never advised H he could use the trust principal for the expenses of the home. The daughter died before H. Upon H's death the daughter's husband asked P to vacate. P brought this action in probate court. The court found T in breach of his duty to H and ordered the husband to convey the home to P and also ordered Farr to reimburse T's daughter's husband from the remaining portion of H's trust for the expenses he and T's daughter had paid for the upkeep of the property. If the trust was insufficient, the court found Farr personally liable. P appeals the denial of attorneys' fees. T's daughter's husband and Farr appeal from the denial of their motions to amend the findings and for a new trial.

b. **Issues.**

1) Does a trustee, holding a discretionary power to pay principal for the "comfortable support and maintenance" of a beneficiary, have a duty to inquire into the financial resources of that beneficiary so as to recognize his needs?

2) If so, was the court's remedy for such failure correct?

c. **Held.** 1) Yes. 2) No. Vacated and remanded.

1) The requirement that a trustee's power must be exercised with sound judgment which follows from a due appreciation of trust responsibility imposes upon a trustee a duty of inquiry into the beneficiary's needs.

2) T also failed to meet his responsibilities of distribution under the trust.

3) The conveyance was supported by sufficient consideration, and T's daughter and her husband had no notice of a breach of trust and were not themselves guilty of breach of fiduciary duty; they cannot be charged as constructive trustees of the property.

4) The remedy for T's failure to expend trust principal in this circumstance is to impress a constructive trust on the amounts which should have been distributed but which were not because of T's error. On remand these amounts will be determined and paid to H's estate.

5) The exculpatory clause in Testator's will, drafted by Farr and holding Farr harmless, was incorrectly invalidated by the probate court since there was no evidence that the insertion of the clause was an abuse of Farr's fiduciary relationship with Testator at the time the will was drawn.

6) Farr's actions were not breaches of trust committed in bad faith or intentionally or with reckless indifference. Nor are they willful neglect or default.

D. SPENDTHRIFT TRUSTS

In a spendthrift trust, the beneficiaries cannot voluntarily alienate their interests, nor can their creditors reach their interests.

Shelley v. Shelley

1. Immunity from Alimony and Child Support--Shelley v. Shelley, 223 Or. 328, 354 P.2d 282 (1960).

a. **Facts.** Hugh Shelley left a trust the income of which was to be paid to his wife, Gertrude Shelley, as long as she lived, and after her death to his son, Grant Shelley. The trust also provided that each beneficiary was prevented from alienating his or her interest in the estate, nor would the interest or estate be subject to claims of creditors. Grant Shelley was first married to Patricia Shelley, and two children were born of this marriage. Thereafter, Patricia divorced Grant, with the divorce decree requiring payment for support. Grant later married Betty Shelley (P), and two children were born of this marriage. P later obtained a divorce from Grant, with the divorce decree requiring both support and alimony. The U.S. National Bank of Portland, Oregon (D) invested the trust assets in securities, which are now held by it together with the undisbursed income from the trust. P obtained an injunction restraining the disbursement of any of the trust assets. Patricia Shelley brought a garnishment proceeding by which she sought to subject the trust to the claim for support money provided for in her divorce decree. D then brought a bill of interpleader, tendering to the court all of the funds held in trust and praying for an order establishing the rights of the parties. The trial court entered a decree subjecting the accrued income of the trust to the claims of P and Patricia Shelley; subjecting future income of the trust to the periodic obligations brought by P and Patricia Shelley; and holding that in the event the trust income was insufficient to satisfy such claims, the corpus of the trust was subject to invasion.

b. **Issue.** Is a spendthrift provision of a trust effective against the claims of the beneficiary's former spouse for alimony and for support of the beneficiary's child?

c. **Held.** No. Affirmed in part and reversed in part.

1) Although a trust is a spendthrift trust or trust for support, the interest of the beneficiary can be reached in satisfaction of an enforceable claim by the spouse or child of a beneficiary for support, or by the spouse for alimony. The privilege of disposing of property is not absolute; it is hedged with various restrictions where there are policy considerations warranting the limitation.

2) Public policy requires that the interest of the beneficiary of a trust should be subject to the claims for child support. It is clear that parents have the obligation to support their children. Were we to bar such claims for support, we would have the spectacle of a parent enjoying the benefits of a trust while the community pays for the support of the children. With regard to alimony for the spouse, the same considerations apply; in many

cases, if the beneficiary's interest cannot be reached, the state may be called upon to support the spouse.

3) We hold that the beneficiary's interest in the income of the trust is subject to the claims of P for alimony and to the claims for support of the children as provided under both divorce decrees. We adopt the view, however, that the claimants may reach only that much of the income which the trial court deems reasonable.

4) The question of the claimant's right to reach the corpus of the trust involves other considerations. There is nothing in the trust here which would indicate the testator's intent to make P either directly or indirectly the beneficiary of the trust. At least with respect to the corpus, an Oregon statute makes the subject matter of the trust free from attachment. It follows that the lower court erred in making the corpus of the trust subject to P's claim for alimony.

5) Whether the children can reach the corpus involves still a different problem. The trust states that disbursements to Grant Shelley's children were to be made "in case of any emergency whereby unusual and extraordinary expenses are necessary. . . ." D claims that the expenses claimed in this case are not unusual or extraordinary. We disagree. We construe the clause to include the circumstances involved here—where the children are deserted by their father and are in need of support.

6) The decree of the lower court, permitting the corpus of the trust to be invaded, was too broad. First, it improperly included P's claim for alimony; and second, it permitted encroachment upon the corpus without reference to whether the trustee has exercised his discretion or whether there has been an emergency as contemplated by the testator. The decree therefore should have permitted an invasion of the corpus only if it was necessary first to reach the income under the circumstances mentioned and such income was then insufficient. Further, the decree should have made such corpus available only in event of the trustee's exercise of discretion under the emergency circumstances provided for in the trust.

2. Creditors' Rights in Support Trusts and Discretionary Trusts.

a. **Support trusts.** A support trust is one in which the trustee is directed to make distributions as necessary for the education and maintenance of the beneficiary, and to expend the income and principal only for that purpose. Creditors of the beneficiary of a support trust cannot reach the beneficiary's interest, except suppliers of necessaries may recover through the beneficiary's right to support.

b. **Discretionary trusts.** A discretionary trust is one in which the trustee is given discretion whether to apply or withhold payments of income or principal to or from a particular beneficiary, or (in some cases) to distribute the same to some other beneficiary. Before the trustee exercises her discretion to make payments to the beneficiary, the beneficiary's interest cannot be reached by his creditors. If, however, the trustee decides to pay over or to apply some amount of trust income or principal to the beneficiary, the right thereto vests in the beneficiary and his creditors may then reach it.

3. **Medicaid Trusts.** To qualify for Medicaid, an individual's financial resources must not exceed a few thousand dollars. Whether trusts that provide support to the individual are counted among the individual's resources for Medicaid purposes depends upon the type of trust.

   a. **Discretionary trusts.** If an individual's assets form all or part of the trust and if the trust was established by the individual, a spouse, or a person acting on the individual's behalf, for purposes of Medicaid, a trust is deemed to be created by the individual. All of the assets of a revocable trust are considered available resources. Any income or principal that may be paid to the individual under any circumstances under the terms of an irrevocable trust are considered resources.

      1) **Exceptions.** A discretionary trust created by will by one spouse for the benefit of the survivor is not deemed an available resource. If a trust is created for a disabled person to provide care for the individual over and above what Medicaid may provide, and there is a provision for the trust to reimburse Medicaid upon the individual's death, the trust is not considered an available resource.

   b. **Third-person trusts.** Income or principal actually or legally available to a beneficiary of a trust established by a third person is considered a resource.

   c. **Careful drafting.** This area of the law demands great caution. Judicial interpretations of trust language are not consistent. Public policy considerations are unsettled. What works in one jurisdiction may not work in another.

E. MODIFICATION AND TERMINATION OF TRUSTS

1. **Modification of Distributive Provisions.** Some courts will permit a deviation of the terms of an express gift in instances where an unforeseen emergency threatens the accomplishment of the testator's purpose.

In re Trust of Stuchell

   a. **Trust modification denied--*In re* Trust of Stuchell,** 801 P.2d 852 (Or. 1990).

      1) **Facts.** Petitioner's (P's) four children were remainder beneficiaries of a trust. One of them, Harrell, was mentally retarded and unable to live without assistance. Harrell lived in a state facility and received Medicaid and Social Security benefits, both of which have income and resource limitations for participants. P requested the court to approve a modification of the trust so as to prevent Harrell's remainder from being distributed to him if he survives the trust's income beneficiaries. The proposed modification was designed to prevent Harrell's disqualification for public assistance. P appeals from the trial court's dismissal of her petition.

2) **Issue.** Should P's proposed modification be approved?

3) **Held.** No. Affirmed.

a) P relies on common law authority for allowing a court to approve the proposed modification. A trust may be terminated under very limited circumstances: (i) all beneficiaries agree, (ii) none is under a legal disability, and (iii) the trust's purposes would not be frustrated in doing so.

b) To extend the rule, P relies on Restatement (Second) Trusts, section 167(1), which provides that a court may permit the trustee to do acts not authorized by the terms of the trust.

c) However, Comment b to section 167(1) states that a court will not permit a deviation from the terms of a trust "merely because such deviation would be more advantageous to the beneficiaries than a compliance with such direction." This limitation precludes permitting the proposed amendment, the only purpose of which is to make the trust more advantageous to the beneficiaries.

b. **Deviation allowed--Hamerstrom v. Commerce Bank of Kansas City,** 808 S.W.2d 434 (Mo. 1991).

Hamerstrom v. Commerce Bank of Kansas City

1) **Facts.** Elizabeth (P) petitioned for a deviation to increase the amount she received monthly from a trust. P's husband and two sons, remainder beneficiaries, consented. A guardian ad litem appointed by the court to represent the interests of unknown and unascertained beneficiaries of the remainder opposed the action. The trial court denied the petition and P's request for attorneys' fees. P appeals.

2) **Issue.** Are the possible issue of P's two sons beneficiaries contemplated within the applicable statute which authorizes a court to vary the terms of a private trust when all adult beneficiaries consent and after making a finding that the variation will benefit minor, unborn, and unascertained beneficiaries?

3) **Held.** No. Reversed and remanded.

a) Missouri follows the rule that if the material purpose of a settlor has not been attained, even if all of the beneficiaries of a trust consent, a trust cannot be terminated prior to the date specified by the trust terms.

b) The statute modifies that rule but precludes a deviation when certain protected beneficiaries exist and it is found that the proposed deviations do not benefit the protected beneficiaries.

c) A beneficiary is one who has any present or future interest, vested or contingent, and also includes the owner of an interest by assignment or other transfer. [UPC §1-201(3)]

d) A testator's intention must be determined by what the will actually says. The trust in the instant case does not provide for the heirs or surviving issue of one of the sons to take if one son dies. Rather, the deceased son's share will be delivered to the surviving brother.

e) Where a challenge is made regarding a trust, solely for a party's own benefit and no benefit to the trust estate is shown, attorneys' fees paid from the trust estate cannot normally be awarded. However, since all beneficiaries can agree to terminate a trust, it is implicit in their extensive powers that they may also authorize the payment of attorneys' fees. All present and contingent adult beneficiaries in the instant case have consented to modify the trust and can also authorize payment of attorneys' fees.

2. **Termination of Trusts.** If the settlor and all beneficiaries consent, a trust may be terminated. The weight of authority provides, however, that a trust cannot be terminated prior to the time fixed for termination, even though all the beneficiaries consent, if termination would be contrary to a material purpose of the settlor.

In re Estate of Brown

a. **Remaining material purpose--*In re* Estate of Brown,** 148 Vt. 94, 528 A.2d 752 (1987).

1) **Facts.** Andrew Brown died in 1977, settling his entire estate in a trust. The relevant portion of the trust instrument provided that the trust would be used for the education of the children of his nephew, Woolson Brown. After this purpose was accomplished, the income from the trust and such part of the principal as was necessary would be used by the trustee for the care, maintenance, and welfare of Woolson Brown and his wife, Rosemary, so that they might live in the style and manner to which they were accustomed during the remainder of their natural lives. Upon their demise, any remainder of the trust was to be paid to their then-living children in equal shares.

The trustee complied with the terms of the trust by using the proceeds to pay for the education of the children of Woolson and Rosemary Brown. After he determined that their education was complete, the trustee began distribution of trust income to the lifetime beneficiaries, Woolson and Rosemary.

In 1983, Woolson and Rosemary petitioned the probate court for termination of trust, arguing that the sole remaining purpose of the trust was to maintain their lifestyle and that distribution of the remaining assets was necessary to accomplish this purpose. The remaindermen (Woolson and Rosemary's children) filed consents to the proposed termination. The probate court denied the petition to terminate, and the petitioners appealed to the Washington Superior Court. The superior court reversed, concluding that continuation of the trust was no longer necessary because the only material purpose, the education of the children, had been accomplished. An appeal by the trustee followed.

2) **Issue.** If any material purpose of the trust remains to be accomplished, may the trust be terminated if all beneficiaries consent?

3) **Held.** No. Judgment reversed.

a) An active trust may not be terminated, even with the consent of all the beneficiaries, if a material purpose of the settlor remains to be accomplished.

b) If either a support trust or a spendthrift trust were involved, termination could not be compelled by the beneficiaries because a material purpose of the settlor would remain unsatisfied.

c) The trust at issue does not qualify as a support trust. A support trust is created where the trustee is directed to use trust income or principal for the benefit of an individual, but only to the extent necessary to support the individual. Because the trustee must, at the very least, pay all of the trust income to beneficiaries Woolson and Rosemary Brown, the trust cannot be characterized as a support trust.

d) The trust also does not qualify as a spendthrift trust. A trust in which by the terms of the trust or by statute a valid restraint on the voluntary and involuntary transfer of the interest of the beneficiary is imposed is a spendthrift trust. The terms of the trust instrument do not manifest Andrew Brown's intention to create such a trust. The mere fact that an interest in a trust is not transferable does not make the trust a spendthrift trust.

e) Termination cannot be compelled here because a material purpose of the settlor remains unaccomplished. The settlor's intention to assure a lifelong income to Woolson and Rosemary Brown would be defeated if termination of the trust were allowed.

b. **Trusts remaining indestructible beyond the perpetuities period.** A trust is not void merely because it can extend beyond the perpetuities period. The Rule Against Perpetuities applies to interests in a trust and requires that they vest or fail within the period provided by the Rule, but it does not limit the duration of the trust. Nonetheless, a trust cannot remain indestructible by the beneficiaries beyond the perpetuities period.

F. CHARITABLE TRUSTS

A charitable trust is one for the benefit of a class of persons, and not for the benefit of the community at large, and must be for relief of poverty, or for the advancement of education, religion, health, or other charitable purpose. A trust is not charitable merely because it is for the benefit of a class of people. The nature of the charitable purpose must be for the relief of poverty or for the advancement of education, religion, health, or other charitable purpose. It must benefit the general public or some particular class of the public that is indefinite in number.

Shenandoah Valley National Bank v. Taylor

1. **Creation of a Charitable Trust--Shenandoah Valley National Bank v. Taylor,** 192 Va. 135, 63 S.E.2d 786 (1951).

   a. **Facts.** The will of the decedent, Charles Henry, provided that the residue of his estate was to be held in trust by the Shenandoah Valley National Bank of Winchester, to be paid by the trustee on the last school days of each calendar year before Christmas and Easter "in as many equal parts as there are children in the first, second, and third grades of the John Kerr School of the City of Winchester, and (the trustee) shall pay one of each such equal parts to each child in such grades, to be used by such child in the furtherance of his or her obtainment of an education." One of the next of kin of the decedent filed suit against the executor and trustee challenging the validity of the will, which undertook to create a charitable trust. The heir argued that the trust did not constitute a charitable trust and was invalid in that it violated the Rule Against Perpetuities. The trial court held that the trust was not charitable but was a private trust, and thus violated the Rule Against Perpetuities and was void.

   b. **Issue.** Must a trust be public in nature before it will be considered a charitable trust?

   c. **Held.** Yes. Affirmed.

      1) A charitable trust is created only if the settlor properly manifests an intention to create a charitable trust. Charitable purposes include the relief of poverty and the advancement of education, religion, health, municipal purposes, and other purposes the accomplishment of which are beneficial to the community. It is essential that the charity be for the benefit of an indefinite number of persons, for if all the beneficiaries are personally designated, the trust lacks the essential element of indefiniteness, which is one characteristic of a legal charity.

      2) Here, the time for payment of the funds to the children is when their minds would be far removed from studies and indicates that no educational purpose was in the testator's mind. Execution of the mandate of the trust accomplishes no educational purpose. It merely places the income forever beyond the range of the trust. The words of the trust import an intent to have the trustee pay each child an allotted share. The testator's intent was to bestow upon each child gifts that would bring happiness on the two holidays, which purpose falls far short of an educational trust.

      3) It is argued that even if the will fails to create a charitable trust for educational purposes, it nonetheless produces a desirable social effect. We disagree. A trust from which the income is to be paid at stated intervals to each member of a designated segment of the public, without regard to whether the recipients are poor or in need, is not for the relief of poverty, nor is it a social benefit to the community.

There is no language in this will that permits the trustee to limit the recipients to the schoolchildren who are in necessitous circumstances. Accordingly, it is mere benevolence—a private trust—and not a charitable trust.

G. MODIFICATION OF CHARITABLE TRUSTS: CY PRES

Where a general charitable bequest is impracticable, some courts will execute a gift cy pres through a scheme framed by the court for the purpose of carrying out the general purpose.

1. General Charitable Purpose--*In re* Neher, 18 N.E.2d 625 (N.Y. 1939).

In re Neher

a. **Facts.** T's will devised certain real property to the village (P), with a direction that P erect a hospital named as a memorial to T's deceased husband. P accepted the property in 1931. In 1937, P petitioned the surrogate's court to construe and reform the relevant provision of T's will, directing that P would receive the property and erect an administration building in T's husband's memory since a nearby hospital adequately served P's needs. P's petition was denied. The appellate division affirmed. P appeals.

b. **Issue.** Was T's devise a general intention to devote the property to charitable purposes instead of a specific intention to limit the use of the property to the operation of a hospital?

c. **Held.** Yes. Reversed and remanded.

1) This was a gift to a whole community. That was the first stated design of beneficence.

2) The direction that a hospital be erected shows an absence of particularity as to type, management, or control, except that P's trustees were to be the governing board. This absence of particularity is a strong showing against the view that the instruction was the substance of the gift.

3) We think T's intention was a general charitable gift with an added graft as to T's desires. Such a graft may be ignored when compliance is altogether impracticable, and the gift may be executed cy pres through a scheme devised by the court to carry out the general charitable purpose.

2. Great Increase in Available Funds--*In re* Estate of Buck, 21 U.S.F.L. Rev. 691 (Cal. Sup. Ct. 1986).

In re Estate of Buck

a. **Facts.** In 1975, Beryl Buck died a resident of Marin County, California. Marin County is the most affluent of the counties in the San Francisco Bay Area and is the nation's second-wealthiest county of more than 50,000 residents. Buck's will left the residue of her estate to the San Francisco Foundation, a community trust administering charitable funds in five counties in the Bay Area. Her will directed that the residue of her estate be used for exclusively nonprofit charitable, religious, or educational purposes in providing care for the needy in Marin County, and for other nonprofit charitable, religious, or educational purposes in that county.

At the time of Buck's death, the largest asset in her estate consisted of a block of stock worth about $9 million. In 1979, Shell Oil won a bidding war and bought the stock in the Buck trust for $260 million, which increased to well over $300 million by 1984. In 1984, the foundation brought suit seeking judicial authorization to spend some portion of Buck trust income in the other four counties of the Bay Area. The foundation's petition for cy pres rested upon the following theory: The enormous increase in the value of principal was a change in circumstances raising substantial doubt whether Buck, had she anticipated such an event, would have limited her beneficence to Marin County. Forty-six individuals and charitable organizations in the other four counties (called "objector-beneficiaries") were allowed to intervene to object to the Marin-only limitation.

b. **Issue.** Does the doctrine of cy pres apply if there is a dramatic, unexpected increase in trust funds and a different use of trust funds would be more advantageous to the community?

c. **Held.** No. Judgment denying the petition for modification.

1) Cy pres applies only where the purpose of a trust has become illegal, impossible, or permanently impracticable of performance, and the testator manifested a general charitable intention. In practice, cy pres has most often been applied in California in such cases where the charitable trust purpose is literally impossible to fulfill or in cases where it has become reasonably impossible of performance. Ineffective philanthropy, inefficiency, and relative inefficiency (*i.e.*, inefficiency of trust expenditures in one location given greater relative needs or benefits elsewhere) do not constitute impracticability.

2) Where both the testator's intent and the charitable gift can, in fact, be effectuated, *i.e.*, the specified trust purpose has not become impossible or impracticable of performance, there is no justification for cy pres. Cy pres may not be invoked upon the belief that the modified scheme would be more desirable or would constitute a better use of the income. Courts have held that terms of a charitable trust may not be modified on the grounds that a different use would be more beneficial to the community or advantageous to the charity. Cy pres does not authorize the court to vary the terms of a trust merely because the variation will meet the desire and suit the convenience of the trustee.

3) The residents of Marin County have substantial unmet needs which are within the scope of the purposes of the Buck Trust. The entire income of the Buck Trust is presently insufficient, and will remain insufficient in the future, to address all of these needs and opportunities.

In re Wilson

3. **Gender-Based Trusts Not Violative of Equal Protection Where No State Involvement--*In re* Wilson,** 59 N.Y.2d 461, 452 N.E.2d 1228 (1983).

a) **Facts.** This case involves two appeals raising equal protection issues. The first appeal arises from the will of Clark Wilson, which provided that the residue of his estate be held in trust and that the income be applied to defraying educational and other expenses of the first year at college of five young men who shall have graduated from Canastota High School, three of whom shall have attained the highest grades in science and two of whom shall have attained the highest grades in chemistry. The trustee of Wilson's will, the Key Bank of Central New York (P), initiated a proceeding to determine the validity of this provision. The trial court found that the provision did not violate the Equal Protection Clause. The appellate court modified the decree, finding that administration of the trust was impossible because the school was under no legal obligation to provide the names of the qualified male candidates.

Under the facts of the second appeal, the will of the decedent, Edwin Johnson, left the residuary estate in trust to be used each year for scholarships and grants for bright and deserving young men who have graduated from the Croton-Harmon High School and whose parents are financially unable to send them to college. The National Organization of Women (P) filed a complaint arguing that the provision constituted illegal gender-based discrimination. During this proceeding, a stipulation was entered into between the executor of the will and the attorney general to avoid administering the will in a discriminatory manner. The attorney general (P) filed a petition to the surrogate court to construe the provision. The court found that the trustee's unwillingness to administer the trust according to its terms rendered administration of the trust impossible. The appellate court reversed, holding that the provision violated the Equal Protection Clause, and in the exercise of its cy pres power reformed the trust by eliminating the gender restriction.

b) **Issue.** Is the Equal Protection Clause violated when a court permits the administration of private charitable trusts according to the testator's intent to finance education of male students and not female students?

c) **Held.** No. Order of appellate court affirmed in *Wilson* and reversed in *Johnson.*

1) A charitable trust will not necessarily fail when the settlor's specific charitable purpose can no longer be accomplished. When a court determines that changed circumstances have rendered the administration of a charitable trust impracticable or impossible, the court may exercise its cy pres power to reform the trust in a manner that will most effectively accomplish its general purposes. Here, the trust's limitations of beneficiaries by gender are not rendered invalid as violative of public policy.

2) Nor do these provisions violate the Equal Protection Clause. The Equal Protection Clause is invoked when the state engages in invidious discrimination. However, discrimination by an otherwise private entity is not violative of the Equal Protection Clause. The Fourteenth Amendment does not require the state to exercise the full extent of its power to eradicate private discrimination. It is only when the state itself discriminates, compels another to discriminate, or allows another to assume its functions and discriminate that such discrimination will implicate the Fourteenth Amendment.

IX. POWERS OF APPOINTMENT: BUILDING FLEXIBILITY INTO THE ESTATE PLAN

A. INTRODUCTION

1. **Types of Powers.** The creator of a power of appointment is called the ***donor***. The person granted the power is called the ***donee***. Those persons to whom the donee may appoint property are the ***objects***.

    a. **General and special powers.** All powers of appointment can be divided into general powers and special powers. A general power is one exercisable in favor of the donee, his estate, his creditors, or the creditors of the estate. A special power is one not exercisable in favor of the donee, his estate, his creditors, or the creditors of his estate.

2. **Does the Appointive Property Belong to the Donor or the Donee?** Under the relation-back doctrine, the donee was thought of as having the power to fill in a blank in the will of the donor; property subject to a power of appointment was viewed as owned by the donor and the power was conceived as merely authority of the donee to do an act for the donor. Special powers are still treated according to this doctrine.

Irwin Union Bank & Trust Co. v. Long

3. **Creditor's Right to Property Subject to a Power of Appointment--Irwin Union Bank & Trust Co. v. Long,** 312 N.E.2d 908 (Ind. Ct. App. 1974).

    a. **Facts.** In 1957, Victoria Long obtained a judgment in the amount of $15,000 against Philip Long as part of a divorce decree. In this action, Victoria seeks satisfaction of that judgment by pursuing funds allegedly owed to Philip as a result of a trust set up by Laura Long, his mother. Victoria alleged that the Irwin Union Bank and Trust Company was indebted to Philip as the result of its position as trustee of the trust created by Laura. The trial court ordered that any income, property, or profits, which were owed to Philip and not exempt from execution should be applied to the divorce judgment. Thereafter, the trial court ordered that 4% of the trust corpus that benefitted Philip was not exempt from execution and could be levied upon by Victoria. The primary issue raised on appeal is whether the trial court erred in allowing execution on the 4% of the trust corpus.

    b. **Issue.** Can a creditor reach property covered by a power of appointment which is unexercised?

    c. **Held.** No. Judgment of trial court reversed and case remanded.

        1) Where a beneficiary was given a power under a testamentary trust to distribute property not his own by electing to withdraw not more than 4% of the trust corpus under certain circumstances, the power given to the beneficiary was a "power of appointment," and the beneficiary's former wife was not entitled as a creditor under a divorce decree to reach property covered by a power of appointment that was unexercised.

2) The beneficiary of a trust had no control over the trust corpus until he exercised his power of appointment and gave notice to the trustee that he wished to receive his 4% of the trust corpus. Until such exercise was made, the trustee had the absolute control and benefit of the trust corpus within the terms of the trust instrument.

4. **Tax Reasons for Creating Powers.** The federal tax laws provide that the holder of a general power of appointment over income or principal is treated as the owner of the property. The income from the property is taxable to the donee. If the donee exercises the power during life, the property transferred by exercise is subject to gift taxation. If the donee dies holding a general power, the property is included in the donee's federal gross estate and is subject to taxation. Note that property subject to a special power of appointment is not treated as owned by the donee.

B. CREATION OF A POWER OF APPOINTMENT

1. **Intent to Create a Power.** To create a power of appointment, the donor must manifest an intent to do so, either expressly or impliedly.

2. **Powers to Consume.** The issue of whether a power to consume principal has been created arises in connection with powers of appointment.

a. **Inconsistent clauses in will--Sterner v. Nelson,** 210 Neb. 358, 314 N.W.2d 263 (1982). Sterner v. Nelson

1) **Facts.** The will of the decedent, Oscar Wurtele, bequeathed to his wife, Mary, all his property "absolutely with full power in her to make such disposition of said property as she may desire." It also provided that upon the death of his wife (or if she predeceased the testator), the property remaining should vest in his foster daughter and her children (Ps). After the death of the decedent, the widow remarried. The widow died testate, leaving property to various individuals, including her husband, but not to Ps referred to in Oscar's will. The trial court held that the language in Oscar's will created a fee simple absolute in the widow. Ps appeal.

2) **Issue.** Where a will conveys absolute title in fee simple, will an inconsistent clause in the instrument attempting merely to limit that title or convey to the same person a limited title be disregarded?

3) **Held.** Yes. The judgment is affirmed.

a) The general rule is that where there is a bequest to one in general terms only, expressing neither fee nor life estate, and there is a subsequent limitation over of what remains at the first taker's death, if there is also given to the first taker an unlimited and unrestricted power of absolute disposal, the bequest is construed to pass a fee. The attempted limitation over is void. If a will conveys an absolute title in fee simple, an inconsistent clause in the instrument attempting to limit that title or convey to the same person a limited title will be disregarded.

b) Here, the grant to Mary Wurtele was clear and unambiguous. She was to have the property "absolutely with full power in her to make such disposition of said property as she may desire." We find no reason why the common law rule should not be applied to this bequest. Accordingly, we hold that the bequest to Mary Wurtele was a fee simple absolute.

b. **Taxation of powers to consume.** If a power to consume permits the donee to appoint the property to himself during life, it is a general power of appointment and hence taxable. However, if the power is limited by ascertainable standards, it falls within an exception and is not taxable.

C. RELEASE OF A POWER OF APPOINTMENT

All powers of appointment except powers in trust or imperative powers have been made releasable in all jurisdictions, either by judicial decision or by statute.

Seidel v. Werner

1. **Contract to Exercise a Power of Appointment--Seidel v. Werner,** 81 Misc. 2d 220, 364 N.Y.S.2d 963 (1975).

a. **Facts.** The decedent, Steven Werner, entered into a separation agreement with his second wife, Harriet, whereby he agreed to make a will in which he would exercise his testamentary power of appointment over his share of a trust, known as the Abraham Werner Trust No. 1, by establishing a trust for the benefit of their children, Anna and Frank Werner. Less than four months after the divorce judgment, of which the separation agreement was made a part, the decedent executed a will which, instead of executing his testamentary power of appointment in favor of Anna and Frank Werner, left everything to his third wife, Edith. The trustees of the trust (Ps) sue for a declaratory judgment to determine who is entitled to the decedent's share of the trust fund.

b. **Issue.** May the donee of a power of appointment which is not presently exercisable contract to make an appointment?

c. **Held.** No. So ordered.

1) The donee of a power of appointment which is not presently exercisable, or of a postponed power which has not become exercisable, cannot contract to make an appointment. Such a contract cannot be the basis of an action for specific performance or damages, but the promisee can obtain restitution of the value given by him for the promise unless the donee has exercised the power pursuant to the contract.

2) However, Harriet, Anna, and Frank Werner argue that at a minimum the agreement should be construed as a release of his power of appointment, and that Anna and Frank should be

permitted to take as on default of appointment. This argument is inapplicable to this case since it is clear that the parties did not intend a release of the power of appointment. Nor is the effect of the promised exercise of the power the same as would follow from release of the power, since the agreement provides for appointment of a greater principal to Anna and Frank than they would get in default of appointment. Also, under the trust instrument, on default of exercise of the power, the property goes to the four children absolutely, whereas under the separation agreement the decedent shall create a trust payable to Harriet as trustee for the support of Anna and Frank. Finally, under the separation agreement, if Anna and Frank fail to qualify, the principal would go to the decedent's estate, whereas under the trust instrument, in default of appointment and an inability of Anna and Frank to take, the decedent's share would go to his other children, if living, and if not, to his next of kin. Under these circumstances, it is too strained to construe the separation agreement as the equivalent of a release of the power of appointment. Accordingly, Edith Werner is entitled to the decedent's share in the principal of the Abraham Werner trust.

D. EXERCISE OF A POWER OF APPOINTMENT

1. **Exercise by Residuary Clause in Donee's Will.** Courts are split over whether a residuary clause should presumptively exercise a general or special power of appointment. The Uniform Probate Code, section 2-610, provides that a general residuary clause in a will, or a will making general disposition of all of the testator's property, does not exercise a power of appointment held by the testator unless specific reference is made to the power or there is some other indication of intention to include the property subject to the power.

   a. **Partial release of general power of appointment--Beals v. State Street Bank & Trust Co.,** 367 Mass. 318, 326 N.E.2d 896 (1975).

Beals v. State Street Bank & Trust Co.

      1) **Facts.** The will of the decedent, Arthur Hunnewell, placed the residue of his property in a trust, the income of which was to be paid to his wife during her life. The will directed that at the death of the wife the trust was to be divided into portions, one for each surviving daughter and for the then-surviving issue of any deceased daughter. The will directed that the income of each portion should be, on a daughter's death, paid and disposed of as she may direct and appoint by her last will. Following the death of her mother, one daughter, Isabella Hunnewell Dexter, requested the trustees to make the principal payments by transferring virtually all of her trust share to the Dexter family office in Boston. Thereafter, Isabella executed an instrument which partially released her general power of appointment under the will of her father. Isabella, who died without issue, did not expressly exercise her power of appointment under her father's will but did leave a will that left the residue of her estate to the issue of her sister Margaret Blake, who had predeceased Isabella. In default of appointment, the Blake issue would take one-half of Isabella's trust share. If Isabella's will should be treated

as effectively exercising her power of appointment, the Blake issue would take the entire trust share and the executors of the will of Isabella's sister Jane would not receive that one-half of the trust share that would otherwise go to Jane in default of appointment. The trustees of the will of Arthur Hunnewell filed a petition for instructions, seeking a determination of the distribution to be made. The trial court reserved decision and reported the case to the appeals court. The case was then transferred to the supreme court.

2) **Issue.** Does the partial release of a general power of appointment obviate the application of the rule of construction that presumes that a general residuary clause exercises a general power of appointment?

3) **Held.** No. So ordered.

a) We are unaware of any decided case which, in this context, has dealt with a testamentary general power reduced to a special power by action of the donee. We conclude that the residuary clause of Isabella's will should be presumed to have exercised the power of appointment. We believe that a presumption of exercise is more appropriate in this case than a presumption of nonexercise.

b) When this court first decided not to extend to a special power of appointment the rule of construction that a general residuary clause executes a general testamentary power unless a contrary intent is shown by the will, we noted significant distinctions between a general power and a special power. A general power was said to be a close approximation of a property interest while a special power lacked this quality.

c) The rationale for the canon of construction applicable to general powers should be applied in this case. The power was a general power at its inception. Isabella had the use and enjoyment of the major portions of the property and this is a factor properly considered as weighing in favor of the exercise of a power of appointment by a will. Here, the partial release of a general power does not obviate the application of that rule of construction which presumes that a general residuary clause exercises a general power of appointment.

2. **Limitations on Exercise of a Special Power.** In almost all jurisdictions, a donee of a general power of appointment can appoint outright or in further trust and can create new powers of appointment. With respect to a special power of appointment, the donee's authority is more limited. A special power must be exercised in accordance with the instrument creating the power, and the donor may impose restrictions upon the way the power may be exercised.

a. **Creation of limited interest.** Unless the donor has expressed a contrary intent, the donee of a special power may appoint limited interests to objects of the power, or appoint in further trust. In some states the donee of a special power may not appoint in further trust unless it appears that the donor intended to allow such an appointment. The rationale for this minority view is that the donor presumptively intended that the trust be terminated and the assets distributed to persons selected by the donee. The special power gives the donee only the right to select the recipients.

b. **Exclusive and nonexclusive powers.** A special power is either exclusive or nonexclusive. If the donor intends that the donee be able to exclude one or more of the class of objects, perhaps appointing all the property to one object, the power is exclusive. If the donor intends that all members of the class benefit, but that the amount of each share shall be determined by the donee, the power is nonexclusive. The presumption is that the donor intends the power to be exclusive. However, courts often have found that the presumption is overcome by particular language in the creating instrument.

3. **Fraud on a Special Power.** The donee of a special power may not appoint to non-objects of the power. If the donee of a special power appoints to a class composed of objects and non-objects, the appointment to the non-objects is void. An appointment to an object with an express condition that the object pay over an amount to a non-object is a fraudulent appointment. The condition is void. If the donee of a special power appoints to an object in consideration of a benefit to a non-object, the appointment is void to the extent it was motivated by the purpose of benefiting non-objects.

4. **Ineffective Exercise of the Power.** When the donee intends to exercise a power of appointment, but the exercise is ineffective for some reason, it may be possible to carry out the donee's intent through the doctrines of allocation and of capture.

a. **Allocation of assets.** Under the doctrine of allocation, when the donee of a power blends her own property with the appointive property, and exercises the power in an invalid way, the donee's own property and the appointive property will be allocated, if possible, to give maximum effect to donee's intent. Thus, the donee's own property may be allocated to the appointees, and the appointive property may be allocated to legatees of the donee's own property.

b. **Capture.** Ordinarily, if the donee of a power makes an ineffective exercise, the property goes in default of appointment. If there is no gift in default, the property reverts to the donor or the donor's estate. An important exception to this is the capture doctrine. If the donee of a general power of appointment ineffectively exercises the power, but manifests an intent to assume control of the appointive property for all purposes, the property is captured in the donee's estate. The question is whether the donee intended to capture the property; if so, the property does not pass in default of appointment. The intent to capture the property can be found in a general blending clause in a will which expresses the donee's intent to dispose of his own property and any property over which he has power of appointment. An intent to capture can also be found in a residuary clause which disposes of donee's property and the appointive assets in the same manner.

E. FAILURE TO EXERCISE A POWER OF APPOINTMENT

If the donee of a general power fails to exercise it, the appointive property passes in default of appointment. The property reverts to the donor's estate if there is no gift in default of appointment. If the donee of a special power fails to exercise it, and there is no gift in default of appointment, the appointive property may pass to the objects of the property if the objects are an ascertainable limited class.

Loring v. Marshall

1. Disposition of Property When Special Power of Appointment Is Not Exercised--Loring v. Marshall, 396 Mass. 166, 484 N.E.2d 1315 (1985).

a. **Facts.** Marian Hovey died in 1898, survived by a brother, a sister, and two nephews. By her will, Marian left the residue of her estate in trust, the income payable in equal shares to her brother and sister during their lives. Upon her brother's death in 1900, his share of the income passed to her sister, and, upon her sister's death in 1922, the income was paid in equal shares to her two nephews. One nephew died in 1928, unmarried and without issue. His share of the income then passed to his brother who remained the sole income beneficiary until his death in 1946.

Marian's will gave Cabot Jackson Morse, the surviving nephew, a special power to appoint the trust principal to his "wife and issue" with the limitation that only income could be appointed to a widow who was living at Marian's death. Cabot was survived by his wife Anna, who was living at Marian's death, and by his only child, Cabot Jr., who died in 1948, two years after his father. Cabot left a will which provided that the power of appointment he had under Marian's will was to be exercised by appointing to his wife the right to the income during her lifetime. Consequently, the trust income following Cabot's death was paid to Anna until her death in 1983, when the principal became distributable. The trustees thereupon sought instructions as to who is entitled to the remainder of the Marian Hovey Trust now that the trust is distributable. Among the claimants are several charities who were to receive the whole trust fund if neither nephew left appointees.

b. **Issue.** If the donee of a special power fails to exercise it and there is no gift in default of appointment, may the appointive property pass to the objects of the power?

c. **Held.** Yes. Judgment so ordered.

1) When a special power of appointment is not exercised and absent specific language indicating an express gift in default of appointment, the property not appointed goes in equal shares to the members of the class to whom the property could have been appointed.

2) Applying this rule of law, there is no specific language in the will indicating a gift in default of appointment in the event Cabot should fail to appoint the principal.

3) Marian's will discloses an intent to keep her property in the family. The interests Marian gave to her sister and brother were life interests, as were the interests given to her nephews. The share of any nephew who died unmarried and without issue, as one did, was added to the share of the other nephew. Each nephew was limited to exercising his power of appointment in favor of his issue and his widow. The apparent intent to keep the assets within the family is sufficiently strong to overcome any claim that Marian's will provides for a gift to the charities in default of appointment.

4) Where a testamentary trust provided that the last surviving income beneficiary had a power of appointment of trust principal and the last surviving income beneficiary of a trust appointed only the trust income, in the absence of any express gift in default of appointment the surviving issue of the donee of the power of appointment (*i.e.*, the estate of Cabot Jr.) was entitled to distribution of the trust principal.

X. FUTURE INTERESTS: DISPOSITIVE PROVISIONS OF THE TRUST INSTRUMENT

A. INTRODUCTION

A future interest is a nonpossessory interest capable of becoming possessory in the future. The law of future interests deals with situations where the beneficial enjoyment of land by a successor occurs at some time in the future. Certainty of beneficial enjoyment is not required; however, there must be at least the possibility of future beneficial enjoyment.

B. CLASSIFICATION OF FUTURE INTERESTS

1. **Future Interests in the Transferor.** There are three types of future interests that may be retained by the transferor: ***reversion, possibility of reverter***, and ***right of entry***. These interests will or may become possessory in the transferor or her successors in interest.

   a. **Reversion.** A reversion is a future interest left in the grantor after she conveys a vested estate of a lesser quantum than she has (usually a life estate).

   b. **Possibility of reverter.** A possibility of reverter arises when a grantor carves out of her estate a determinable estate of the same quantum (the determinable estate will end if some future event occurs).

   c. **Right of entry.** A right of entry occurs when a grantor creates an estate subject to a condition subsequent and retains the power to cut short or terminate the estate upon the happening of that condition.

2. **Future Interests in Transferees.** There are three types of future interests in transferees: vested remainders, contingent remainders, and executory interests.

   a. **Remainders.** A remainder is a future interest created in a grantee that is capable of becoming a present possessory estate upon the expiration of a prior possessory estate created in the same conveyance in which the remainder is created. A ***vested*** remainder is created in an ascertained person in being and is not subject to a condition precedent (*i.e.*, it is capable of becoming possessory whenever the preceding estate terminates). A ***contingent*** remainder, on the other hand, is created in an unascertained person or is subject to a condition precedent (*i.e.*, it is contingent on something happening before it can become possessory).

   b. **Executory interests.** Any interest in a transferee that cannot be a remainder must be an executory interest. An executory interest is a future interest that must, in order to become possessory, divest or cut short some interest in another transferee (a shifting executory interest) or divest the transferor following a certain period of time during which no transferee is entitled to possession (a springing executory interest).

3. **Destructibility of Contingent Remainders.** This doctrine holds that if a legal contingent remainder in land does not vest before or at the termination of the preceding freehold estate, the remainder is destroyed. In about three-fourths of the states, the destructibility rule has been abolished by statute or judicial decision.

C. CONSTRUCTION AND DRAFTING PROBLEMS

1. **Preference for Vested Interests.** If an interest might be classified as vested or contingent, the common law preference is to classify it as vested.

   a. **Transferability and taxation.** Over 40 states have made contingent interests transferable by statute or judicial decision. Reversions, remainders, and executory interests are descendible and devisable at death in the same manner as possessory interests. The federal government subjects to gift or estate taxation any gratuitous transfer of a property interest.

   b. **Acceleration into possession.**

      1) **Renunciation valid--*In Re* Estate of Gilbert,** 592 N.Y.S.2d 224 (1992). *In re* Estate of Gilbert

         a) **Facts.** Lester Gilbert renounced his share of two wholly discretionary trusts under his father's will. The estate was worth $40 million dollars. Lester, age 32, had no children and was a member of a group of people who shared a similar religious doctrine. The executor petitions this court to declare Lester's renunciation null and void.

         b) **Issues.**

            (1) Would permitting the renunciation violate the testator's intent to provide for Lester?

            (2) Does Lester possess a current property interest which he can renounce?

         c) **Held.** (1) No. (2) Yes.

            (1) Decedent's intention is not controlling. The law does not compel a man to accept an estate against his will.

            (2) The controlling statutes provide that a beneficiary of a disposition may renounce all or part of his interest in a transfer of property by a person during his lifetime or by will. Property is "anything that may be the subject of ownership."

            (3) Lester's renunciation applies to his remainder interest in one elective share trust, contingent upon Lester surviving his mother, and to his current interest in a trust under which Lester may have the right to

compel the trustees to distribute trust property to him under certain circumstances.

(4) The filing of a renunciation has the same effect with respect to the renounced interest as if Lester had predeceased his father without issue.

Edwards v. Hammond

2) **Age ignored as a condition precedent--Edwards v. Hammond,** 3 Lev. 132, 83 Eng. Rep. 614 (1683).

a) **Facts.** A father bequeathed land to himself for life, and then to his eldest son (who was not an heir of this type of property) and his heirs, if his son lived to the age of 21, but if his eldest son died before reaching 21, then to the father and his heirs. The father died, the eldest son at the time being 17 years old. This son brought an action for ejectment, arguing that the bequest created a present devise subject to divestment. The defendant argued that the bequest created a condition precedent and that the estate should descend to the youngest son, an heir, in the meantime.

b) **Issue.** Where an age condition in a bequest is stated both as a condition precedent and as a divesting contingency, will the condition precedent be ignored as surplusage?

c) **Held.** Yes.

(1) Where an age condition in a bequest is stated both as a condition precedent and as a divesting contingency, the condition precedent will be ignored as surplusage. Here, the eldest son takes even though he has not reached the age of 21. If he fails to reach that age, his interest is subject to divestment.

c. **Requiring survival to time of possession.** Generally, a remainderman need not live to the time of possession. If the remainderman predeceases the life tenant, the remainder passes to the remainderman's estate. The testator may, however, expressly require survival, and in some cases courts will infer a requirement of survival.

First National Bank of Bar Harbor v. Anthony

1) **Present vested interest--First National Bank of Bar Harbor v. Anthony,** 557 A.2d 957 (Me. 1989).

a) **Facts.** Anthony (T) created a revocable inter vivos trust providing for income to be paid to him for life, then his widow, should she survive him, and upon her death the corpus to be divided in equal shares to T's three children, John, Peter, and Dencie. T's wife and John predeceased T. Upon T's death, his will was admitted to probate and left two-thirds of T's estate to Peter and one-third to Dencie; the heirs of John were expressly omitted. The bank, as trustee, filed a complaint in superior court requesting construction of the trust. John's children, T's grandchildren, filed a motion for summary judgment, asserting John's interest in the trust was vested, not contingent, at the time of its creation. The summary judgment motion was granted against John's children, who appeal.

b) **Issue.** Was John's remainder interest a present, vested interest at the time of the creation of the inter vivos trust?

c) **Held.** Yes. Judgment vacated.

(1) Because a will is not operative until a testator's death, an interest in a testamentary trust cannot vest prior to the death. An inter vivos trust is operative from the date of creation.

(2) The terms of T's trust included T's right to change beneficiaries, an absence of control over how the children might dispose of their shares, and no condition of survival of any children. This plan effectively eliminated any further interest of T unless he chose to intervene.

(3) T's failure to change the trust terms suggests a disposition to a predeceased child's estate rather than a reversion.

(4) Other states have held that an inter vivos trust reserving to the settlor income for life plus power to revoke, with a remainder over at settlor's death, creates a vested interest in the remaindermen subject to defeasance by exercise of the revocation power. Enjoyment is postponed until termination of the life estates, but upon execution of the trust instrument, there is a present right to the remainder.

2) **Heirs determined as of the date of death of the testator--Security Trust Co. v. Irvine,** 33 Del. Ch. 375, 93 A.2d 528 (1953).

Security Trust Co. v. Irvine

a) **Facts.** The will of the decedent, James Wilson, devised all real property to the Security Trust Company (P) in trust for his two sisters, Martha and Mary Wilson, during their joint lives and during the lifetime of the survivor of them, and further provided that if his sister Margaret Irvine should be left a widow, then she should share equally with the other two sisters. Upon the death of Martha and Mary, the estate would be divided equally among the testator's brothers and sisters, share and share alike, with the issue of any deceased brother or sister to take his or her parent's share. Testator was survived by five brothers and sisters. From these, Mary Wilson was the last surviving life tenant. P brought an action to determine: (i) whether the residuary estate left to the brothers and sisters of the testator vested as of the date of death of the last life tenant or as of the date of his death; and (ii) whether Martha and Mary take as members of the class of brothers and sisters should it be decided that the estate vested as of the date of death of the testator.

b) **Issues.**

(1) In the absence of a contrary intent, will the heirs be determined as of the date of death of the testator?

(2) In the event of the death of devisees leaving no issue, are the interests of such devisees divested by their death?

c) **Held.** (1) Yes. (2) No. So ordered.

(1) The law favors early vesting of devised estates and will presume that words of survivorship relate to the death of the testator. In the absence of a clear intent to the contrary, the heirs will be determined as of the date of death of the testator and not at some future date. The fact that a life tenant is a member of a class does not prevent the life tenant from participating in the remainder of the testator's estate as part of the class. Here, the life tenants should participate in the remainder devised by testator to his brothers and sisters.

(2) The weight of authority in other states is to the effect that in the event of the death of the devisees leaving no issue, the interest of such devisees is not divested by their death. The interests of Martha and Mary Wilson and Margaret Irvine were not divested by their death without issue and that their interests in the estate of the testator should go to their respective estates.

Lawson v. Lawson

3) **Time of vesting of contingent estates--Lawson v. Lawson,** 267 N.C. 643, 148 S.E.2d 546 (1966).

a) **Facts.** The will of the decedent, J. Rad Lawson, devised land to his daughter, Opal Lawson Long, for life and at her death to her children, if any, in fee simple; if no children, then to the brothers and sisters of Opal Lawson Long. The whole brothers and sisters (Ps) bring a petition for partition and allege that Ds, the only children of two whole brothers of Opal who died before her (but who survived the testator), have no interest in the property. The trial court held that Ps own the property in fee simple and that Ds have no interest in the land. Ds appeal.

b) **Issue.** Do contingent remainder interests limited upon a single precedent estate vest before the death of the life tenant?

c) **Held.** No. Judgment affirmed.

(1) This case presents a typical example of a contingent remainder. Alternative remainders limited upon a single precedent estate are always contingent. Such remainders are created by a limitation to one for life, with remainder in fee to his children.

(2) Here, the interests of the whole brothers and sisters were contingent and could not vest before the death of the life tenant, for not until then could it be determined that the life tenant would leave no issue surviving. Only those who can answer the roll immediately upon the happening of the event acquire any estate in the properties granted. Since Ds' parents, having predeceased the life tenant, could not answer the roll as of the death of the life tenant, Ds cannot acquire any of the properties granted.

Clobberie's Case

4) **Common law rule where bequest is to be paid at certain age--Clobberie's Case,** 2 Vent. 342, 86 Eng. Rep. 476 (1677).

a) **Facts.** A sum of money was bequeathed to a woman to be paid to her with interest upon her reaching the age of 21 or upon the day of her marriage. She died before either condition was satisfied.

b) **Issue.** Where a bequest is to be paid on the express condition that the beneficiary reach a certain age, which condition does not occur, does the bequest pass to the estate of the beneficiary?

c) **Held.** Yes.

(1) Where a sum of money is to be paid to a woman upon her reaching the age of 21 or upon her day of marriage, and she dies before either condition is met, the bequest passes to her executor as part of her estate. However, if the money were bequeathed to one "at" the age of 21, then the bequest would lapse.

2. Gifts to Classes.

a. Gifts to children or issue.

1) **Meaning of "children" and "issue."** The word "children" means only immediate offspring and does not include grandchildren. The word "issue" includes grandchildren and more remote descendants.

2) **UPC Section 2-705.** Adopted persons and persons born out of wedlock are included in class gift terminology in accordance with rules for determining relationships for purposes of intestate succession. However, a person born out of wedlock is not treated as the child of the father unless he is openly and notoriously so treated by the father.

a) **Adopted adult not considered an "heir"--Minary v. Citizens Fidelity Bank & Trust Co.,** 419 S.W. 2d 340 (Ky. 1967).

Minary v. Citizens Fidelity Bank & Trust Co.

(1) **Facts.** The will of the decedent, Amelia S. Minary, devised her residuary estate in trust to pay the income to her husband and three sons for their respective lives. The trust was to terminate upon the death of the last surviving beneficiary, at which time the trust was to be distributed to the testator's surviving heirs and if no heirs, then to the First Christian Church. Two of the three sons left no surviving issues, but a third son, Alfred, married and thereafter adopted his wife. Myra Minary (P), the wife of Alfred, brought suit against the Citizens Fidelity Bank (D), contending that the trust should be awarded to her since she, having been adopted by her husband, becomes an "heir" for purposes of the will. The trial court held for P. D appeals.

(2) **Issue.** Will adoption of an adult for the purpose of bringing that person under the provisions of a preexisting testamentary instrument be permitted?

(3) **Held.** No. The judgment is reversed.

(a) Even though the adoption statute provides that an adult person may be adopted in the same manner as a child, we are constrained to view this practice as an act of subterfuge which thwarts the testator's intent. Here, were we to give strict effect to the adoption statute, we would thwart the efforts of the deceased to dispose of her property as she saw fit. Adoption of an adult for the purpose of bringing that person under the provisions of a preexisting testamentary instrument when she clearly was not intended to be so covered should not be permitted, and we do not view this as doing any great violence to our adoption laws.

3) **Gifts over on death without issue.** In these cases, the question to be determined is whether the expression means (i) death without issue at any time or (ii) death without issue during testator's lifetime. The first construction is preferred by a majority of courts if a possessory fee simple may be divested. The second construction is preferred if a remainder may be divested.

b. **Gifts to heirs**

Estate of Woodworth

1) **Determining identity of heirs--Estate of Woodworth,** 22 Cal.Rptr.2d 676 (1993).

a) **Facts.** Testator's (T's) testamentary trust established by T's will provided for a portion of T's estate to go to T's wife (W) as life tenant and to terminate upon W's death. The remaining trust estate was to go to T's daughter (D) if she survived and if not, then to D's heirs at law. Upon D's death in 1980, she was survived by her husband (H), a niece, and a nephew. H died testate in 1988, leaving the residue of his estate to the Regents (Rs) for the University's Berkeley campus. W died in 1991. The trustee bank petitioned the probate court to determine D's heirs at law. The court determined the niece and nephew to be D's heirs. Rs appeal.

b) **Issue.** Absent evidence of T's intent to the contrary, must the identity of "heirs" entitled to trust assets be determined at the date of death of the named ancestor who predeceased the life tenant, and not at the date of death of the life tenant?

c) **Held.** Yes. Reversed.

(1) There is a common law preference for vested rather than contingent remainders, unless an instrument discloses a different intent. Thus, a remainder to a class became vested in the class when one or more of its members came into existence and could be ascertained, even though the class is subject to open.

(2) When a gift is made to "heirs," the donor is saying he wants the property distributed as if the named person died intestate. Thus, the death of the named individual is the normal time for applying the statute of descent or distribution, absent a manifested intent by T that the statute be applied earlier or later.

(3) None of the exceptions to the early vesting rule reflected in *Wells Fargo Bank v. Title Insurance & Trust Co.*, 99 Cal. Rptr. 464 (1971), apply here. This is not a situation where the "life tenant is the sole heir, but the will devises the remainder to the testator heirs."

(4) We have nothing before us which reveals T's intent and nothing forecloses the possibility that T took into account that D might predecease and H might outlive W.

(5) There is no language in the decree which contains any expression of futurity in the description of the ancestor's heirs, such as "my then living heirs at law." The word "then" here merely indicates time of enjoyment.

2) **The doctrine of worthier title.** The doctrine of worthier title provides that when a settlor transfers property in trust, with a life estate in the settlor or in another, and purports to create a remainder in the settlor's heirs, it is presumed that the settlor intended to retain a reversion in himself and not create a remainder in his heirs. The doctrine is a rule of construction, not a rule of law. It raises a presumption that no remainder in the settlor's heirs has been created, but this presumption can be rebutted by evidence of a contrary intent of the grantor. The doctrine may still exist in some states.

3) **The rule in *Shelley's Case*.** The rule in *Shelley's Case* states that if one instrument creates a freehold in land in A and purports to create a remainder in A's heirs and the estates are both legal or both equitable, then the remainder becomes a remainder in fee simple in A. It is a rule of law, and it applies regardless of the intent of the transferor. The rule has been abolished in practically all states.

c. **Decrease in class: death of one beneficiary.**

1) **Construing class gift to testator's grandchildren--Dewire v. Haveles,** 404 Mass. 274, 534 N.E.2d 782 (1989). Dewire v. Haveles

a) **Facts.** A petition for a declaration of rights was brought seeking construction of a will creating a class gift on behalf of the testator's grandchildren. Thomas Dewire died in January 1941 survived by his widow, his son (Thomas Jr.), and three grandchildren. His will placed substantially all of his estate in a residuary trust. The trust income was payable to his widow for life and on her death to Thomas Jr. and Thomas Jr.'s widow and children. After testator's death, Thomas Jr. had three more children by a second wife. Thomas Jr. died in 1978, a widower, survived by all six of his children. Thomas III, who had served as trustee since 1978, died in 1987 leaving a widow and one child, Jennifer. The question presented is whether Jennifer takes her deceased father's share in the trust income or whether the remaining class members (the other five grandchildren) take that income share equally by right of survivorship.

In his will, testator provided that his grandchildren share equally in the net income of his estate. There is no explicit provision in the will concerning the distribution of income on the death of a grandchild, nor is there any statement as to what the trustee should do with trust income between the death of the last grandchild and the date assigned for termination of the trust 21 years after that event.

b) **Issue.** Is the daughter of testator's deceased grandchild entitled to succeed by right of representation to the granchild's income interest in a trust created by a class gift?

c) **Held.** Yes. Judgment accordingly.

(1) The gift of net income to the testator's grandchildren, divided equally or to be shared equally, is a class gift. The class includes all six grandchildren, three of whom were born before and three of whom were born after testator's death.

(2) In the absence of a contrary intent expressed in the will or a controlling statute stating otherwise, members of a class are joint tenants with rights of survivorship.

(3) Testator's will violated the Rule Against Perpetuities because Thomas Jr. could (and did) have children after testator's death; the trust was thus scheduled to terminate 21 years after a life not necessarily yet in being. Nevertheless, the language of this void provision can be used to determine the testator's intention as to dispositions that do not violate the Rule.

(4) The testator provided that the trust should terminate 21 years after the death of his last grandchild. It is unlikely that the testator intended that trust income should be accumulated for 21 years. He must have expected that someone would receive the income during those years. The only logical recipients would be the issue (by right of representation) of deceased grandchildren, the same group of people who would take the trust assets on termination of the trust (assuming no violation of the Rule Against Perpetuities).

(5) Where every other provision in the will concerning the distribution of trust income and principal (after the death of testator and his wife) points to equal treatment of testator's issue per stirpes, there is a sufficient contrary intent shown to overcome the rule of construction that the class gift of income to grandchildren is given to them as joint tenants with the right of survivorship. Thus, Jennifer in her lifetime is entitled to one-sixth of the net income of the trust during the period of the class gift of income.

d. **The rule of convenience.** Under the rule of convenience, a class will close whenever any member of the class is entitled to possession and enjoyment of her share. The class will close when a beneficiary has the right to demand distribution, and not when the beneficiary actually demands distribution or when distribution occurs. If no members of the class have been born before the testator's death, the class does not close until the death of the designated ancestor of the class. Where there is an immediate bequest of a separate fixed sum to each member of a class, the class closes at testator's death, regardless of whether there are any members of the class then alive. If the gift is postponed in possession after a life estate, the class will not close under the rule of convenience until the time for taking possession.

1) **Class closes when all existing members reach stated age--Lux v. Lux,** 109 R.I. 592, 288 A.2d 701 (1972). Lux v. Lux

a) **Facts.** The will of the decedent, Philomena Lux, provided that in the event that her husband, Anthony Lux, predeceased her, the residue of her estate should go to her grandchildren, share and share alike. It further provided that any real estate included in the residue shall be maintained for the benefit of the grandchildren and shall not be sold until the youngest of the grandchildren has reached 21 years of age. The testator was survived by one son (Anthony) and five grandchildren. The youngest grandchild was born after the execution of the will but before the testator's death. The son informed the trial court that he and his wife plan to have more children. The trial court appointed a guardian ad litem to represent the interests of the grandchildren. It also appointed an attorney to represent the rights of individuals who are unknown but who may have an interest under the will.

b) **Issue.** When all existent members of a class have attained the stated age, should the class be closed and the distribution be made?

c) **Held.** Yes. So ordered.

(1) We hold that the distribution of the trust corpus shall be made at any time when the youngest of the then-living grandchildren has attained the age of 21. When all existent members of the class have attained the stated age, considerations of convenience require that distribution shall then be made and that the property shall not be kept from further utilization to await the uncertain conception of further members of the group.

(2) Should it become necessary due to a decline in rental income to sell the property, the trustee has the discretionary power to sell the real estate. The proceeds from the sale shall, because of the doctrine of the substitute res, replace the realty as the trust corpus. Income would be payable to the beneficiaries as it accrues. Should additional children be born, the amount of each share of income received by a grandchild would be reduced as each new member of the class joins his brothers and sisters.

XI. DURATION OF TRUSTS: THE RULE AGAINST PERPETUITIES

A. INTRODUCTION

1. **Development of the Rule.** The Rule Against Perpetuities states: "No interest is good unless it must vest, if at all, not later than 21 years after some life in being at the creation of the interest." An early formulation of the Rule was announced in the *Duke of Norfolk's Case* in 1682, and the Rule was further refined over the next few centuries as courts sought to prevent long-term restrictions on the alienability of land.

2. **Policies Underlying the Rule.** The Rule is designed to further marketability of property and prevent an undue concentration of wealth in the hands of the few. The Rule also encourages the socially desirable result that wealth be controlled by the living and not by the dead. It also curtails trusts, which can protect wealthy beneficiaries from bankruptcies and creditors.

3. **When the Lives in Being Are Ascertained.** The validity of an interest is determined as of the time of the purported creation of the interest. "Lives in being" must be persons alive at that time. Generally, the perpetuities period (lives in being plus 21 years) begins to run whenever the transferor makes an irrevocable transfer. If the interest is created by will, the period begins at testator's death. If the interest is created by deed, or by an irrevocable deed of trust, the period begins at the time the deed is delivered with intent to pass title. If a trust is revocable by the settlor, the period begins at the date the trust becomes irrevocable.

4. **The Validating Life.** For an interest to be valid, the necessary proof must be made from among persons who can affect vesting. Alternatively, the interest must vest at creation, or vest or fail within 21 years after creation.

B. THE REQUIREMENT OF NO POSSIBILITY OF REMOTE VESTING: THE WHAT-MIGHT-HAPPEN RULE

Under the common law rule, any possibility of remote vesting voids the interest. About half the states have reformed this what-might-happen rule. One of the reforms is the wait-and-see doctrine (covered below).

1. **The "Fertile Octogenarian."** The law conclusively presumes that a person can have children as long as the person is alive. A few states have enacted legislation to deal with the conclusive presumption of fertility, prescribing that any person who has attained the age of 65 shall be deemed incapable of having a child.

2. **The "Unborn Widow."** The law presumes that a person's surviving spouse might turn out to be a person not now alive.

   a. **Example.** O devises "to A for life, then to A's wife for life, then to A's children who survive A's widow." It is possible that A may marry someone not in being (not yet born) at O's death (which is the time of the transfer). She could live beyond lives in being (O's life and A's life) plus 21 years. Therefore, the devise to the children is void. This is the case of the "unborn widow."

b. **Application--Dickerson v. Union National Bank of Little Rock,** 268 Ark. 292, 595 S.W.2d 677 (1980).

Dickerson v. Union National Bank of Little Rock

1) **Facts.** The testator was survived by her two children. Cecil, 50, was single, and Martin, 45, was married. At that time the two sons had a total of seven children, who were the testator's grandchildren. The testator named the bank as executor and directed that at the close of administration proceedings the bank transfer to itself as trustee all the assets of the estate. The will required the trust to continue until the death of both sons and Martin's widow, and the youngest child of either son has reached the age of 25. At that time, the trust was to distribute and pay over the entire balance of the trust fund to the bodily heirs of both of her sons.

The testator died in 1967. The probate court entered a routine order reciting that the will had been properly executed and approving the executor's first and final accounting and closing the administration of the estate. The order makes no reference to the validity of the trust or the manner in which the assets of the estate were to be distributed.

In 1977, Cecil filed a complaint against the bank and its trust officer. The complaint asserted that the trust was void under the Rule Against Perpetuities. The complaint charges the trust officer with violations of his fiduciary duties in failing to deliver all the estate assets to the heirs of the testator and in failing to ask the probate court to construe the will with respect to violations of the Rule Against Perpetuities. The chancery court rejected Cecil's attack on two grounds. First, Cecil should have raised the question of the validity of the trust in the probate court in connection with the probate of the will and the administration of the estate. His failure to do so makes the issue res judicata. Second, on the merits, the trust does not violate the Rule Against Perpetuities.

2) **Issue.** Is a trust created by a will void under the Rule Against Perpetuities because it is possible that the interest of the various beneficiaries might not vest within the period allowed by that rule?

3) **Held.** Yes. Chancery court judgment reversed and case remanded.

a) Failure of a will beneficiary to challenge the validity of a trust as violative of the Rule Against Perpetuities in probate proceedings did not preclude him from raising that issue in a later action, where the validity of the trust was not necessarily within the issues before the probate court and the probate court made no pertinent decisions as to the validity of the trust.

b) Where the bank was both executor of the estate and trustee of the trust established in the will, the bank was a fiduciary and owed a duty of good faith and loyalty to all beneficiaries of the estate and of the trust. Therefore, the bank could not ignore the possible invalidity of the trust both in probate court and in ex parte chancery court proceedings and then take advantage, to its own pecuniary benefit, of the beneficiaries' similar course of conduct by asserting that the beneficiaries' failure to challenge the validity of the trust in probate proceedings precluded Cecil from raising that issue in a later action.

c) A bare possibility that a beneficiary's interest will not vest within the period allowed by the Rule Against Perpetuities is enough to render that interest void.

d) The terms of this trust present an instance of the "unborn widow." This trust is not to terminate until the deaths of Cecil, Martin, and Martin's widow, but the identity of Martin's widow cannot be known until his death. Martin might marry an 18-year-old woman 20 years after his mother's death, have additional children by her, and then die. Cecil might also die. Martin's young widow, however, might live for another 40 or 50 years, after which the interests would finally vest. But since Cecil and Martin would have been the last measuring lives in being at the death of the testator, the trust property would not vest until many years past the maximum time allowed by the Rule. The trust is therefore void because there is a possibility that the estate will not vest within a period measured by a life or lives in being at the testator's death, plus 21 years.

c. **Split contingencies.** If the transferor makes a gift upon either of two contingencies, one of which must occur within the perpetuities period, and the other of which might not, the gift is valid if the first contingency occurs, and void if the second contingency occurs.

First Portland National Bank v. Rodrique

1) **Rule not violated--First Portland National Bank v. Rodrique,** 172 A.2d 107 (Me. 1961).

a) **Facts.** T's 1926 will provided for a trust whereby T's second wife (W) was to receive a life income and T's four children by his first wife and their issue were given an interest which comes into possession upon the occurrence of two alternative conditions, either upon W's death, if the trust has continued for 25 years, or if not, when 25 years has elapsed. T's residuary clause devised the remainder of T's property equally to T's four children and T's stepdaughter. W brings suit for construction of T's will.

b) **Issue.** Does the trust provision in T's will violate the Rule Against Perpetuities?

c) **Held.** No. Remanded for entry of a decree in accord with this opinion.

(1) W, the life annuitant, has survived the date of the void limitation, and the trust will terminate and all interests vest not later than her death.

(2) Where a gift is made upon alternative contingencies, one of which must occur, if at all, within the perpetuities period, and the other of which may not, the gift is valid if the first contingency occurs although it is invalid if the second contingency occurs.

C. APPLICATION OF THE RULE TO CLASS GIFTS

1. **The Basic Rule: All or Nothing.** Under the Rule, a class gift cannot be partially valid. It must be valid for all members of the class, or it is valid for none. If the gift to one member of the class might vest too remotely to satisfy the Rule, the entire class gift is void.

   a. **Class gifts--Ward v. Van der Loeff,** [1924] A.C. 653.

   Ward v. Van der Loeff

      1) **Facts.** The will of the decedent, William Burnyeat, left his estate in trust for his wife with the remainder to his children. In the event that he had no children, he gave his wife a power to appoint the trust fund among the children of his brothers and sisters; in default of appointment, the trust fund was to go in equal shares to the children of his brothers and sisters. A codicil to the will provided: (i) that the life interest to his wife shall be terminable on her remarriage unless such remarriage shall be with a natural-born British subject; (ii) that the power of appointment be revoked; and (iii) that, after the death of his wife, the trustees would hold the trust for any or all of the children of his brothers and sisters who shall be living at the death of his wife or born at any time afterward before any one of such children attains a vested interest and attains the age of 21 (if a son) or attains that age or marries (if a daughter), in equal shares. The testator was survived by his wife but no children, by his father and mother, aged 67, and by two brothers and two sisters, each of whom had children living at the testator's death. Phillip Burnyeat, another nephew of the testator, was born after the testator's death and after the remarriage of his widow to a Dutch subject.

      2) **Issue.** Will a gift to a class violate the Rule Against Perpetuities where the bequest is to the children of brothers and sisters born at any time after the death of a life in being?

      3) **Held.** Yes.

         a) (Lord Haldane) In construing the words of a will, the effect of the Rule Against Perpetuities must in the first instance be left out of sight, and then having in this way defined the intention expressed, the court must apply the Rule to the meaning thus ascertained. Here, the codicil is void since it speaks of the testator's brothers and sisters generally and there is no expression which excludes the children of other possible brothers and sisters of the whole or half blood who might in contemplation of law be born.

         b) However, the codicil does not operate to revoke the gift to the children of brothers and sisters contained in the will. The revocation in the codicil is confined to the power of appointment to the wife. The provision in the will stands undisturbed. The time when distribution of the estate occurs—here, when the widow remarried—is when the class of children who will take will be ascertained. Phillip

Burnyeat is excluded since he was born after the widow remarried.

c) (Lord Dunedin) There are only two classes of cases where the primary meaning of a class gift can be departed from. First, where it is impossible under the circumstances that any person indicated by the prima facie meaning can take under the bequest. Here, this is not the case since the law presumes that other brothers and sisters could still come into existence. Second, where something in the will itself excludes the prima facie interpretation. Here, this also is not the case.

b. **Consequences of violating the rule.** Violation of the Rule will result in the violating interest being stricken, with all other valid interests left standing.

2. **Gifts to Subclasses.** One exception to the all or nothing class gift rule is the doctrine of subclasses. Under this doctrine, a remainder held to be invalid as violative of the Rule Against Perpetuities does not taint and invalidate all other remainders where the ultimate takers are not described as a single class but as a group of subclasses.

American Security & Trust Co. v. Cramer

a. **Remainders to other subclasses not invalidated--American Security & Trust Co. v. Cramer,** 175 F. Supp. 367 (D.D.C. 1959).

1) **Facts.** The will of the decedent, Abraham Hazen, bequeathed the residue of his estate in trust to his wife for life; after her death half of the corpus was to be given to the testator's sister and brothers and the other half was to remain in trust for the decedent's adopted daughter, Hannah Duffey. Upon the death of Hannah, the income was to go to the children of Hannah, if alive, and if dead then to their issue, and upon the death of each, the share of each was to go to those who are heirs according to the law of descent and distribution. The heirs of the testator brought this action to have the will stricken as in violation of the Rule Against Perpetuities. The lower court held that the interests of Hannah's children were valid. The court of appeals affirmed. At the time of the testator's death, Hannah had two children—Mary and Hugh Duffey—and after the testator's death had two more—Depue and Horace Duffey. After the death of Hugh, the trustee brought a bill for instructions regarding the validity of the remainder over to Hugh's heirs; again, the remainder was held valid. Thereafter, Depue died and again a suit was brought. While this action was pending, Horace died and a supplemental bill for instructions was filed. Although Mary is still living, this court will pass on the validity of the remainder regarding all parties concerned.

2) **Issues.**

a) If a class gift is to be valid, must the class close within the period provided by the Rule Against Perpetuities?

b) Where one remainder is held to be invalid as violative of the Rule Against Perpetuities, does this taint and invalidate all other remainders where the ultimate takers are not described as a single class but as a group of subclasses?

3) **Held.** a) Yes. b) No. Counsel will submit an appropriate order.

a) A gift will fail unless the members of the class are finally determined within a life or lives in being plus 21 years and actual periods of gestation; stated differently, the class must close within the period provided by the Rule, if the class is to be held valid. Here, the remainders to the heirs of Hugh and Mary Duffey are valid—both Hugh and Mary were lives in being at the testator's death, and the remainders limited to their heirs had to vest, if at all, within the period provided by the Rule. The remainders to the heirs of Horace and Depue are invalid—they both were born after the testator died, and hence the remainders to their heirs could vest later than the period provided by the Rule. It does not help to show that the Rule might be complied with, or that, the way things turned out, it actually was complied with.

b) The invalidity of these remainders does not taint the valid remainders to the heirs of Mary and Hugh. If the ultimate takers are not described as a single class—*i.e.*, A's children that reach age 25—but rather as a group of subclasses—*i.e.*, the heirs of each of A's children—and if the share to which each separate subclass is entitled will finally be determined within the period of the Rule, the gifts to the different subclasses are separable for the purpose of the Rule. We read the language here as a devise of remainders to subclasses and not as a single class: "upon the death of 'each' the share of the 'one' so dying shall go to . . . her or his heirs at law." Accordingly, the invalidity of one does not invalidate them all.

c) The Rule in *Shelley's Case* does not save the two invalid remainders since the remainders were not limited to "heirs" but instead went to "her or his heirs at law according to the laws of descent now in force." When a remainder in fee after a life estate fails, there is a reversion in the heirs of the testator. The two one-sixth shares held invalid shall therefore pass to the successors in interest of the heirs of the testator.

3. **Specific Sum to Each Class Member.** Another exception to the all or nothing class gift rule is where there is a gift of a stated sum to each member of the class. The reason for this exception is that the amount intended by the conveyor to be received by each member of the class is ascertainable without reference to the number of persons in the class.

4. **Does Vest = Vest = Vest?** Difficulties arise regarding the meaning of the word vest, since orthodox doctrine has insisted that whether an interest is vested or contingent depends upon the form of words set forth in the limitation.

D. APPLICATION OF THE RULE TO POWERS OF APPOINTMENT

To apply the Rule Against Perpetuities to powers of appointment, the powers must be separated into (i) general powers presently exercisable, which are treated as absolute ownership for purposes of the Rule, and (ii) general testamentary powers and all special powers.

1. General Powers Presently Exercisable.

a. **Validity of power.** A general inter vivos power is valid if there is certainty that the power will become exercisable, or fail, within the perpetuities period. Once the power becomes exercisable, the property is no longer tied up. The fact that the donee may exercise the power after lives in being plus 21 years is irrelevant.

b. **Validity of interests created by exercise of a general power presently exercisable.** The validity of an interest created by exercise of a general power is determined on the same basis as if the donee owned the property in fee. The perpetuities period runs from the exercise of the power.

2. General Testamentary Powers and Special Powers.

a. **Validity of power.** A testamentary of special power is valid if it may not be exercised beyond the perpetuities period which begins at the creation of the power. If the power may be exercised beyond the perpetuities period, it is void ab initio.

b. **Validity of exercise.** General testamentary powers are treated like special powers in determining the validity of the appointment. The perpetuities period begins at the date the power was created.

1) **The "Delaware tax trap."** Delaware law provides that *all* interests created by the exercise of all powers, special as well as general, must vest within 21 years of the death of some life in being at the time the power is exercised. This provision theoretically would permit life estates to be created in indefinite succession through the exercise of successive special powers of appointment, thus avoiding federal tax liability (since property subject to a special power of appointment is not taxable at the donee's death). However, section 2041(a)(3) of the Internal Revenue Code taxes the assets in the donee's estate if the donee exercises a special power by creating another power of appointment that can be exercised without regard to the date of creation of the first power.

2) **The second-look doctrine.** Under the second-look doctrine, the exercise of the power is read back into the original instrument but facts existing on the date of the exercise are taken into account. Thus, on the basis of facts existing at the date of the appointment, the court will determine whether the appointive interests will vest within the time prescribed by the Rule.

c. **Rule applied to unconditional power of revocation--Second National Bank of New Haven v. Harris Trust & Savings Bank,** 29 Conn. Supp. 275, 283 A.2d 226 (1971).

Second National Bank of New Haven v. Harris Trust & Savings Bank

1) **Facts.** Caroline Trowbridge created an inter vivos trust naming the Second National Bank of New Haven (P) as trustee, with the income of the trust to be paid to the settlor's daughter, Margaret Marsh, who was also given a general testamentary power of appointment over half of the corpus. The remaining half would be distributed to Margaret's surviving children, and if none then to another daughter of the settlor, Mary Brewster Murray, or to her surviving issue per stirpes. The settlor reserved the power to revoke, modify, or alter the terms of the trust respecting payment of the income. Margaret Marsh left a will purporting to exercise the power by creating another trust giving the income to her daughter, Mary Washburne, for a period of 30 years, after which time the trust would be distributed to her or, if Mary died prior to this, then to her surviving children. At issue was whether the exercise of the testamentary power of appointment by Margaret's will is invalid as violative of the Rule Against Perpetuities.

2) **Issue.** Where a settlor reserves an unconditional power of revocation, for purposes of the Rule Against Perpetuities does the period of the Rule begin from when a power of appointment is first created?

3) **Held.** No. Judgment accordingly.

   a) When a power of appointment is in fact exercised, the validity of the appointment is determined by precisely the same rule as if the original testator who created the power had made in his own will the same provision in favor of the same appointee. The appointment is read back into the instrument creating the power. As far as perpetuities are concerned, the period of the Rule is reckoned from the date of creation of the power, not from the date of its exercise.

   b) However, there is an exception to this general rule where an unconditional power of revocation is reserved. In those instances, the period of perpetuities is calculated from the time the power of revocation ceased, usually at the death of the grantor.

   c) Here, the power to revoke reserved by the settlor Caroline Trowbridge does not qualify for the exception applicable to a full and unconditional power of revocation, since she reserved the power to revoke only as to the payment of income. Thus, the remoteness of the future interests created could not be affected by any exercise of the power.

   d) Here, both the gift of the income to Mary Washburne for 30 years and the gift of the remainder after the 30 years to Mary's children vested in interest at the death of Margaret Marsh within the period of the Rule. Postponement of enjoyment beyond the period of the Rule would not invalidate them. Accordingly, Mary has a valid income interest in the half of the trust subject to the power of appointment for

30 years and is then entitled to the principal. If she dies before then, the principal would be distributed to her estate because her remainder has become indefeasibly vested.

e) If Mary dies before the 30-year period expires, the principal goes to her estate; it does not pass to her surviving children under the terms of Margaret's trust. That trust's contingent remainder to Mary's children violates the Rule Against Perpetuities because it might vest more than 21 years after Margaret's death. The result in cases where future interests are voided by the Rule is that the prior interests become what they would have been had the limitation of the future interest been omitted from the instrument. Where a divesting interest is void, the interest that would otherwise have been divested becomes absolute.

E. SAVING CLAUSE

A saving clause takes care of any possible violation of the Rule. Such a clause should be included even in those jurisdictions that have adopted a cy pres or "wait-and-see" doctrine.

1. **Attorney Liability for Violating Rule.** Courts are divided as to whether an attorney who drafts a will that violates the Rule is liable for negligence.

F. PERPETUITIES REFORM

Three kinds of reform have emerged to alleviate some of the harsh effects of the Rule: the wait-and-see doctrine, the equitable reformation or cy pres doctrine, and remedying the most objectionable applications of the Rule with specific remedies.

1. **The "Wait-and-See Doctrine."** Under this doctrine, the validity of interests is judged by actual events as they happen, and not by events that might happen. [*See In re* Estate of Anderson, 541 So. 2d 423 (Miss. 1989)]

Merchants National Bank v. Curtis

a. **No violation of rule--Merchants National Bank v. Curtis,** 97 A.2d 207 (N.H. 1953).

1) **Facts.** T devised a life estate to her children (Cs), remainder to T's only grandchild (G) and her heirs forever. T also provided in Clause Sixth that if G or other grandchildren survive Cs and leave no heirs of her or their body, T's estate would pass to T's brothers and sisters and/or their children by representation and to T's husband's niece.

2) **Issue.** Is the gift over to the designated relatives in Clause Sixth void under the Rule Against Perpetuities?

3) **Held.** No. Case discharged.

a) New Hampshire has refused to apply in unmodified form common law principles which defeat normal and reasonable estate plans.

b) Such judicial techniques as (i) a constructional preference for considering interests vested rather than contingent, (ii) earlier vesting, (iii) alternative contingencies, and (iv) the "wait and see" doctrine have the salutary effect of avoiding the punitive aspects of the rule while at the same time confirming its policy and purpose.

c) Since Clause Sixth is capable of one construction that actually occurred and is within the period of perpetuities, *i.e.,* that the contingency occur, if at all, on the death of G, the gift is valid.

d) The other contingency would occur, if at all, on the death of the unborn grandchildren. If there had been another grandchild who died after G, without leaving heirs of her body, this event would have occurred beyond the period of perpetuities.

e) There is no justification for deciding the problems as of the date of death of the testator on facts that might have happened rather than on facts which actually happened.

f) At the death of the survivor of the life tenants, both of whom were lives in being at T's death, it became certain that no grandchildren of T would be born after T's death. Thus, it was certain that upon the death of G, also a life in being, the gift of Clause Sixth would vest.

2. **Cy Pres or Equitable Reformation.** Under this doctrine, an invalid interest is reformed within the limits of the Rule to approximate most closely the intention of the creator of the interest.

G. THE RULE AGAINST SUSPENSION OF THE POWER OF ALIENATION: NEW YORK LAW

1. **A Brief Explanation of the Suspension Rule.** The rule prohibiting suspension of the power of alienation proceeds upon a policy assumption that the power of alienation is suspended only when there are not persons in being who can convey an absolute fee. The rule applies only to interests that are contingent because the taker is unborn or unascertainable. Subsequent modifications of the statute have made it similar in scope to the common law Rule Against Perpetuities, with the exception that trusts that might last beyond the statutory period are more likely to be held invalid under the statute than they would be under the Rule.

2. **Application of the Suspension Rule to Statutory Spendthrift Trusts.** If a transfer is made in trust, the power of alienation is suspended if either the legal fee simple to the specific property held in trust cannot be transferred or the owners of all the equitable interests cannot convey an absolute fee in possession.

XII. TRUST ADMINISTRATION: THE FIDUCIARY OBLIGATION

A. GENERAL FIDUCIARY DUTIES AND LIABILITIES

1. **Duty of Loyalty: Herein of Self-Dealing.** A trustee has a duty to give undivided loyalty to the beneficiaries. The duty of loyalty requires trustees to avoid any conflicts of interest between personal interests and the interests of the trust or estate. Thus, ***any*** transactions between the individual and the trust or estate should be avoided. If the trustee engages in self-dealing, good faith and fairness to the beneficiaries are not enough to save the trustee from liability. The only defense the trustee has to self-dealing is that the beneficiaries consented after full disclosure; even then the transaction must be fair and reasonable.

   a. **Trustee's wife acts as purchaser--Hartman v. Hartle,** 122 A. 615 (N.J. 1923). Hartman v. Hartle

      1) **Facts.** Testator (T) named two sons-in-law executors and directed them to sell her real estate and divide the proceeds equally among T's five children. The executors sold part of the real estate to one of T's sons, who bought the property for his sister, the wife of one of the executors. She sold the property two months later for a $1,600 profit. One of T's daughters filed a bill charging the sale to have been improper and fraudulent.

      2) **Issue.** Is the sale of property by an executor to his wife, without previous authority from the court, illegal and void?

      3) **Held.** Yes.

         a) The settled law in this state is a trustee cannot purchase from himself at his own sale, and his wife is subject to the same disability.

         b) Because the property is now owned by innocent purchasers, the executors and the wife will be held accountable for complainant's one-fifth share of the profits on resale.

   b. **Conflict of interest--*In re* Rothko,** 43 N.Y.2d 305, 372 N.E.2d 291 (1977). *In re* Rothko

      1) **Facts.** The decedent, Mark Rothko, an internationally known painter, died testate, leaving an estate consisting principally of 798 paintings. Bernard Reis, Theodoros Stamos, and Morton Levine were appointed coexecutors. Within three weeks of their appointment, the executors agreed to sell to Marlborough A.G., a Liechtenstein corporation, 100 paintings to be paid for in interest-free installments over a 12-year period after an initial payment of $200,000. They also consigned to Marlborough Gallery, Inc., a domestic corporation, some 700 other paintings listed in a schedule to be prepared. It later came to light that Reis was a director, secretary, and treasurer of Marlborough

Gallery in addition to being coexecutor of the estate; that Stamos was a not-too-successful artist financially and that it was to his advantage to curry favor with Marlborough Gallery; and that Levine failed to exercise ordinary prudence because he was aware of Reis's conflict of interest. Kate Rothko, the decedent's daughter, later joined by her brother, Christopher Rothko, and the attorney general of the state (Ps), brought suit to remove the executors, to enjoin the sale of the paintings, to rescind the agreements entered into, to have returned the paintings still in possession of the corporations, and for damages. The trial court held for Ps. The appellate court affirmed. This appeal followed, the executors contending that they acted in good faith and that the plan was fair.

2) **Issue.** While a trustee is administering a trust, must he refrain from placing himself in a position where his personal interest may conflict with the interest of the beneficiaries?

3) **Held.** Yes. Affirmed.

a) The duty of loyalty imposed on a fiduciary prevents him from accepting employment from a third party who is entering into a business transaction with the trust. While the fiduciary as trustee is administering the trust, he must refrain from placing himself in a position where his personal interest or that of a third person does or may conflict with the interest of the beneficiaries. Here, to assert that there was no conflict of interest on the part of Reis and Stamos is to indulge in sheer fantasy. Reis was not only a director and officer of Marlborough Gallery but had financial inducements to favor Marlborough through sales of his own extensive art collection. So too did Stamos benefit as an artist under contract with Marlborough.

b) Levine argues that, having acted prudently and upon the advice of counsel, a complete defense is established. We disagree. An executor who knows that his coexecutor is committing breaches of trust and who not only fails to exert efforts directed toward prevention but accedes to the breaches is legally accountable even though he was acting on the advice of counsel.

c) We now turn to the proper measure of damages. In general, where a trustee is authorized to sell trust property, but in breach of trust sells it for less than he should receive, he is liable for the value of the property at the time of the sale less the amount that he received. If the breach of trust consists only in selling it for too little, the trustee is not chargeable with the amount of any subsequent increase in value of the property. However, where the breach consists of some misfeasance other than solely selling for too low a price, appreciation damages may be appropriate. A trustee may be held liable for appreciation damages if it was his or her duty to retain the property. The same rule should apply here where there is a serious conflict of interest.

c. **Co-trustees.** One of several trustees does not have the power alone to transfer or deal with the property. Nor may a trustee delegate decision-making powers to a co-trustee. These powers can only be exercised by the co-trustees together.

d. **Good faith required of fiduciary--*In re* Heidenreich,** 85 Misc. 2d 135, 378 N.Y.S.2d 982 (1976). *In re* Heidenreich

1) **Facts.** Decedent died in 1965 owning 1,309 shares of stock in Federation Bank and Trust Co. The residue of her estate, including this stock, was to be held in trust for her daughter and three grandchildren. Following a bank merger and reorganization, the stock was exchanged in 1969 for 1,341 shares of stock in Franklin New York Corp., the parent of Franklin National Bank. When one of the individual trustees died in 1973, Franklin National Bank was appointed successor trustee. Franklin reviewed the trust portfolio and decided to retain its own stock, which subsequently became worthless. Upon decedent's daughter's death, the guardian ad litem of two of decedent's grandchildren objects to the accounting, and argues that the bank should be surcharged for (i) retaining the stock of its parent corporation, (ii) depositing trust funds in a savings account at Franklin National Bank, and (iii) leaving $6,450 in a checking account at another bank for almost a year.

2) **Issue.** Will a surcharge be imposed upon a fiduciary who retains stock of its own corporation where retention is authorized by the will of a decedent and where the fiduciary acts in good faith?

3) **Held.** No. The objection of the guardian is overruled.

a) A fiduciary has an obligation to extricate itself from a conflict of interest either by not qualifying to act as trustee or by selling an unauthorized retention of stock of its own corporation. Here, the will of the testator authorized the fiduciary to retain any property, however acquired. Accordingly, the court finds that the trustees were authorized to retain the stock in spite of the conflict of interest.

b) However, in spite of this power to retain, the court could still surcharge the fiduciary if it found that the fiduciary did not act in good faith. The court finds that the trustees made a considered judgment regarding the retention of the stock, and they should not be second-guessed.

c) As for the funds in the savings account, we find that the trustees were making short-term deposits in order to have liquid assets ready for investment.

d) Finally, the funds in the checking account represented commissions due to the trustees. Although left as trust assets, the funds were adequately earmarked to be taken at a later date. The trustees have demonstrated that they used proper judgment, and there is no basis for a surcharge.

e. **Insider trading.** Under Securities Exchange Commission Rule 10b-5, a person with inside information about a stock cannot buy or sell the stock unless he first discloses this information. A fiduciary will be bound by this rule since the obligations of a fiduciary do not include the performing of an illegal act.

2. Fiduciary Duties Relating to Care of the Trust Property.

a. **Duty to collect and protect trust property.** A trustee has the duty of obtaining possession of the trust assets without unnecessary delay and ascertaining that the executor has tendered the appropriate property.

b. **Duty to earmark trust property.** A trustee has a duty to earmark property. The trustee is liable for any loss that results from the failure to earmark.

c. **Duty not to mingle trust funds with trustee's own.** A trustee has a duty to not commingle the trust funds with his own. As with the failure to earmark, the trustee will be liable for losses resulting from commingling.

d. **Duty not to delegate.** A trustee has a duty not to delegate to others the doing of acts which the trustee can reasonably be required to perform personally. He may delegate certain nondiscretionary functions, but he has a duty to supervise those to whom he delegates.

Shriners Hospitals for Crippled Children v. Gardiner

1) **Delegation of investment power--Shriners Hospitals for Crippled Children v. Gardiner,** 733 P.2d 1110 (Ariz. 1987).

a) **Facts.** Laurabel Gardiner established a trust to provide income to her daughter and grandchildren, Charles and Robert, and a daughter-in-law. The remainder passes to Shriners (P) upon the death of the income beneficiaries. Daughter was appointed trustee; Charles was named first alternate trustee; and Robert second alternate trustee. Daughter, not an experienced investor, placed the trust assets with Dean Witter. Charles, an investment counselor and stockbroker, made all investment decisions and embezzled in excess of $300,000. P brought a petition to surcharge Daughter for the full amount. The trial court denied the petition; a divided court of appeals reversed. Daughter appeals.

b) **Issues.**

(1) Is Daughter's delegation of investment power to Charles a breach of fiduciary duty?

(2) Was Daughter's delegation of investment power to Charles the proximate cause of the loss?

(3) Can Robert properly continue to act as successor trustee and as guardian and conservator for the predecessor trustee Daughter?

c) **Held.** (1) Yes. Reversed and remanded. (2) Remanded for findings of fact by trial court. (3) If trial court finds Daughter liable, Robert would have to be removed since, as her guardian and conservator, his interest would conflict with his fiduciary duty as trustee to enforce the surcharge.

(1) A trustee breaches the prudent man standard when she delegates her responsibilities to act prudently and personally perform her duties.

(2) Charles was a surrogate trustee, and Daughter unreasonably delegated her investment authority to him. It is of no import that Charles was named as an alternate trustee.

(3) Daughter was under a duty to exercise control over Charles's investments and evaluate Charles's advice and then make her own decisions.

e. **Liability for contracts and torts.** The traditional rule is that a trustee is personally liable on any contract the trustee makes, in the absence of express provision in the contract limiting the trustee's liability. A trustee is similarly liable in tort. A trustee is personally liable to the same extent that a beneficial owner of the trust property would be liable.

3. **Duty of Impartiality: Allocation to Income and Principal.** A trustee has the duty to deal with both the income beneficiary and the remainderman impartially. The trust property must produce a reasonable income while being preserved for the remainderman.

a. **Trustee's duty of impartiality--Dennis v. Rhode Island Hospital Trust Co.,** 744 F.2d 893 (1st Cir. 1984).

Dennis v. Rhode Island Hospital Trust Co.

1) **Facts.** Plaintiffs (Ps) are remaindermen of a trust established by their great-grandmother, and as such, entitled to income until 1991 when the trust ceases and Ps receive the principle. Ps claimed in the district court that the bank trustee (T) had breached various fiduciary obligations. The court found T had failed to act impartially as between the trust's income beneficiaries and remaindermen. T sold the trust's real estate at the lowest point of value. Both Ps and Ds appeal different aspects of the judgment.

2) **Issue.** Did T act unfairly as between the income beneficiaries and the remaindermen?

3) **Held.** Yes. Affirmed as modified.

a) The district court found T failed to keep up the real estate, to renovate, modernize, or to take other reasonable steps that might have given the remaindermen property roughly capable of continuing to produce reasonable income. The record provides adequate support for these conclusions, and we will not overturn a district court's factual determination unless it is clearly erroneous, particularly in a diversity case where a reasonable construction of state law is involved.

b) T did not appraise the property periodically, did not keep proper records, and made no accounting for 55 years. An impartial trustee must view the overall picture, not close its eyes to relevant facts.

c) T could have sold the property in 1950 and reinvested the proceeds so as not to create a "partiality" problem. The Restatement (Second) of Trusts says a trustee is under a duty to the beneficiary ultimately entitled to principal not to retain property certain or likely to depreciate, even though the property yields a high income, unless T makes adequate provision for amortizing the income.

d) State case law allows the court considerable discretion in fiduciary breach cases to fashion a remedy based on a hypothetical sale. The year 1950 is not an unreasonable remedial choice because that date marks a reasonable outer bound of the time the trustee could plead ignorance of the serious fairness problem.

e) The district court's surcharge calculation is approved except for the additional percentage to reflect "appreciation." There is no reason to believe T would have outperformed inflation.

f) T's removal is primarily a matter for the district court. T can be removed even if charges of misconduct are not made out. Ill feeling might interfere here with the trust administration.

National Academy of Sciences v. Cambridge Trust Co.

4. **Constructive Fraud--National Academy of Sciences v. Cambridge Trust Co.,** 370 Mass. 303, 346 N.E.2d 879 (1976).

a. **Facts.** The will of the decedent, Leonard T. Troland, left all of his property to be held in trust by the Cambridge Trust Company (D), with the net income to be paid to his wife for life as long as she remained unmarried. It further provided that his wife should not devote any major portion of her income to the support or benefit of people other than herself. The testator further provided that on his wife's death D would transfer the trusteeship to the National Research Council of Washington, D.C., an agency of the National Academy of Sciences (P), to constitute a trust for research in psycho-physics. The widow subsequently remarried but failed to notify D of this. The National Academy of Sciences (P) brought a petition seeking a revocation of the accounts of D and restoration by D of the $106,000 that was paid to the widow after her remarriage. The probate court held for P, ordering revocation of the accounts and charging D for the amounts erroneously distributed. D appeals.

b. **Issue.** Does the failure to make any reasonable effort to ascertain the true set of facts constitute a sufficient basis on which to hold a trustee responsible for a constructive fraud on beneficiaries of a trust?

c. **Held.** Yes. Judgment affirmed.

1) If a person makes a representation of fact in relation to subject matter susceptible of knowledge and such representation is not true, and if another party to whom it is made relies and acts upon it, it is fraud and deceit for which the party making it is responsible. We hold that the "fraud" in the applicable statute contemplates this standard of constructive fraud, at least to the extent that the fiduciary has made no reasonable efforts to ascertain the true state of facts that it has

misrepresented in the accounts. Here, the probate court found that D made no effort at all to ascertain if the widow had remarried. The judgment is affirmed.

5. **Changing Trustees.** Unless the trustee has been guilty of breach of trust or has shown unfitness, the beneficiaries cannot remove the trustee and have a new one appointed. The settlor's special confidence in the designated trustee has priority.

B. POWERS OF THE TRUSTEE

1. **General Managerial Powers.** In the absence of a statute, the administrative powers of a trustee are derived exclusively from the instrument creating the trust. The trustee is obligated to carry out the settlor's intent, which varies from trust to trust. Certain administrative powers can be implied as necessary to accomplish the purposes of the trust. Some states have enacted legislation to broaden trustees' powers.

2. **Powers of Investment.** Under the UPC, a trustee must observe the standards in dealing with the trust assets that would be observed by a prudent person dealing with the property of another. If the trustee has special skills or is named trustee on the basis of representations of special skills or expertise, he is under a duty to use those skills. The trustee must consider the following factors before investing: (i) safety of principal, (ii) liquidity, and (iii) rate of return.

   a. **Duty to diversify--Estate of Collins,** 72 Cal. App. 3d 663, 139 Cal. Rptr. 644 (1977). Estate of Collins

      1) **Facts.** The will of the decedent, Ralph Collins, authorized the trustees (Ds), decedent's business partner and lawyer, to purchase every kind of property and make every kind of investment, and further provided that all discretion conferred upon the trustees shall be absolute. After the will was admitted to probate and distribution of the estate made, there was $50,000 remaining for Ds to invest. They loaned the money to two real estate developers, Downing and Ward, who assured Ds that they were not in default on any of their loans. Thereafter, Downing and Ward Construction Company went bankrupt, resulting in a loss to the trust fund of $60,000. Ds filed a petition for approval and for settling of the first and final account and for their discharge. The beneficiaries under the trust (Ps) objected on the basis that Ds had improperly invested the $50,000. The trial court held for Ds. Ps appeal.

      2) **Issue.** Is a trustee under a duty to the beneficiaries to distribute the risk of loss by a reasonable diversification of investments?

      3) **Held.** Yes. Reversed.

         a) A trustee is under a duty to distribute the risk of loss by reasonable diversification. Here, Ds invested two-thirds of the trust principal in a single investment.

b) The general rule is that second or other junior mortgages are not proper trust investments. Here, Ds invested in real property secured only by a second deed of trust.

c) Also, in buying a mortgage for trust investments, the trustee should give careful attention to the valuation of the property, in order to make certain that the margin of security is adequate. Here, Ds invested without adequate investigation of either the borrowers or the collateral.

b. **Balancing gains and losses.** Courts typically apply the prudent person standard to each investment decision of the trustee rather than to the trust portfolio as a whole. Thus, the trustee is not permitted to balance gains and losses if the breaches of trust are separate and distinct.

c. **ERISA.** The Employment Retirement Income Security Act of 1974 provides rules governing investment of pension funds by the trustees managing the funds and imposes a prudent investor rule. The trustee must discharge his duties solely in the interest of the beneficiaries.

C. LIABILITY TO THIRD PARTIES

City of Phoenix v. Garbage Services Co.

1. **Third-Party Liability--City of Phoenix v. Garbage Services Co.,** 827 F. Supp. 600 (D. Ariz. 1993).

a. **Facts.** Estes retained an option to purchase a landfill when he conveyed it in 1965. Estes's will nominated VNB (T) as executor and trustee of a testamentary trust and conveyed the balance of his property, including the option, to T. T exercised the option as trustee in 1966. At time of purchase and subsequently Garbage Services Co. ("GSC") managed the property. Estes had owned 100% of GSC's stock and T now held the stock as a trust asset. In 1972, the landfill closed. In 1980, the City of Phoenix, (P), filed this action to recover response costs for cleanup of hazardous substances pursuant to the Comprehensive Environmental Response, Compensation, and Liability Act ("CERCLA"). This court in a previous order held T can be liable as an owner because it held title as trustee. T now moves for partial summary judgment, seeking an order limiting its liability.

b. **Issue.** Is T's liability limited to the extent that the trust's assets are sufficient to indemnify it?

c. **Held.** No. Motion denied.

1) A trustee is liable as holder of legal title as an "owner" under CERCLA, but there is nothing in the statute or legislative history to determine whether Congress intended a trustee to bear personal liability.

2) In developing federal common law to supplement the statute, we must balance two concerns: (i) the extent to which a uniform federal rule is required to further federal objectives, and (ii) the

need to avoid disrupting existing commercial relationships. Here, CERCLA's important federal policies require us to fashion a uniform federal rule from the existing common law on trustee liability.

3) The Restatement (Second) of Trusts, section 264, provides a trustee is subject to personal liability for torts committed in the course of trust administration to the same extent he would be if he held the property free of trust. Section 265 limits third-person trustee personal liability to the extent to which the trust estate indemnifies him.

4) CERCLA imposes liability for response costs on (i) owners of a facility or (ii) any person who at the time of disposal owned any facility at which hazardous substances were disposed of.

5) If a trustee was held liable under 4)(i), as a current owner, his liability would arise solely because he held title and would be limited to trust assets.

6) When a property owner allows his site to be used for disposal of hazardous substances, CERCLA imposes strict liability for damages.

7) The extent of the trustee's personal liability depends on whether he had power to control the use of the trust property at the time it was contaminated.

8) Where a trustee had power to control the use of trust property and knowingly allowed the property to be used for hazardous substance disposal, then the trustee is personally liable to the extent he would be if he held the property free of trust.

9) Here, T had full power to manage and control trust property, was vested with all the powers of an absolute owner, made the decision to purchase the landfill, and decided to continue leasing to GSC.

10) If contamination of trust property occurred entirely before the creation of the trust, the liability would be limited to trust assets.

XIII. WEALTH TRANSFER TAXATION: TAX PLANNING

A. INTRODUCTION

1. **A Brief History of the Federal Estate Tax.** Under the Tax Reform Act of 1976, Congress united the gift and estate taxes. The same rate schedule was applied to both gifts and estates, thus removing the tax incentive to make gifts before death. A single "unified credit" was enacted which, in effect, operates cumulatively to both lifetime and death transfers. Moreover, the new unified tax computation requires the estate tax to take into account lifetime gratuitous transfers, so that all gratuitous transfers are now taxed cumulatively. Federal wealth transfer taxation consists of three different taxes: (i) gift tax, (ii) estate tax, and (iii) generation-skipping transfer tax.

2. **Estate and Inheritance Taxes Distinguished.** An estate tax is a tax upon the value of all property owned by a decedent which is transferred to decedent's heirs or beneficiaries upon the decedent's death. On the other hand, an inheritance tax is a tax upon the value of property received by an heir or beneficiary on account of a decedent's death.

    a. **Estate tax computation.** A single set of deductions, exemptions, and graduated rates are applied to the decedent's estate; with few exceptions, it does not matter how many heirs or beneficiaries share in the estate, or who they are.

    b. **Inheritance tax computation.** Separate exemptions and rates are applied to the share received by each beneficiary and, typically, the rates of tax and allowable exemptions vary according to the relationship of the beneficiaries to the decedent.

3. **The Unified Federal Estate and Gift Tax.** Under the unified system, unified taxes are imposed on the estates of decedents dying after December 31, 1976, and for gifts made after that date. The rates are progressive on the basis of cumulative lifetime and death transfers.

4. **Liability for Payment of Taxes.**

    a. **Payment of gift tax.** The donor is primarily liable for payment of the gift tax. However, if the donor fails to pay the tax, the government has a lien on the donated property to the extent of the tax due, and also has the right to hold the donee liable for the unpaid gift tax, to the extent of the value of the property received by the donee.

    b. **Payment of estate tax.** The executor is primarily responsible for payment of the estate tax. The executor is personally liable for payment of the tax until he has been discharged from liability, but he is generally entitled to reimbursement out of the decedent's estate.

B. THE FEDERAL GIFT TAX

1. **Nature of a Taxable Gift.** Section 2501(a) of the Internal Revenue Code of 1986 imposes a gift tax on the transfer of property by gift. The courts have held that a "gift" occurs where the donor gives up complete dominion

and control. In a revocable trust, a taxable transfer does not occur until the power of revocation ceases.

a. **Discretionary power in trustee--Holtz's Estate v. Commissioner,** 38 T.C. 37 (1962).

Holtz's Estate v. Commissioner

1) **Facts.** A trust instrument of the decedent, Leon Holtz, provided that the trustee should distribute the net income to the settlor as the trustee thinks desirable, and upon the settlor's death, if his wife survived him, the income of the trust should be paid to her for life, and upon the death of both the settlor and his wife, the trust would terminate and the remaining principal would be paid to the estate of the survivor. The settlor transferred property having a value of $384,000 into the trust and thereafter he transferred an additional $50,000 to the trust. The Commissioner (D) determined that as a result of these transfers, Holtz made taxable gifts in the amount of $263,000, which were subject to the gift tax. The estate of the settlor (P) petitions the court and contends that the transfers were not completed gifts and that no part thereof was subject to the gift tax.

2) **Issue.** Does the placing of discretionary power in the trustee to invade corpus make the gift of corpus incomplete and hence not subject to the gift tax?

3) **Held.** Yes. Decision for the petitioner.

a) The placing of discretionary power in the trustee to invade the corpus makes the gift of the corpus incomplete under certain circumstances. The rule of thumb is generally that if the trustee is free to exercise his unfettered discretion and there is nothing to compel him to invade the corpus, then the settlor retains a mere expectancy that does not make the gift incomplete. However, if the exercise of the trustee's discretion is governed by some external standard that a court may apply in compelling compliance with the conditions of the trust agreement, and the trustee's power to invade is unlimited, then the gift of corpus is incomplete.

b) Here, the trustee had unfettered power to use all of the corpus for the benefit of the settlor if it thought that it was desirable for the welfare, comfort, and needs of the settlor. It is reasonable to assume that the trustee would, and could be required to, invade the corpus if this was desirable for the welfare, comfort, and needs of the settlor. It was thus possible that the entire corpus might be distributed during the settlor's lifetime. Hence, the settlor had not abandoned sufficient dominion and control over the property transferred to make the gift consummate.

b. **Income tax basis.** Under the federal income tax, a tax is levied upon capital gain realized upon the sale of property. The amount of the tax varies according to the amount of gain, which is the difference between the "basis" and the selling price.

2. **The Annual Exclusion.** Under section 2503(b) of the Code, a taxpayer is permitted to exclude from taxable gifts the first $10,000 given to any person during the year. The Code also provides an unlimited exclusion for tuition fees and medical expenses paid on behalf of another. The annual exclusion is not available for gifts of future interests.

a. **Transfer for the benefit of minor.** Section 2503(c) of the Code provides a way to avoid having a gift to a minor classified as a future interest. An annual exclusion for property transferred to a trust for a minor is authorized if at all times the property and the income therefrom may be expended for the benefit of the minor before he attains age 21, as long as the property and any accumulated income will be distributed to the minor at age 21 or, if the child dies before attaining age 21, to his estate or appointee.

Estate of Crisofani v. Commissioner

b. **Gifts of a present interest in property--Estate of Cristofani v. Commissioner,** 97 T.C. 74 (1991).

1) **Facts.** Decedent (D) had two children (Cs) and five grandchildren (Gs). D executed an irrevocable trust; D's children were trustees. Both Cs and Gs had the right under the trust terms, during a 15-day period following a contribution, to withdraw an amount not to exceed the amount specified for the federal gift tax exclusion under section 2503(b). The trustees could apply as much of the principal as necessary for proper support, health, maintenance, and education of D's children as necessary, taking into account several factors including D's desire to consider Cs the primary beneficiaries and Gs the secondary beneficiaries. D intended to fund the trust with a one-third individual interest in certain real property for 1984, 1985, and 1986. D did this for two years, transferring an interest valued at $70,000 each year. D died prior to making the 1986 transfer. D did not report the transfers on federal gift tax returns. D claimed seven annual exclusions under section 2503(b) for 1984 and 1985 with respect to Cs and Gs. Gs did not exercise their rights to withdraw under the trust during those years. The IRS allowed D's estate, petitioner (P), to claim the exclusions with respect to Cs but disallowed it for Gs for 1984 and 1985, determining that Gs' claimed exclusions were not transfers of present interests. P appeals.

2) **Issue.** Do transfers of property to a trust, where the beneficiaries possess the right to withdraw an amount not in excess of the section 2503(b) exclusion within 15 days of such transfers, constitute gifts of a present interest in property within the meaning of section 2503(b)?

3) **Held.** Yes. Decision entered for P.

a) For purposes of the exclusion, a trust beneficiary is considered a donee of a gift in trust.

b) The exclusion applies to present interests in property, an unrestricted right to the immediate use, possession, or enjoyment of property or income from property.

c) In *Crummy v. Commissioner,* 397 F.2d 82 (9th Cir. 1968), the court focused on the minor beneficiaries' legal right to demand payment from the trustee, not on the likelihood that they would actually receive present enjoyment of the property. If the beneficiaries had a legal right to make a demand upon the trustee which could not be resisted, the court determined the beneficiaries received a present interest.

d) Revenue rulings are not authority for this court but this ruling shows the IRS's recognition of what constitutes a present interest.

e) Here, the exclusions were allowed for Cs, who possessed the same right of withdrawal as Gs. Gs' legal right to withdraw specified amounts constitutes a gift of a present interest.

f) It is not required that trust beneficiaries have a vested present interest or a vested remainder interest in the trust corpus or income in order to qualify for the exclusion.

3. **Gifts Between Spouses and From One Spouse to a Third Person.** Under the Economic Recovery Tax Act of 1981, a husband and wife are permitted to treat their property as assets of a marital unit, transferable between husband and wife without the payment of any transfer taxes. Only when the assets pass from one of the spouses to a third person is a transfer tax imposed.

C. THE FEDERAL ESTATE TAX

1. **A Thumbnail Sketch of the Federal Estate Tax.** The basic purpose of the federal estate tax is to tax the value of property owned or passing at death, plus the value of property given away during lifetime.

2. **The Gross Estate: Property Passing by Will or Intestacy.**

a. **Section 2033: Property owned at death.** Under this section, the value of the gross estate includes the value of property to the extent of the decedent's interest at the time of death; it reaches all property owned at death that passes by will or intestacy. It does not reach a decedent's life estate created by another person.

b. **Section 2034: Dower or curtesy.** Section 2034 of the Code includes in decedent's gross estate "the value of all property to the extent of any interest therein of the surviving spouse, existing at the time of the decedent's death as dower or curtesy, or by virtue of the statute creating an estate in lieu of dower or curtesy." Section 2034 does not apply to community property. In community property states, on the death of either spouse only his or her half is includable in the gross estate; the other half belongs to the surviving spouse and is not includable. Note that the importance of section 2034 is greatly offset by the marital deduction, which operates to take out of the taxable estate most of the property included therein under section 2034.

3. **The Gross Estate: Nonprobate Property.**

a. **Section 2040: Joint tenancy.**

1) **Joint tenancy between persons other than husband and wife.** Section 2040(a) requires the inclusion of the entire value of the property held in joint tenancy, except such part of the entire value as is attributable to the amount of consideration furnished by the other joint tenant.

2) **Joint tenancy and tenancy by the entirety between husband and wife.** Section 2040(b) provides that with respect to property held by the decedent and decedent's spouse as joint tenants with right of survivorship or as tenants by the entirety, half the value of the property is includable in decedent's gross estate regardless of which spouse furnished the consideration for the property's acquisition. Since each spouse is deemed to own half of the amount of the joint tenancy with right of survivorship or tenancy by the entirety, the decedent's spouse's half interest in the property included in the gross estate will receive a stepped-up basis at death.

b. **Section 2039: Employee death benefits.** Under section 2039, there is included in the decedent's estate the value of amounts receivable by a beneficiary under an agreement where the decedent, during life, was receiving or had a right to receive payments under the agreement. If the decedent has no power to select the beneficiary of his employee benefits (*i.e.*, a statute requires death benefits to be payable to decedent's spouse or children), the death benefits are not includable in decedent's estate. If benefits are payable to a beneficiary at a scheduled time or upon the happening of an event, irrespective of whether decedent is then living or dead, they are not taxable under section 2039, even though the decedent may be dead at the time scheduled for payment.

c. **Section 2042: Life insurance.** Section 2042 provides that the gross estate shall include the value of insurance proceeds on the life of the decedent if the decedent possessed at death any of the incidents of ownership under the policies or if the policy proceeds were payable to the insured's executor or estate.

4. **The Gross Estate: Lifetime Transfers with Rights Retained.**

a. **Section 2036: Transfers with life estate or power of control retained.** Section 2036(a)(1) applies when the decedent retains a life estate in the transferred property. The transfer is subject to estate taxation because the decedent retained the most important incident of property ownership: the right to possess and enjoy the property or the right to income from it. Section 2036(a)(2) exposes to estate tax any property transferred by the decedent wherein there was retained the right, either alone or in conjunction with another person, to control the beneficial enjoyment of the property or income therefrom. The tax will attach despite the fact that the transferor could not have exercised the power so as to secure a personal economic benefit.

1) **No bona fide sale--Estate of Maxwell v. Commissioner,** 3 F.3d 591 (2d Cir. 1993). Estate of Maxwell v. Commissioner

a) **Facts.** Decedent (D) conveyed her home to her son and his wife in 1984 for $270,000. D leased the premises for five years at $1,800 per month. D forgave $20,000 of the purchase price as part of the annual gift tax exclusion and held a mortgage for the remaining $250,000. The buyers paid expenses. The rent essentially canceled out the mortgage payments, and buyers were never called upon to pay mortgage principal. Upon D's death, buyers sold the home for $550,000. On D's estate tax return, the estate reported $210,000 remaining on the mortgage debt. The Commissioner (R) found that the 1984 transaction constituted a transfer with a retained life estate and assessed a deficiency to adjust for the difference between the fair market value and the reported amount. The estate (P) appealed to the tax court which affirmed R. P appeals.

b) **Issues.**

(1) Did D retain possession or enjoyment of the property following the transfer?

(2) If she did, was the transfer a bona fide sale for an adequate and full consideration in money or money's worth?

c) **Held.** (1) Yes. (2) No. Affirmed.

(1) Section 2036(a) requires inclusion in the value of the gross estate of all property transferred under which decedent retained a life estate, *i.e.*, possession, enjoyment, or right to income from the property.

(2) Possession or enjoyment is retained when there is an express or implied understanding to that effect among the parties to the transfer.

(3) The mortgage note had no value if there was, as the tax court determined from the conduct of the parties, no intention that it would ever be paid.

(4) The forgiveness of the initial $20,000 strongly suggests the existence of an understanding between D and buyers that D would forgive $20,000 each year until her death and the balance would be forgiven by D's will.

2) **Requirement of an ascertainable standard--Old Colony Trust Co. v. United States,** 423 F.2d 601 (1st Cir. 1970). Old Colony Trust Co. v. United States

a) **Facts.** The decedent had established a trust for the benefit of his son and named himself as a trustee. The trust permitted the trustees to increase the percentage of income payable to the son beyond the prescribed 80% when in their opinion such increase was needed in case of sickness or was desirable in view of changed circumstances. In addition, the trustees were given the discretion to cease paying income to the son. Another article gave broad administrative and management powers to the trustees. A deficiency was assessed against the estate. The executor paid the tax and sued for its recovery in district court. The court ruled for the government. Old Colony Trust Company appeals.

b) **Issue.** If there is no ascertainable standard with which a settlor-trustee must comply in his distribution of trust income, will the settlor's estate be taxed according to the value of the principal that the settlor contributed?

c) **Held.** Yes. Affirmed.

(1) If there is an ascertainable standard, the trustee can be compelled to follow it. If there is not, even though he is a fiduciary, it is not unreasonable to say that his retention of an unmeasurable freedom of choice is equivalent to retaining some of the incidents of ownership. Hence, if there is an ascertainable standard, the settlor-trustee's estate is not taxed, but if there is not, it is taxed.

(2) Here, the settlor retained the unrestricted power to distribute the trust income. Accordingly, the tax was properly assessed.

b. **Section 2038: Revocable transfers.** Section 2038 provides that the value of the gross estate shall include the value of all property of which the decedent has at any time made a transfer by trust or otherwise, where the enjoyment was subject to any change through the decedent's exercise of a power to alter, amend, revoke, or terminate. Unless the decedent has the right to exercise the power, a transfer subject to such power is not taxable in her estate. This is true even where the power is vested in one who lacks a substantial adverse interest to the decedent, such as a trustee or even a subordinate party (*e.g.*, transferor's spouse).

c. **Section 2037: Transfers with reversionary interest retained.** Under section 2037, the value of property transferred during life is includable in the transferor's gross estate if possession can be obtained only by surviving the decedent, and the decedent has retained a reversionary interest in the property, and the value of such reversionary interest immediately before the death of the decedent exceeds 5% of the value of the property.

5. **The Gross Estate: Transfers Within Three Years of Death.** Under section 2035, certain inter vivos transfers made within three years prior to death are brought within the decedent's gross estate.

6. **The Gross Estate: Powers of Appointment Given Decedent by Another.** Under section 2041, the gross estate includes the value of property over which the decedent at the time of death held a general power of appointment. The donee of a general power of appointment is treated as owner of the property subject to the power. If a donee exercises or releases a general power of appointment, the donee makes a taxable gift. If decedent merely possessed a general power of appointment at the time of his death, the property is taxable whether the power was exercised or unexercised. Property subject solely to a special power is not taxable in the donee's estate under section 2041.

a. **Comfort limited by ascertainable standard--Estate of Vissering v. Commissioner,** 990 F.2d 578 (10th Cir. 1993).

Estate of Vissering v. Commissioner

1) **Facts.** Decedent's (D's) mother created a trust controlled by Florida law. D and a bank served as trustees. D received all the income from the trust after his mother's death and on D's death the assets were to be divided in equal parts for D's two children. D developed Alzheimer's disease and entered a nursing home in 1984 but never resigned as trustee. At D's death, he possessed a power of appointment that permitted him to benefit himself, his estate, his creditors or the estate's creditors for his "continued comfort." The tax court held that D held at his death a general power defined by I.R.C. section 2041, requiring the trust assets to be included in D's gross estate. D's estate appeals.

2) **Issue.** Did D hold powers permitting him to invade the principal of the trust for his own benefit, unrestrained by an ascertainable standard relating to health, education, support, or maintenance?

3) **Held.** No. Reversed and remanded.

a) State law determines legal interests and rights created by the trust instrument, but federal law determines tax consequences.

b) Florida law would hold that a trust document permitting invasion of principal for "comfort," without qualifying language, creates a general power of appointment.

c) However, there is modifying language in the trust here—"to the extent required for continued comfort"—that we believe would lead Florida to hold does not permit an unlimited power of invasion.

d) Examples in the Treasury Regulation, such as "support in reasonable comfort," "maintenance in health and reasonable comfort," and "support in his accustomed manner of living," deemed to be limited by an ascertainable standard are no different from the language in D's trust provision.

e) If D sought to use the trust assets to significantly increase his standard of living, his cotrustee would have been obligated to withhold consent and the remainder beneficiaries could have petitioned the court to disallow such expenditures as inconsistent with the settlor's intent.

b. **Power of appointment derived from will establishing testamentary trust for benefit of widow--De Oliveira v. United States,** 767 F.2d 1344 (9th Cir. 1985).

De Oliveira v. United States

1) **Facts.** Testator died testate in 1956. His will created a testamentary trust to hold his half of the community property and named his wife, Serafina, as lifetime beneficiary and trustee. The will also gave the trustee certain powers. In 1972, Serafina executed a document entitled "Power of Attorney." Under that document Serafina agreed to confer with the family members and to abide by a majority vote on any proposed sale, lease, loan, or transaction regarding any of the family property.

Serafina died testate in 1978. Her son, Jose Jr., was appointed executor of her estate. The federal estate tax return filed for the estate did not include as assets of the estate the property in the testamentary trust established by the testator, Jose Sr. On audit, the IRS determined that the provisions of the testator's will creating the trust gave Serafina the power, exercisable in favor of herself, to consume, appropriate, or dispose of the corpus of the trust. The IRS therefore concluded that Serafina possessed a general power of appointment and that the trust assets were required to be included in her gross estate for estate tax purposes. The district court entered judgment for the government.

2) **Issue.** Are trust assets properly included in the gross estate of testator's widow where a power of appointment is derived from provisions in the will establishing a testamentary trust for the benefit of the widow and naming her as trustee with a power to consume, invade, or appropriate property for her benefit?

3) **Held.** Yes. Judgment affirmed.

a) State law determines the property rights and interests created by a will, but federal law determines the tax consequences of those rights and interests.

b) Section 2041 of the Internal Revenue Code includes within the gross estate of a decedent the value of property over which the decedent possessed a general power of appointment. Serafina's power to consume, invade, or appropriate property is limited only by the requirement that it be exercised for her "benefit." Thus, Serafina's power remains one exercisable in favor of her, her estate, or the creditors of her estate and therefore is a general power.

c) The paragraph in the will stating that all provisions for support of Serafina shall take effect on the day of testator's death did not alter the conclusion that the power of appointment given to Serafina was a general power. Despite the contention that the support paragraph was intended to limit the power of appointment to an "ascertainable standard," its true purpose was to free the widow from a need to seek a court-ordered maintenance.

d) A power of attorney executed by the widow that required her to exercise the power of appointment only upon authorization by a majority of her children did not have the effect of making the general power of appointment created by the will not a general power of appointment for purposes of Serafina's gross estate.

7. The Marital Deduction.

a. **Introduction.** Section 2056 allows a marital deduction for certain dispositions of property to a decedent's spouse. Unlimited amounts of property (other than certain "terminable interests") can now be transferred between spouses without the imposition of either a gift tax or an estate tax.

b. Interests that qualify for the deduction. For an interest to qualify as a marital deduction, the following requirements must be met:

(i) The decedent must have been a citizen of the United States;

(ii) The decedent must have been survived by his or her spouse;

(iii) The value of the interest deducted must be includable in the decedent's gross estate;

(iv) The interest must pass from the decedent to the surviving spouse; and

(v) The interest must be a deductible interest (*i.e.*, the interest passing to the surviving spouse must be such that it is subject to taxation in the spouse's estate to the extent not consumed or disposed of by the spouse during her lifetime).

1) Scrivener's error--Loeser v. Talbot, 589 N.E.2d 301 (Mass. 1992).

Loeser v. Talbot

a) Facts. Settlor (S) executed a trust, intending to create three subtrusts: a marital trust, a terminable interest trust, and a family trust. The terminable interest trust granted S's wife special and general testamentary powers over trust income and principal respectively. Trustees (Ts) contend the powers are reversed due to a scrivener's error, which is apparent when the purposes of the trust are considered. Ts argue the trust's purpose was to qualify the trust property for the I.R.C. section 2056(b)(7) marital deduction and to keep the property within the family line. Ts filed a complaint for reformation of the trust. The trust beneficiaries assented. Because the I.R.S. may not abide by a lower court decision, the probate court reserved and reported the case to the appeals court. We granted the parties' application for direct appellate review.

b) Issue. Should the powers of appointment granted S's wife be reversed so that S's wife possesses a general power over income and a special power, limited to issue, over the terminable interest trust principal?

c) Held. Yes.

(1) We have held that a trust instrument may be reformed when, because of mistake or inadvertence of the scrivener, the settlor's intention is not embodied in the trust language. Full, clear, and decisive proof of mistake is required for reformation.

(2) A major aspect of S's intent was to qualify for the marital deduction. Throughout the trust, the terminable interest trust is referred to; another trust article provides for the terminable interest trust to be funded only with qualifying assets and provides the trustees are authorized to manage the terminable interest trust property in a way that ensures that the trust qualifies for the marital deduction. Based on these provisions, we are confident of S's intent.

(3) The powers granted to S's wife were an integral part of S's plan. S intended these powers to achieve specific tax consequences.

(4) We are further convinced that this is not a situation where S intended the actual language in the trust but misunderstood its legal effect.

(5) Absent reformation, the powers thwart an otherwise coherent estate plan. If the powers are reversed, the special power will serve additional estate planning objectives; it will ensure the trust principal passes only to S's issue. This goal was as important to S as minimizing estate tax.

c. **Tax planning.** Each spouse has an exemption from estate and gift taxation, in the form of a unified credit, which is $600,000. By taking advantage of both spouses' exemptions, $1.2 million can be passed to the couple's children, free of estate taxation. Because of the graduated tax rates, the total estate tax payable on the death of a husband and wife will be lower if the two estates are equal. Equalization is not necessarily the best solution in all cases. Formula clauses remain useful in producing precisely the right amount to put in a credit shelter trust or a marital deduction trust. A credit shelter trust is a trust designed to hold an amount equal to the exemption of the first spouse to die (*i.e.,* the amount not taxable on his death) in such a manner as not to be taxable on the surviving spouse's death.

8. **The Charitable Deduction.** Section 2055 of the Code allows an unlimited deduction for transfers for public, charitable, or religious purposes.

9. **Executor's Elections: Post-Death Tax Planning.**

a. **Valuation of estate assets.** For estate tax purposes, assets are valued at their fair market value as of the date of death, or as of the alternate valuation date, which is the date six months after death (except for assets distributed, sold, exchanged, or otherwise disposed of during the six-month period, for which it is the date of distribution or sale).

b. **Sections 2053 and 2054 deductions.** Section 2053 allows a deduction for funeral expenses, administration expenses, claims against the estate, and unpaid mortgages. Section 2054 allows a deduction for losses incurred during the settlement of estates arising from fires, storms, shipwrecks, or other casualties, or from theft, when such losses are not compensated for by insurance or otherwise.

D. THE GENERATION-SKIPPING TAX.

The Tax Reform Act of 1986 prevents wealthy persons from making transfers in trust, either during lifetime or by will, in a manner that would insulate the transferred property from estate or gift taxation over several generations. The underlying principle of the generation-skipping tax is that a transfer tax (gift, estate, or generation-skipping) should be paid once a generation and that it should not be possible for an owner of property to avoid a generational transfer tax by giving the next generation only a life estate or skipping its members entirely. If a trust turns out to produce a generation-skipping transfer, the tax is payable in the future when such transfer occurs. All generation-skipping transfers are taxed at a flat rate, which is the highest rate applicable under the federal estate tax. The amount taxed and the person liable for the tax depend upon the type of transfer. Section 2631(a) provides an exemption of up to $1 million for each person making generation-skipping transfers. A husband and wife can give away $2 million in generation-skipping transfers without incurring any tax.

E. STATE WEALTH TRANSFER TAXES.

All states except Nevada have death taxes, but less than a dozen impose a gift tax on lifetime transfers.

TABLE OF CASES

(Page numbers of brief cases in bold)

Notes

Publications Catalog

Publishers of America's Most Popular Legal Study Aids!

All Titles Available At Your Law School Bookstore.

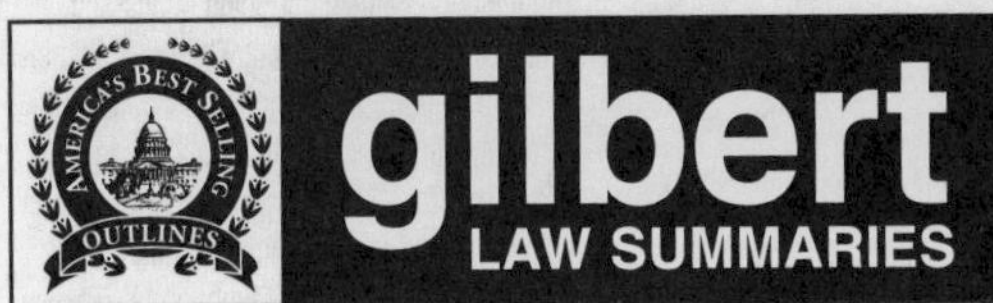

Gilbert Law Summaries are the best selling outlines in the country, and have set the standard for excellence since they were first introduced more than twenty-five years ago. It's Gilbert's unique combination of features that makes it the one study aid you'll turn to for all your study needs!

Accounting and Finance for Lawyers
Professor Thomas L. Evans, University of Texas
Basic Accounting Principles; Definitions of Accounting Terms; Balance Sheet; Income Statement; Statement of Changes in Financial Position; Consolidated Financial Statements; Accumulation of Financial Data; Financial Statement Analysis.
ISBN: 0-15-900382-2 Pages: 232 $19.95

Administrative Law
By Professor Michael R. Asimow, U.C.L.A.
Separation of Powers and Controls Over Agencies; (including Delegation of Power) Constitutional Right to Hearing (including Liberty and Property Interests Protected by Due Process, and Rulemaking- Adjudication Distinction); Adjudication Under Administrative Procedure Act (APA); Formal Adjudication (including Notice, Discovery, Burden of Proof, Finders of Facts and Reasons); Adjudicatory Decision Makers (including Administrative Law Judges (ALJs), Bias, Improper Influences, Ex Parte Communications, Familiarity with Record, Res Judicata); Rulemaking Procedures (including Notice, Public Participation, Publication, Impartiality of Rulemakers, Rulemaking Record); Obtaining Information (including Subpoena Power, Privilege Against Self-incrimination, Freedom of Information Act, Government in Sunshine Act, Attorneys' Fees); Scope of Judicial Review; Reviewability of Agency Decisions (including Mandamus, Injunction, Sovereign Immunity, Federal Tort Claims Act); Standing to Seek Judicial Review and Timing.
ISBN: 0-15-900000-9 Pages: 306 $20.95

Agency and Partnership
By Professor Richard J. Conviser, Chicago Kent
Agency: Rights and Liabilities Between Principal and Agent (including Agent's Fiduciary Duty, Right to Indemnification); Contractual Rights Between Principal (or Agent) and Third Persons (including Creation of Agency Relationship, Authority of Agent, Scope of Authority, Termination of Authority, Ratification, Liability on Agents, Contracts); Tort Liability (including Respondeat Superior, Master-Servant Relationship, Scope of Employment). Partnership: Property Rights of Partner; Formation of Partnership; Relations Between Partners (including Fiduciary Duty); Authority of Partner to Bind Partnership; Dissolution and Winding up of Partnership; Limited Partnerships.
ISBN: 0-15-900327-X Pages: 172 $17.95

Antitrust
By Professor Thomas M. Jorde, U.C. Berkeley, Mark A. Lemley, University of Texas, and Professor Robert H. Mnookin, Harvard University
Common Law Restraints of Trade; Federal Antitrust Laws (including Sherman Act, Clayton Act, Federal Trade Commission Act, Interstate Commerce Requirement, Antitrust Remedies); Monopolization (including Relevant Market, Purposeful Act Requirement, Attempts and Conspiracy to Monopolize); Collaboration Among Competitors (including Horizontal Restraints, Rule of Reason vs. Per Se Violations, Price Fixing, Division of Markets, Group Boycotts); Vertical Restraints (including Tying Arrangements); Mergers and Acquisitions (including Horizontal Mergers, Brown Shoe Analysis, Vertical Mergers, Conglomerate Mergers); Price Discrimination—Robinson-Patman Act; Unfair Methods of Competition; Patent Laws and Their Antitrust Implications; Exemptions From Antitrust Laws (including Motor, Rail, and Interstate Water Carriers, Bank Mergers, Labor Unions, Professional Baseball).
ISBN: 0-15-900328-8 Pages: 236 $18.95

Bankruptcy
By Professor Ned W. Waxman, College of William and Mary
Participants in the Bankruptcy Case; Jurisdiction and Procedure; Commencement and Administration of the Case (including Eligibility, Voluntary Case, Involuntary Case, Meeting of Creditors, Debtor's Duties); Officers of the Estate (including Trustee, Examiner, United States Trustee); Bankruptcy Estate; Creditor's Right of Setoff; Trustee's Avoiding Powers; Claims of Creditors (including Priority Claims and Tax Claims); Debtor's Exemptions; Nondischargeable Debts; Effects of Discharge; Reaffirmation Agreements; Administrative Powers (including Automatic Stay, Use, Sale, or Lease of Property); Chapter 7-Liquidation; Chapter 11-Reorganization; Chapter 13-Individual With Regular Income; Chapter 12-Family Farmer With Regular Annual Income.
ISBN: 0-15-900442-X Pages: 368 $21.95

Business Law
By Professor Robert D. Upp, Los Angeles City College
Torts and Crimes in Business; Law of Contracts (including Contract Formation, Consideration, Statute of Frauds, Contract Remedies, Third Parties); Sales (including Transfer of Title and Risk of Loss, Performance and Remedies, Products Liability, Personal Property Security Interest); Property (including Personal Property, Bailments, Real Property, Landlord and Tenant); Agency; Business Organizations (including Partnerships, Corporations); Commercial Paper; Government Regulation of Business (including Taxation, Antitrust, Environmental Protection, and Bankruptcy).
ISBN: 0-15-900005-X Pages: 289 $17.95

California Bar Performance Test Skills
By Professor Peter J. Honigsberg, University of San Francisco
Hints to Improve Writing; How to Approach the Performance Test; Legal Analysis Documents (including Writing a Memorandum of Law, Writing a Client Letter, Writing Briefs); Fact Gathering and Fact Analysis Documents; Tactical and Ethical Considerations; Sample Interrogatories, Performance Tests, and Memoranda.
ISBN: 0-15-900152-8 Pages: 229 $18.95

Civil Procedure
By Professor Thomas D. Rowe, Jr., Duke University, and Professor Richard L. Marcus, U.C. Hastings
Territorial (Personal) Jurisdiction, including Venue and Forum Non Conveniens; Subject Matter Jurisdiction, covering Diversity Jurisdiction, Federal Question Jurisdiction; Erie Doctrine and Federal Common Law; Pleadings including Counterclaims, Cross-Claims, Supplemental Pleadings; Parties, including Joinder and Class Actions; Discovery, including Devices, Scope, Sanctions, and Discovery Conference; Summary Judgment; Pretrial Conference and Settlements; Trial, including Right to Jury Trial, Motions, Jury Instruction and Arguments, and Post-Verdict Motions; Appeals; Claim Preclusion (Res Judicata) and Issue Preclusion (Collateral Estoppel).
ISBN: 0-15-900447-0 Pages: 460 $22.95

Commercial Paper and Payment Law
By Professor Douglas J. Whaley, Ohio State University
Types of Commercial Paper; Negotiability; Negotiation; Holders in Due Course; Claims and Defenses on Negotiable Instruments (including Real Defenses and Personal Defenses); Liability of the Parties (including Merger Rule, Suits on the Instrument, Warranty Suits, Conversion); Bank Deposits and Collections; Forgery or Alteration of Negotiable Instruments; Electronic Banking.
ISBN: 0-15-900367-9 Pages: 194 $19.95

Community Property
By Professor William A. Reppy, Jr., Duke University
Classifying Property as Community or Separate; Management and Control of Property; Liability for Debts; Division of Property at Divorce; Devolution of Property at Death; Relationships Short of Valid Marriage; Conflict of Laws Problems; Constitutional Law Issues (including Equal Protection Standards, Due Process Issues).
ISBN: 0-15-900422-5 Pages: 188 $18.95

Call To Order: 1-800-787-8717 or Order On-Line at http://www.gilbertlaw.com

Conflict of Laws
By Dean Herma Hill Kay, U.C. Berkeley

Domicile; Jurisdiction (including Notice and Opportunity to be Heard, Minimum Contacts, Types of Jurisdiction); Choice of Law (including Vested Rights Approach, Most Significant Relationship Approach, Governmental Interest Analysis); Choice of Law in Specific Substantive Areas; Traditional Defenses Against Application of Foreign Law; Constitutional Limitations and Overriding Federal Law (including Due Process Clause, Full Faith and Credit Clause, Conflict Between State and Federal Law); Recognition and Enforcement of Foreign Judgments.

ISBN: 0-15-900424-1 Pages: 273 $20.95

Constitutional Law
By Professor Jesse H. Choper, U.C. Berkeley

Powers of Federal Government (including Judicial Power, Powers of Congress, Presidential Power, Foreign Affairs Power); Intergovernmental Immunities, Separation of Powers; Regulation of Foreign Commerce; Regulation of Interstate Commerce; Taxation of Interstate and Foreign Commerce; Due Process, Equal Protection; "State Action" Requirements; Freedoms of Speech, Press, and Association; Freedom of Religion.

ISBN: 0-15-900375-X Pages: 355 $21.95

Contracts
By Professor Melvin A. Eisenberg, U.C. Berkeley

Consideration (including Promissory Estoppel, Moral or Past Consideration); Mutual Assent; Defenses (including Mistake, Fraud, Duress, Unconscionability, Statute of Frauds, Illegality); Third-Party Beneficiaries; Assignment of Rights and Delegation of Duties; Conditions; Substantial Performance; Material vs. Minor Breach; Anticipatory Breach; Impossibility; Discharge; Remedies (including Damages, Specific Performance, Liquidated Damages).

ISBN: 0-15-900014-9 Pages: 326 $21.95

Corporations
By Professor Jesse H. Choper, U.C. Berkeley, and Professor Melvin A. Eisenberg, U.C. Berkeley

Formalities; "De Jure" vs. "De Facto"; Promoters; Corporate Powers; Ultra Vires Transactions; Powers, Duties, and Liabilities of Officers and Directors; Allocation of Power Between Directors and Shareholders; Conflicts of Interest in Corporate Transactions; Close Corporations; Insider Trading; Rule 10b-5 and Section 16(b); Shareholders' Voting Rights; Shareholders' Right to Inspect Records; Shareholders' Suits; Capitalization (including Classes of Shares, Preemptive Rights, Consideration for Shares); Dividends; Redemption of Shares; Fundamental Changes in Corporate Structure; Applicable Conflict of Laws Principles.

ISBN: 0-15-900342-3 Pages: 319 $21.95

Criminal Law
By Professor George E. Dix, University of Texas

Elements of Crimes (including Actus Reus, Mens Rea, Causation); Vicarious Liability; Complicity in Crime; Criminal Liability of Corporations; Defenses (including Insanity, Diminished Capacity, Intoxication, Ignorance, Self-Defense); Inchoate Crimes; Homicide; Other Crimes Against the Person; Crimes Against Habitation (including Burglary, Arson); Crimes Against Property; Offenses Against Government; Offenses Against Administration of Justice.

ISBN: 0-15-900217-6 Pages: 317 $20.95

Criminal Procedure
By Professor Paul Marcus, College of William and Mary, and Professor Charles H. Whitebread, U.S.C.

Exclusionary Rule; Arrests and Other Detentions; Search and Seizure; Privilege Against Self-Incrimination; Confessions; Preliminary Hearing; Bail; Indictment; Speedy Trial; Competency to Stand Trial; Government's Obligation to Disclose Information; Right to Jury Trial; Right to Counsel; Right to Confront Witnesses; Burden of Proof; Insanity; Entrapment; Guilty Pleas; Sentencing; Death Penalty; Ex Post Facto Issues; Appeal; Habeas Corpus; Juvenile Offenders; Prisoners' Rights; Double Jeopardy.

ISBN: 0-15-900449-7 Pages: 271 $20.95

Estate and Gift Tax
By Professor John H. McCord, University of Illinois

Gross Estate; Allowable Deductions Under Estate Tax (including Expenses, Indebtedness, and Taxes, Deductions for Losses, Charitable Deduction, Marital Deduction); Taxable Gifts; Deductions; Valuation; Computation of Tax; Returns and Payment of Tax; Tax on Generation-Skipping Transfers.

ISBN: 0-15-900425-X Pages: 327 $20.95

Evidence
By Professor Jon R. Waltz, Northwestern University, and Roger C. Park, University of Minnesota

Direct Evidence; Circumstantial Evidence; Rulings on Admissibility; Relevancy; Materiality; Character Evidence; Hearsay and the Hearsay Exceptions; Privileges; Competency to Testify; Opinion Evidence and Expert Witnesses; Direct Examination; Cross-Examination; Impeachment; Real, Demonstrative, and Scientific Evidence; Judicial Notice; Burdens of Proof; Parol Evidence Rule.

ISBN: 0-15-900385-7 Pages: 387 $22.95

Federal Courts
By Professor William A. Fletcher, U.C. Berkeley

Article III Courts; "Case or Controversy" Requirement; Justiciability; Advisory Opinions; Political Questions; Ripeness; Mootness; Standing; Congressional Power Over Federal Court Jurisdiction; Supreme Court Jurisdiction; District Court Subject Matter Jurisdiction (including Federal Question Jurisdiction, Diversity Jurisdiction); Pendent and Ancillary Jurisdiction; Removal Jurisdiction; Venue; Forum Non Conveniens; Law Applied in the Federal Courts (including Erie Doctrine); Federal Law in the State Courts; Abstention; Habeas Corpus for State Prisoners; Federal Injunctions Against State Court Proceedings; Eleventh Amendment.

ISBN: 0-15-900232-X Pages: 313 $21.95

Future Interests & Perpetuities
By Professor Jesse Dukeminier, U.C.L.A.

Reversions; Possibilities of Reverter; Rights of Entry; Remainders; Executory Interest; Rules Restricting Remainders and Executory Interest; Rights of Owners of Future Interests; Construction of Instruments; Powers of Appointment; Rule Against Perpetuities (including Reforms of the Rule).

ISBN: 0-15-900218-4 Pages: 185 $19.95

Income Tax I - Individual
By Professor Michael R. Asimow, U.C.L.A.

Gross Income; Exclusions; Income Splitting by Gifts, Personal Service Income, Income Earned by Children, Income of Husbands and Wives, Below-Market Interest on Loans, Taxation of Trusts; Business and Investment Deductions; Personal Deductions; Tax Rates; Credits; Computation of Basis, Gain, or Loss; Realization; Nonrecognition of Gain or Loss; Capital Gains and Losses; Alternative Minimum Tax; Tax Accounting Problems.

ISBN: 0-15-900421-7 Pages: 312 $21.95

Income Tax II - Partnerships, Corporations, Trusts
By Professor Michael R. Asimow, U.C.L.A.

Taxation of Partnerships (including Current Partnership Income, Contributions of Property to Partnership, Sale of Partnership Interest, Distributions, Liquidations); Corporate Taxation (including Corporate Distributions, Sales of Stock and Assets, Reorganizations); S Corporations; Federal Income Taxation of Trusts.

ISBN: 0-15-900384-9 Pages: 238 $19.95

Labor Law
By Professor James C. Oldham, Georgetown University, and Robert J. Gelhaus

Statutory Foundations of Present Labor Law (including National Labor Relations Act, Taft-Hartley, Norris-LaGuardia Act, Landrum-Griffin Act); Organizing Campaigns, Selection of the Bargaining Representative; Collective Bargaining (including Negotiating the Agreement, Lockouts, Administering the Agreement, Arbitration); Strikes, Boycotts, and Picketing; Concerted Activity Protected Under the NLRA; Civil Rights Legislation; Grievance; Federal Regulation of Compulsory Union Membership Arrangements; State Regulation of Compulsory Membership Agreements; "Right to Work" Laws; Discipline of Union Members; Election of Union Officers; Corruption.

ISBN: 0-15-900340-7 Pages: 260 $19.95

Legal Ethics
By Professor Thomas D. Morgan, George Washington University

Regulating Admission to Practice Law; Preventing Unauthorized Practice of Law; Contract Between Client and Lawyer (including Lawyer's Duties Regarding Accepting Employment, Spheres of Authority of Lawyer and Client, Obligation of Client to Lawyer, Terminating the Lawyer-Client Relationship); Attorney-Client Privilege; Professional Duty of Confidentiality; Conflicts of Interest; Obligations to Third Persons and the Legal System (including Counseling Illegal or Fraudulent Conduct, Threats of Criminal Prosecution); Special Obligations in Litigation (including Limitations on Advancing Money to Client, Duty to Reject Certain Actions, Lawyer as Witness); Solicitation and Advertising; Specialization; Disciplinary Process; Malpractice; Special Responsibilities of Judges.

ISBN: 0-15-900026-2 Pages: 258 $20.95

Legal Research, Writing and Analysis
By Professor Peter J. Honigsberg, University of San Francisco

Court Systems; Precedent; Case Reporting System (including Regional and State Reporters, Headnotes and the West Key Number System, Citations and Case Finding); Statutes, Constitutions, and Legislative History; Secondary Sources (including Treatises, Law Reviews, Digests, Restatements); Administrative Agencies (including Regulations, Looseleaf Services); Shepard's Citations; Computers in Legal Research; Reading and Understanding a Case (including Briefing a Case); Using Legal Sourcebooks; Basic Guidelines for Legal Writing; Organizing Your Research; Writing a Memorandum of Law; Writing a Brief; Writing an Opinion or Client Letter.

ISBN: 0-15-900436-5 Pages: 187 $17.95

Multistate Bar Examination
By Professor Richard J. Conviser, Chicago Kent

Structure of the Exam; Governing Law; Effective Use of Time; Scoring of the Exam; Jurisdictions Using the Exam; Subject Matter Outlines; Practice Tests, Answers, and Subject Matter Keys; Glossary of Legal Terms and Definitions; State Bar Examination Directory; Listing of Reference Materials for Multistate Subjects.

ISBN: 0-15-900246-X Pages: 776 $24.95

Personal Property
Gilbert Staff

Acquisitions; Ownership Through Possession (including Wild Animals, Abandoned Chattels); Finders of Lost Property; Bailments; Possessory Liens; Pledges, Trover; Gift; Accession; Confusion (Commingling); Fixtures; Crops (Emblements); Adverse Possession; Prescriptive Rights (Acquiring Ownership of Easements or Profits by Adverse Use).

ISBN: 0-15-900360-1 Pages: 140 $14.95

Professional Responsibility
(see Legal Ethics)

Call To Order: 1-800-787-8717 or Order On-Line at http://www.gilbertlaw.com

Property
By Professor Jesse Dukeminier, U.C.L.A.

Possession (including Wild Animals, Bailments, Adverse Possession); Gifts and Sales of Personal Property; Freehold Possessory Estates; Future Interests (including Reversion, Possibility of Reverter, Right of Entry, Executory Interests, Rule Against Perpetuities); Tenancy in Common; Joint Tenancy; Tenancy by the Entirety; Condominiums; Cooperatives; Marital Property; Landlord and Tenant; Easements and Covenants; Nuisance; Rights in Airspace and Water; Right to Support; Zoning; Eminent Domain; Sale of Land (including Mortgage, Deed, Warranties of Title); Methods of Title Assurance (including Recording System, Title Registration, Title Insurance).

ISBN: 0-15-900426-8 Pages: 515 $22.95

Remedies
By Professor John A. Bauman, U.C.L.A., and Professor Kenneth H. York, Pepperdine University

Damages; Equitable Remedies (including Injunctions and Specific Performance); Restitution; Injuries to Tangible Property Interests; Injuries to Business and Commercial Interests (including Business Torts, Inducing Breach of Contract, Patent Infringement, Unfair Competition, Trade Defamation); Injuries to Personal Dignity and Related Interests (including Defamation, Privacy, Religious Status, Civil and Political Rights); Personal Injury and Death; Fraud; Duress, Undue Influence, and Unconscionable Conduct; Mistake; Breach of Contract; Unenforceable Contracts (including Statute of Frauds, Impossibility, Lack of Contractual Capacity, Illegality).

ISBN: 0-15-900325-3 Pages: 390 $22.95

Sale and Lease of Goods
By Professor Douglas J. Whaley, Ohio State University

UCC Article 2; Sales Contract (including Offer and Acceptance, Parol Evidence Rule, Statute of Frauds, Assignment and Delegation, Revision of Contract Terms); Types of Sales (including Cash Sale Transactions, Auctions, "Sale or Return" and "Sale on Approval" Transactions); Warranties (including Express and Implied Warranties, Privity, Disclaimer, Consumer Protection Statutes); Passage of Title; Performance of the Contract; Anticipatory Breach; Demand for Assurance of Performance; Unforeseen Circumstances; Risk of Loss; Remedies; Documents of Title; Lease of Goods; International Sale of Goods.

ISBN: 0-15-900219-2 Pages: 234 $19.95

Secured Transactions
By Professor Douglas J. Whaley, Ohio State University

Coverage of Article 9; Creation of a Security Interest (including Attachment, Security Agreement, Value, Debtor's Rights in the Collateral); Perfection; Filing; Priorities; Bankruptcy Proceedings and Article 9; Default Proceedings; Bulk Transfers.

ISBN: 0-15-900231-1 Pages: 224 $18.95

Securities Regulation
By Professor David H. Barber, and Professor Niels B. Schaumann, William Mitchell College of Law

Jurisdiction and Interstate Commerce; Securities Act of 1933 (including Registration Requirements and Exemptions); Securities Exchange Act of 1934 (including Rule 10b-5, Tender Offers, Proxy Solicitations Regulation, Insider Transactions); Regulation of the Securities Markets; Multinational Transactions; State Regulation of Securities Transactions.

ISBN: 0-15-9000437-3 Pages: 478 $22.95

Torts
By Professor Marc A. Franklin, Stanford University

Intentional Torts; Negligence; Strict Liability; Products Liability; Nuisance; Survival of Tort Actions; Wrongful Death; Immunity; Release and Contribution; Indemnity; Workers' Compensation; No-Fault Auto Insurance; Defamation; Invasion of Privacy; Misrepresentation; Injurious Falsehood; Interference With Economic Relations; Unjustifiable Litigation.

ISBN: 0-15-900220-6 Pages: 452 $22.95

Trusts
By Professor Edward C. Halbach, Jr., U.C. Berkeley

Elements of a Trust; Trust Creation; Transfer of Beneficiary's Interest (including Spendthrift Trusts); Charitable Trusts (including Cy Pres Doctrine); Trustee's Responsibilities, Power, Duties, and Liabilities; Duties and Liabilities of Beneficiaries; Accounting for Income and Principal; Power of Settlor to Modify or Revoke; Powers of Trustee Beneficiaries or Courts to Modify or Terminate; Termination of Trusts by Operation of Law; Resulting Trusts; Purchase Money Resulting Trusts; Constructive Trusts.

ISBN: 0-15-900465-9 Pages: 274 $20.95

Wills
By Professor Stanley M. Johanson, University of Texas

Intestate Succession; Simultaneous Death; Advancements; Disclaimer; Killer of Decedent; Elective Share Statutes; Pretermitted Child Statutes; Homestead; Formal Requisites of a Will; Revocation of Wills; Incorporation by Reference; Pour-Over Gift in Inter Vivos Trust; Joint Wills; Contracts Relating to Wills; Lapsed Gifts; Ademption; Exoneration of Liens; Will Contests; Probate and Estate Administration.

ISBN: 0-15-900040-8 Pages: 312 $21.95

Gilbert Law Summaries FIRST YEAR PROGRAM

Includes Five Gilbert Outlines:

- **Civil Procedure**
  By Professor Thomas D. Rowe, Jr. Duke University Law School, and Professor Richard L. Marcus U.C. Hastings School Of Law
- **Contracts**
  By Professor Melvin A. Eisenberg U.C. Berkeley School Of Law
- **Criminal Law**
  By Professor George E. Dix University Of Texas School Of Law
- **Property**
  By Professor Jesse Dukeminier U.C.L.A. Law School
- **Torts**
  By Professor Marc A. Franklin Stanford University Law School

Plus—

- **Gilbert's Dictionary Of Legal Terms**
- **The 8 Secrets Of Top Exam Performance In Law School**
  By Professor Charles H. Whitebread USC Law School

All titles are packaged in a convenient carrying case with handle. $130 if purchased separately. $95 if purchased as a set. Save $35.

ISBN: 0-15-900254-0 Set $95

Gilbert's Pocket Size Law Dictionary
Gilbert

A dictionary is useless if you don't have it when you need it. If the only law dictionary you own is a thick, bulky one, you'll probably leave it at home most of the time — and if you need to know a definition while you're at school, you're out of luck!

With Gilbert's Pocket Size Law Dictionary, you'll have any definition you need, when you need it. Just pop Gilbert's dictionary into your pocket or purse, and you'll have over 4,000 legal terms and phrases at your fingertips. Gilbert's dictionary also includes a section on law school shorthand, common abbreviations, Latin and French legal terms, periodical abbreviations, and governmental abbreviations.

With Gilbert's Pocket Size Law Dictionary, you'll never be caught at a loss for words!

Available in your choice of 5 colors

- **Brown** ISBN: 0-15-900252-4 $7.95
- **Blue** ISBN: 0-15-900362-8 $7.95
- **Burgundy** ISBN: 0-15-900366-0 $7.95
- **Green** ISBN: 0-15-900365-2 $7.95

Limited Edition: Simulated Alligator Skin Cover

- **Black** ISBN: 0-15-900364-4 $7.95

The Eight Secrets Of Top Exam Performance In Law School
Charles Whitebread

Wouldn't it be great to know exactly what your professor's looking for on your exam? To find out everything that's expected of you, so that you don't waste your time doing anything other than maximizing your grades?

In his easy-to-read, refreshing style, nationally recognized exam expert Professor Charles Whitebread will teach you the eight secrets that will add precious points to every exam answer you write. You'll learn the three keys to handling any essay exam question, and how to add points to your score by making time work for you, not against you. You'll learn flawless issue spotting, and discover how to organize your answer for maximum possible points. You'll find out how the hidden traps in "IRAC" trip up most students… but not you! You'll learn the techniques for digging up the exam questions your professor will ask, before your exam. You'll put your newly-learned skills to the test with sample exam questions, and you can measure your performance against model answers. And there's even a special section that helps you master the skills necessary to crush any exam, not just a typical essay exam — unusual exams like open book, take home, multiple choice, short answer, and policy questions.

"The Eight Secrets of Top Exam Performance in Law School" gives you all the tools you need to maximize your grades — quickly and easily!

ISBN: 0-15-900323-7 $9.95

Call To Order: 1-800-787-8717 or Order On-Line at http://www.gilbertlaw.com

Criminal Procedure
By Professor Charles H. Whitebread
USC School of Law

TOPICS COVERED: Incorporation Of The Bill Of Rights; Exclusionary Rule; Fruit Of The Poisonous Tree; Arrest; Search & Seizure; Exceptions To Warrant Requirement; Wire Tapping & Eavesdropping; Confessions (Miranda); Pretrial Identification; Bail; Preliminary Hearings; Grand Juries; Speedy Trial; Fair Trial; Jury Trials; Right To Counsel; Guilty Pleas; Sentencing; Death Penalty; Habeas Corpus; Double Jeopardy; Privilege Against Compelled Testimony.
3 Audio Cassettes
ISBN: 0-15-900281-8 $39.95

Evidence
By Professor Faust F. Rossi
Cornell Law School

TOPICS COVERED: Relevance; Insurance; Remedial Measures; Settlement Offers; Causation; State Of Mind; Rebuttal; Habit; Character Evidence; "MIMIC" Rule; Documentary Evidence; Authentication; Best Evidence Rule; Parol Evidence; Competency; Dead Man Statutes; Examination Of Witnesses; Present Recollection Revived; Past Recollection Recorded; Opinion Testimony; Lay And Expert Witness; Learned Treatises; Impeachment; Collateral Matters; Bias, Interest Or Motive; Rehabilitation; Privileges; Hearsay And Exceptions.
5 Audio Cassettes
ISBN: 0-15-900282-6 $45.95

Family Law
Professor Roger E. Schechter
George Washington University Law School

TOPICS COVERED: Marital Relationship; Formalities And Solemnization; Common Law Marriage; Impediments; Conflict Of Laws; Non-Marital Relationship; Void And Voidable Marriages; Annulment; Divorce; Separation; Full Faith And Credit; Temporary Orders; Property Division; Community Property Principles; Equitable Distribution And Reimbursement; Marital And Separate Property; Alimony; Child Support; Enforcement Of Orders; Antenuptial And Postnuptial Agreements; Separation And Settlement Agreements; Custody; Visitation Rights; Termination Of Parental Rights; Adoption; Illegitimacy; Paternity Actions.
3 Audio Cassettes
ISBN: 0-15-900283-4 $39.95

Federal Courts
Professor John C. Jeffries
University of Virginia School of Law

TOPICS COVERED: History Of The Federal Court System; "Court Or Controversy" And Justiciability; Congressional Power Over Federal Court Jurisdiction; Supreme Court Jurisdiction; District Court Subject Matter Jurisdiction—Federal Question Jurisdiction, Diversity Jurisdiction And Admiralty Jurisdiction; Pendent And Ancillary Jurisdiction; Removal Jurisdiction; Venue; Forum Non Conveniens; Law Applied In The Federal Courts; Federal Law In The State Courts; Collateral Relations Between Federal And State Courts; The Eleventh Amendment And State Sovereign Immunity.
3 Audio Cassettes
ISBN: 0-15-900372-5 $39.95

Federal Income Tax
By Professor Cheryl D. Block
George Washington University Law School

TOPICS COVERED: Administrative Reviews; Tax Formula; Gross Income; Exclusions For Gifts; Inheritances; Personal Injuries; Tax Basis Rules; Divorce Tax Rules; Assignment Of Income; Business Deductions; Investment Deductions; Passive Loss And Interest Limitation Rules; Capital Gains & Losses; Section 1031, 1034, and 121 Deferred/Non Taxable Transactions.
4 Audio Cassettes
ISBN: 0-15-900284-2 $45.95

Future Interests
By Dean Catherine L. Carpenter
Southwestern University Law School

TOPICS COVERED: Rule Against Perpetuities; Class Gifts; Estates In Land; Rule In Shelley's Case; Future Interests In Transferor and Transferee; Life Estates; Defeasible Fees; Doctrine Of Worthier Title; Doctrine Of Merger; Fee Simple Estates; Restraints On Alienation; Power Of Appointment; Rules Of Construction.
2 Audio Cassettes
ISBN: 0-15-900285-0 $24.95

Law School Exam Writing
By Professor Charles H. Whitebread
USC School of Law

TOPICS COVERED: With "Law School Exam Writing," you'll learn the secrets of law school test taking. Professor Whitebread leads you step-by-step through his innovative system, so that you know exactly how to tackle your essay exams without making point draining mistakes. You'll learn how to read questions so you don't miss important issues; how to organize your answer; how to use limited exam time to your maximum advantage; and even how to study for exams.
1 Audio Cassette
ISBN: 0-15-900287-7 $19.95

Professional Responsibility
By Professor Erwin Chemerinsky
USC School of Law

TOPICS COVERED: Regulation of Attorneys; Bar Admission; Unauthorized Practice; Competency; Discipline; Judgment; Lawyer-Client Relationship; Representation; Withdrawal; Conflicts; Disqualification; Clients; Client Interests; Successive And Effective Representation; Integrity; Candor; Confidences; Secrets; Past And Future Crimes; Perjury; Communications; Witnesses; Jurors; The Court; The Press; Trial Tactics; Prosecutors; Market; Solicitation; Advertising; Law Firms; Fees; Client Property; Conduct; Political Activity.
3 Audio Cassettes
ISBN: 0-15-900371-7 $39.95

Real Property
By Professor Paula A. Franzese
Seton Hall Law School

TOPICS COVERED: Estates—Fee Simple, Fee Tail, Life Estate; Co-Tenancy—Joint Tenancy, Tenancy In Common, Tenancy By The Entirety; Landlord-Tenant Relationship; Liability For Condition Of Premises; Assignment & Sublease; Easements; Restrictive Covenants; Adverse Possession; Recording Acts; Conveyancing; Personal Property.
4 Audio Cassettes
ISBN: 0-15-900289-3 $45.95

Remedies
By Professor William A. Fletcher
University of California at Berkeley, Boalt Hall School of Law

TOPICS COVERED: Damages; Restitution; Equitable Remedies; Tracing; Rescission and Reformation; Injury and Destruction of Personal Property; Conversion; Injury to Real Property; Trespass; Ouster; Nuisance; Defamation; Trade Libel; Inducing Breach of Contract; Contracts to Purchase Personal Property; Contracts to Purchase Real Property (including Equitable Conversion); Construction Contracts; and Personal Service Contracts.
4 Audio Cassettes
ISBN: 0-15-900353-9 $45.95

Sales & Lease of Goods
By Professor Michael I. Spak
Chicago Kent College of Law

TOPICS COVERED: Goods; Contract Formation; Firm Offers; Statute Of Frauds; Modification; Parol Evidence; Code Methodology; Tender; Payment; Identification; Risk Of Loss; Warranties; Merchantability; Fitness; Disclaimers; Consumer Protection; Remedies; Anticipatory Repudiation; Third Party Rights.
3 Audio Cassettes
ISBN: 0-15-900291-5 $39.95

Secured Transactions
By Professor Michael I. Spak
Chicago Kent College of Law

TOPICS COVERED: Collateral; Inventory; Intangibles; Proceeds; Security Agreements; Attachment; After-Acquired Property; Perfection; Filing; Priorities; Purchase Money Security Interests; Fixtures; Rights Upon Default; Self-Help; Sale; Constitutional Issues.
3 Audio Cassettes
ISBN: 0-15-900292-3 $39.95

Securities Regulation
By Professor Therese H. Maynard
Loyola Marymount School of Law

TOPICS COVERED: Securities Markets; IPOs; Brokers-Dealers; Securities Acts (1933, 1934); Self-Regulatory Organizations; Insider Trading; the SEC; Securities—*Howey* Test; Publicly Held Corporation; Underwriting; Who is Subject to Section 5 of 1933 Securities Act; Offers; Prospectuses; Registration Statements; Liability for Material Misstatements; Exemptions from Section 5 Registration; Foreign Issuers and Offshore Offerings; Regulations A and D; Rules 504, 505, 506, 701; Liability Provisions of 1933 Act; Due Diligence Defense; Damages; Liability Under Sections 12 (a)(1) and (2).
5 Audio Cassettes
ISBN: 0-15-900359-8 $45.95

Torts
By Professor Richard J. Conviser
Chicago Kent College of Law

TOPICS COVERED: Essay Exam Techniques; Intentional Torts—Assault, Battery, False Imprisonment, Intentional Infliction Of Emotional Distress, Trespass To Land, Trespass To Chattels, Conversion; Defenses. Defamation—Libel, Slander; Defenses; First Amendment Concerns; Invasion Of Right Of Privacy; Misrepresentation; Negligence—Duty, Breach, Actual And Proximate Causation, Damages; Defenses; Strict Liability, Products Liability; Nuisance; General Tort Considerations.
4 Audio Cassettes
ISBN: 0-15-900293-1 $45.95

Wills & Trusts
By Professor Stanley M. Johanson
University of Texas School of Law

TOPICS COVERED: Attested Wills; Holographic Wills; Negligence; Revocation; Changes On Face Of Will; Lapsed Gifts; Negative Bequest Rule; Nonprobate Assets; Intestate Succession; Advancements; Elective Share; Will Contests; Capacity; Undue Influence; Creditors' Rights; Creation Of Trust; Revocable Trusts; Pourover Gifts; Charitable Trusts; Resulting Trusts; Constructive Trusts; Spendthrift Trusts; Self-Dealing; Prudent Investments; Trust Accounting; Termination; Powers Of Appointment.
4 Audio Cassettes
ISBN: 0-15-900294-X $45.95

Law School Legends Series
FIRST YEAR PROGRAM

Includes Five Law School Legends Titles:

- **Civil Procedure**
  By Professor Richard D. Freer
  Emory University Law School
- **Contracts**
  By Professor Michael I. Spak
  Chicago Kent College Of Law
- **Criminal Law**
  By Professor Charles H. Whitebread
  USC School of Law
- **Real Property**
  By Professor Paula A. Franzese
  Seton Hall Law School
- **Torts**
  By Professor Richard J. Conviser
  Chicago Kent College of Law

Plus—

- **Law School Exam Writing**
  By Professor Charles H. Whitebread
  USC Law School

All titles are packaged in a convenient carry case. $250 if purchased separately. $195 if purchased as a set. Save $55.

ISBN: 0-15-900306-7 Set $195

If you accidentally damage a tape within five years from the date of purchase we'll replace it for FREE— No questions asked!

Call To Order: 1-800-787-8717 or Order On-Line at http://www.gilbertlaw.com

100% Comprehensive, 100% Authoritative, 100% of What You Need

CASEBRIEFS
FOR WINDOWS

Detailed Briefs Of Every Major Case— At Your Fingertips!

Casebriefs Interactive Software For Windows

As a law student you can't afford to waste a minute. That's why you need Casebriefs Software. With Casebriefs you simply click on the name of the case you're looking for, and you instantly have an expert brief of it at your fingertips! The facts. The issue. The holding. The rationale. Expert commentary. You'll get everything you need, whether you're preparing for class or studying for your final exam!

When you use Casebriefs, you can focus solely on the cases covered in your casebook, or you can use the Case Library, which includes briefs of all of the major cases from every major casebook. The Case Library is ideal for researching cases for writing assignments, moot court briefs, law review and other periodicals.

With Casebriefs, searching for cases is a breeze. You can search by topic. You can search alphabetically. You can search the cases in the order in which they appear in your casebook. You can even enter the date you'll cover different cases in class, and sort them by those dates. No matter how you want to look for a case, Casebriefs will help you find it instantly!

For each brief, you can add your own notes, or leave it "as is." Whether you customize the briefs or not, you can print them out and take them to class with you. You can even configure Casebriefs to access Lexis/Nexis and Westlaw directly from the Casebriefs screen (with Lexis/Nexis or Westlaw software and account). Whether you want to compare your own briefs to expert briefs, fill in gaps in your class notes, or research cases for your legal writing class, moot court, law review or other periodicals— Casebriefs is the source you'll turn to, over and over again!

Administrative Law
Includes briefs of all of the major cases from the Breyer, Gellhorn and Schwartz casebooks, many of the major cases from the Bonfield and Mashaw casebooks, plus a Case Library.
ISBN# 0-15-900190-0 $27.95

Antitrust
Includes briefs of all of the major cases from the Areeda and Handler casebooks, many of the major cases from the Sullivan casebook, plus a Case Library.
ISBN# 0-15-900400-4 $27.95

Civil Procedure
Includes briefs of all of the major cases from the Cound, Field, Hazard, Rosenberg and Yeazell casebooks, many of the major cases from the Marcus and Levin casebooks, plus a Case Library.
ISBN# 0-15-900191-9 $27.95

Commercial Law
Includes briefs of all of the major cases from the Farnsworth casebook, plus a Case Library.
ISBN# 0-15-900407-1 $27.95

Conflict Of Laws
Includes briefs of all of the major cases from the Cramton and Reese casebooks, many of the major cases from the Brilmayer casebook, plus a Case Library.
ISBN# 0-15-900192-7 $27.95

Constitutional Law
Includes briefs of all of the major cases from the Brest, Cohen, Gunther, Lockhart, Rotunda and Stone casebooks, plus a Case Library.
ISBN# 0-15-900193-5 $27.95

Contracts
Includes briefs of all of the major cases from the Calamari, Dawson, Farnsworth, Fuller, Kessler and Murphy casebooks, many of the major cases from the Burton, Crandall, Hamilton, Knapp, and Rosett casebooks, plus a Case Library.
ISBN# 0-15-900194-3 $27.95

Corporations
Includes briefs of all of the major cases from the Cary, Choper, Hamilton and Vagts casebooks, many of the major cases from the O'Kelley and Solomon casebooks, plus a Case Library.
ISBN# 0-15-900195-1 $27.95

Criminal Law
Includes briefs of all of the major cases from the Boyce, Dix, Johnson, Kadish and La Fave casebooks, many of the major cases from the Dressler, Johnson, Kaplan, Moenssens and Weinreb casebooks, plus a Case Library.
ISBN# 0-15-900196-X $27.95

Criminal Procedure
Includes briefs of all of the major cases from the Kamisar casebook, many of the major cases from the Allen, Haddad and Saltzburg casebooks, plus a Case Library.
ISBN# 0-15-900197-8 $27.95

Domestic Relations
Includes briefs of all of the major cases from the Clark and Wadlington casebooks, plus a Case Library.
ISBN# 0-15-900408-X $27.95

Estate & Gift Taxes
Includes briefs of all of the major cases from the Surrey casebook, plus a Case Library.
ISBN# 0-15-900396-2 $27.95

Evidence
Includes briefs of all of the major cases from the Sutton, Waltz, and Weinstein casebooks, many of the major cases from the Strong and Mueller casebooks, plus a Case Library.
ISBN# 0-15-900198-6 $27.95

Family Law
Includes briefs of all of the major cases from the Areen casebook, many of the major cases from the Clark, Ellman, Krause and Wadlington casebooks, plus a Case Library.
ISBN# 0-15-900199-4 $27.95

Federal Courts
Includes briefs of all of the major cases from the McCormick casebook, many of the major cases from the Bator, Currie, Low and Redish casebooks, plus a Case Library.
ISBN# 0-15-900409-8 $27.95

Income Tax
Includes briefs of all of the major cases from the Freeland and Klein casebooks, many of the major cases from the Burke and Graetz casebooks, plus a Case Library.
ISBN# 0-15-900200-1 $27.95

Labor Law
Includes briefs of all of the major cases from the Cox and Merrifield casebooks, many of the major cases from the Harper, Leslie and Meltzer casebooks, plus a Case Library.
ISBN# 0-15-900410-1 $27.95

Property
Includes briefs of all of the major cases from the Casner, Cribbet, Dukeminier and Rabin casebooks, many of the major cases from the Donahue, Johnson, Kurtz, and Singer casebooks, plus a Case Library.
ISBN# 0-15-900201-X $27.95

Remedies
Includes briefs of all of the major cases from the Re and York casebooks, many of the major cases from the Leavell and Shoben casebooks, plus a Case Library.
ISBN# 0-15-900202-8 $27.95

Securities Regulation
Includes briefs of all of the major cases from the Jennings casebook, many of the major cases from the Cox casebook, plus a Case Library.
ISBN# 0-15-900411-X $27.95

Torts
Includes briefs of all of the major cases from the Epstein, Franklin, Henderson, Keeton and Prosser casebooks, many of the major cases from the Christie, Dobbs and Shulman casebooks, plus a Case Library.
ISBN# 0-15-900203-6 $27.95

Wills, Trusts & Estates
Includes briefs of all of the major cases from the Dukeminier casebook, many of the major cases from the Wagoner casebook, plus a Case Library.
ISBN# 0-15-900204-4 $27.95

Call To Order: 1-800-787-8717 or Order On-Line at http://www.gilbertlaw.com

Employment Guides

A collection of best selling titles that help you identify and reach your career goals.

Guerrilla Tactics for Getting the Legal Job of Your Dreams
Kimm Alayne Walton, J.D.

Whether you're looking for a summer clerkship or your first permanent job after school, this revolutionary book is the key to getting the job of your dreams!

Guerrilla Tactics for Getting the Legal Job of Your Dreams leads you step-by-step through everything you need to do to nail down that perfect job! You'll learn hundreds of simple-to-use strategies that will get you exactly where you want to go. You'll Learn:

- The seven magic opening words in cover letters that ensure you'll get a response.
- The secret to successful interviews every time.
- Killer answers to the toughest interview questions they'll ever ask you.
- Plus Much More!

Guerrilla Tactics features the best strategies from the country's most innovative law school career advisors. The strategies in *Guerrilla Tactics* are so powerful that it even comes with a guarantee: Follow the advice in the book, and within one year of graduation you'll have the job of your dreams ... or your money back!

Pick up a copy of *Guerrilla Tactics* today ... you'll be on your way to the job of your dreams!

ISBN: 0-15-900317-2 $24.95

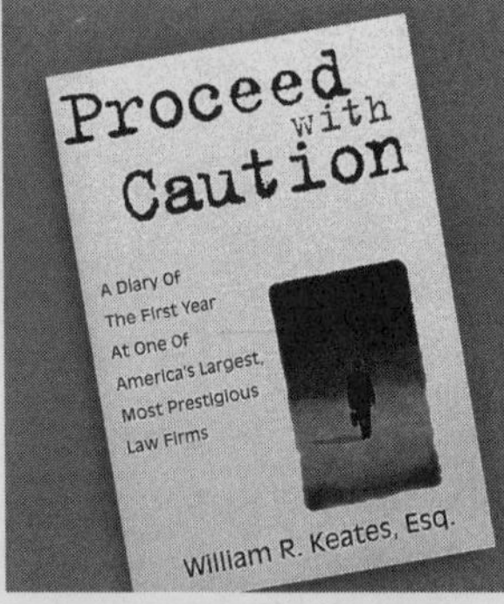

Proceed With Caution: A Diary Of The First Year At One Of America's Largest, Most Prestigious Law Firms
William R. Keates

Prestige. Famous clients. High-profile cases. Not to mention a starting salary approaching six figures.

In *Proceed With Caution*, the author takes you behind the scenes, to show you what it's really like to be a junior associate at a huge law firm. After graduating from an Ivy League law school, he took a job as an associate with one of New York's blue-chip law firms.

He also did something not many people do. He kept a diary, where he spelled out his day-to-day life at the firm in graphic detail.

Proceed With Caution excerpts the diary, from his first day at the firm to the day he quit. From the splashy benefits, to the nitty-gritty on the work junior associates do, to the grind of long and unpredictable hours, to the stress that eventually made him leave the firm — he tells story after story that will make you feel as though you're living the life of a new associate.

Whether you're considering a career with a large firm, or you're just curious about what life at the top firms is all about — *Proceed With Caution* is a must read!

ISBN: 0-15-900181-1 $17.95

The Official Guide To Legal Specialties
National Association for Law Placement

With *The Official Guide To Legal Specialties* you'll get a behind the scenes glimpse at dozens of legal specialties. Not just lists of what to expect, real life stories from top practitioners in each field. You'll learn exactly what it's like to be in some of America's most desirable professions. You'll get expert advice on what it takes to get a job in each field. How much you'll earn and what the day-to-day life is really like, the challenges you'll face, and the benefits you'll enjoy. With *The Official Guide To Legal Specialties* you'll have a wealth of information at your fingertips!

Includes the following specialties:

Banking	Intellectual Property
Communications	International
Corporate	Labor/Employment
Criminal	Litigation
Entertainment	Public Interest
Environmental	Securities
Government Practice	Sports
Health Care	Tax
Immigration	Trusts & Estates

ISBN: 0-15-900391-1 $19.95

Beyond L.A. Law: Inspiring Stories of People Who've Done Fascinating Things With A Law Degree
National Association for Law Placement

Anyone who watches television knows that being a lawyer means working your way up through a law firm — right?

Wrong!

Beyond L.A. Law gives you a fascinating glimpse into the lives of people who've broken the "lawyer" mold. They come from a variety of backgrounds — some had prior careers, others went straight through college and law school, and yet others have overcome poverty and physical handicaps. They got their degrees from all different kinds of law schools, all over the country. But they have one thing in common: they've all pursued their own, unique vision.

As you read their stories, you'll see how they beat the odds to succeed. You'll learn career tips and strategies that work, from people who've put them to the test. And you'll find fascinating insights that you can apply to your own dream, whether it's a career in law or anything else!

From Representing Baseball In Australia. To International Finance. To Children's Advocacy. To Directing a Nonprofit Organization. To Entrepreneur.

If You Think Getting A Law Degree Means Joining A Traditional Law Firm — Think Again!

ISBN: 0-15-900182-X $17.95

America's Greatest Places To Work With A Law Degree
Kimm Alayne Walton, J.D.

"Where do your happiest graduates work?" That's the question that author Kimm Alayne Walton asked of law school administrators around the country. Their responses revealed the hundreds of wonderful employers profiled in *America's Greatest Places To Work With A Law Degree.*

In this remarkable book, you'll get to know an incredible variety of great places to work, including:

- Glamorous sports and entertainment employers — the jobs that sound as though they would be great, and they are!
- The 250 best law firms to work for between 20 and 600 attorneys.
- Companies where law school graduates love to work and not just as in-house counsel.
- Wonderful public interest employers – the "white knight" jobs that are so incredibly satisfying.
- Court-related positions, where lawyers entertain fascinating issues, tremendous variety, and an enjoyable lifestyle.
- Outstanding government jobs, at the federal, state, and local level.

Beyond learning about incredible employers, you'll discover:

- The ten traits that define a wonderful place to work ... the sometimes surprising qualities that outstanding employers share.
- How to handle law school debt, when your dream job pays less than you think you need to make.
- How to find — and get! — great jobs at firms with fewer than 20 attorneys.

And no matter where you work, you'll learn expert tips for making the most of your job. You'll learn the specific strategies that distinguish people headed for the top ... how to position yourself for the most interesting, high-profile work ... how to handle difficult personalities ... how to negotiate for more money ... and what to do now to help you get your next great job!

ISBN: 0-15-900180-3 $24.95

About The Author

Kimm Alayne Walton is the author of numerous books and articles including two national best seller's — *America's Greatest Places To Work With A Law Degree* and *Guerrilla Tactics For Getting The Legal Job Of Your Dreams.* She is a renowned motivational speaker, lecturing at law schools and bar associations nationwide, and in her spare time, she has taken up travel writing, which has taken her swimming with crocodiles in Kakadu, and scuba diving with sharks on the Great Barrier Reef.

E-mail the Job Goddess with your own legal job search questions!

Visit www.gilbertlaw.com for details.

Call To Order: 1-800-787-8717 or Order On-Line at http://www.gilbertlaw.com

Employment Guides

A collection of best selling titles that help you identify and reach your career goals.

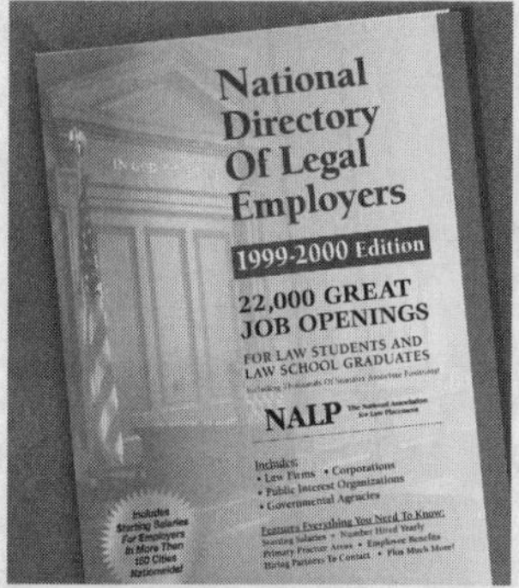

The National Directory Of Legal Employers

National Association for Law Placement

The National Directory of Legal Employers brings you a universe of vital information about 1,000 of the nation's top legal employers— *in one convenient volume!*

It includes:

- Over 22,000 job openings.
- The names, addresses and phone numbers of hiring partners.
- Listings of firms by state, size, kind and practice area.
- What starting salaries are for full time, part time, and summer associates, plus a detailed description of firm benefits.
- The number of employees by gender and race, as well as the number of employees with disabilities.
- A detailed narrative of each firm, plus much more!

The National Directory Of Legal Employers has been the best kept secret of top legal career search professionals for over a decade. Now, for the first time, it is available in a format specifically designed for law students and new graduates.

Pick up your copy of the Directory today!

ISBN: 0-15-900434-9 **$39.95**

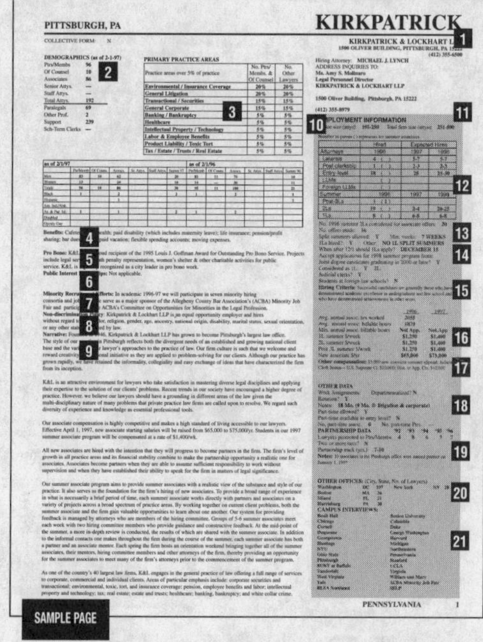

PITTSBURGH, PA

KIRKPATRICK

KIRKPATRICK & LOCKHART LLP

1500 OLIVER BUILDING, PITTSBURGH, PA 15222

PENNSYLVANIA

SAMPLE PAGE

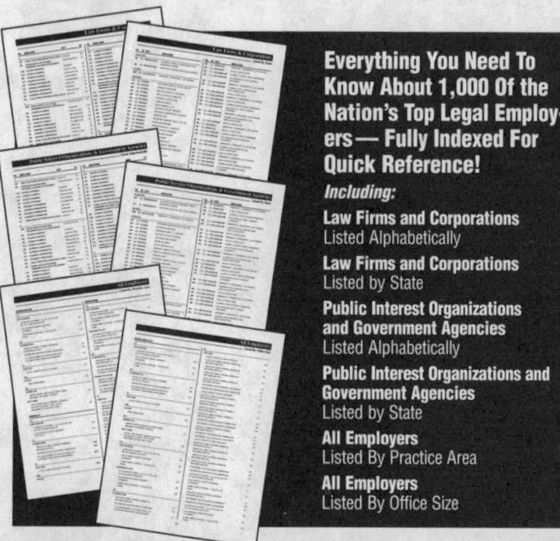

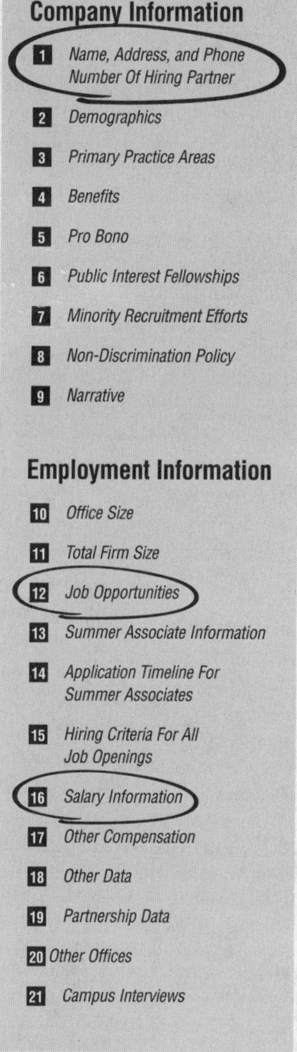

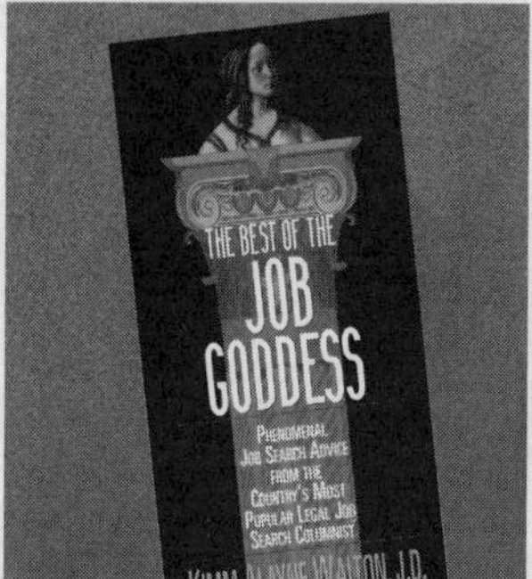

The Best Of The Job Goddess

Kimm Alayne Walton, J.D.

In her popular **Dear Job Goddess** column, legal job-search expert Kimm Alayne Walton provides the answers to even the most difficult job search dilemmas facing law students and law school graduates. Relying on career experts from around the country, the Job Goddess provides wise and witty advice for every obstacle that stands between you and your dream job!

ISBN: 0-15-900393-8 **$14.95**

SAMPLE COLUMN

Business Card Resumes: Good Idea, Or Not?

Dear Job Goddess,

One of my friends showed me something called a "business card resume." What he did was to have these business cards printed up, with his name and phone number on one side, and highlights from his resume on the other side. He said a bunch of people are doing this, so that when they meet potential employers they hand over these cards. Should I bother getting some for myself?

Curious in Chicago

Dear Curious,

Sigh, You know, Curious, that the Job Goddess takes a fairly dim view of resumes as a job-finding tool, even in their full-blown bond-papered, engraved 8-1/2x11" incarnation. And here you ask about a business card resume, two steps further down the resume food chain. So, no, you *shouldn't* bother with business card resumes. Here's why.

Think for a moment, Curious, about the kind of circumstance in which you'd be tempted to whip out one of these incredible shrinking resumes. You're at a social gathering. You happen to meet Will Winken, of the law firm Winken, Blinken, and Nod, and it becomes clear fairly quickly that Will is a) friendly, and b) a potential employer. The surest way to turn this chance encounter into a job is to use it as the basis for future contact. As Carolyn Bregman, Career Services Director at Emory Law School, points out, "Follow up with a phone call or note, mentioning something Winken said to you." You can say that you'd like to follow up on whatever it is he said, or that you've since read more about him and found that he's an expert on phlegm reclamation law and how that's a topic that's always fascinated you, and invite him for coffee at his convenience so you can learn more about it. What have you done? *You've taken a social encounter and turned it into a potential job opportunity.* And that makes the Job Goddess very proud.

But what happens if you, instead, whip out your business card resume, and say, "Gee, Mr. Winken, nice meeting you. Here's my business card resume, in case you ever need anybody like me." *Now* what have you done? You have, with one simple gesture, wiped out any excuse to follow up! Instead of having a phone call or a note from you that is personalized to Winken, you've got a piddling little standardized card with your vital statistics on it. Ugh. I know you're much more memorable, Curious, than anything you could possibly fit on the back of a business card.

So there you have it, Curious. Save the money you'll spend on a business card resume, and spend it later, when you have a *real* business card to print, reading, "Curious, Esq. Winken, Blinken, and Nod, Attorneys at Law."

Yours Eternally,

The Job Goddess

Call To Order: 1-800-787-8717 or Order On-Line at http://www.gilbertlaw.com